The Sound of Navajo Country

· ·

Critical Indigeneities

J. Kēhaulani Kauanui and Jean M. O'Brien,
series editors

SERIES ADVISORY BOARD

Chris Anderson, University of Alberta

Irene Watson, University of South Australia

Emilio del Valle Escalante, University of North
     Carolina at Chapel Hill

Kim TallBear, University of Texas at Austin

Critical Indigeneities publishes pathbreaking scholarly
books that center Indigeneity as a category of critical
analysis, understand Indigenous sovereignty as ongoing
and historically grounded, and attend to diverse forms
of Indigenous cultural and political agency and expression.
The series builds on the conceptual rigor, methodological
innovation, and deep relevance that characterize the best
work in the growing field of critical Indigenous studies.

The Sound of Navajo Country

Music, Language, and Diné Belonging

Kristina M. Jacobsen

THE UNIVERSITY OF NORTH CAROLINA PRESS ⋮ CHAPEL HILL

Publication of this book was supported in part by
a generous gift from Florence and James Peacock.

Designed by April Leidig
Set in Times Roman by Copperline Book Services

The University of North Carolina Press has been a
member of the Green Press Initiative since 2003.

Cover illustration: Chucki Begay, Gray Mountain
(Dzip Pibáhí), Navajo Nation, Arizona.
Photograph by Terry Jackson, © 2007.

Library of Congress Cataloging-in-Publication Data
Names: Jacobsen, Kristina M., author.
Title: The sound of Navajo country : music, language,
and Diné belonging / Kristina M. Jacobsen.
Other titles: Critical indigeneities.
Description: Chapel Hill : The University of North Carolina Press, [2017] |
Series: Critical indigeneities | Includes bibliographical references and index.
Identifiers: LCCN 2016036180 | ISBN 9781469631851 (cloth : alk. paper) |
ISBN 9781469631868 (pbk : alk. paper) | ISBN 9781469631875 (ebook)
Subjects: LCSH: Navajo Indians—Music—Social aspects. | Navajo
Indians—Music—Political aspects. | Country music—Social aspects. |
Navajo Indians—Ethnic identity.
Classification: LCC E99.N3 J28 2017 | DDC 979.1004/9726—dc23
LC record available at https://lccn.loc.gov/2016036180

A version of chapter 3 was originally published as
"Radmilla's Voice: Music Genre, Blood Quantum,
and Belonging on the Navajo Nation," *Cultural
Anthropology* 29, no. 2 (2014): 385–410,
http://dx.doi.org/10.14506/ca29.2.11.

Contents

....

A photographic essay begins on page 109.

Maps and Figures

Maps

Figures

Acknowledgments

· ·

To my Navajo moms: Inez, Shirley, Jane and Helen. Ahéhee,' Shimá! And to the late David McAllester, my first Navajo language teacher, who started me on this journey so many years ago. Irish dancing into his eighties and singing skip dance songs to me in the basement of the Simon's Rock Library, David modeled for me what living life fully, doing research with a keen attention to ethics, and combining a love for music and language might look like. Ahéhee', shicheiiyéé'.

On the Navajo Nation, I am tremendously thankful to the Craig, Tom, and Bia families, who have guided me in so many ways along this journey, both personally and professionally. Lee Begay and Stillwater, Alvin Miles, Fenders II and the late Spanky Mike Jr. were some of the first Native bands and promoters I worked with while doing my master's thesis, and their time and generosity has carried forward—including Alvin's fabulous line-dancing classes—into the current project. Wilson Hunter, Inez Paddock, Wanda Ahasteen, Aileema Benally, Kenneth Watchman, and Kelvin Watchman opened up the world of Chinle and Canyon de Chelly (*Tségi'*) and introduced me to the first "rez band" I ever heard, Aces Wild, for which I will be forever grateful. At KTNN Radio Station in Window Rock, deejays Ray Tsosie and Darlene Lee expertly guided me through the ropes as a station intern in my early twenties, and introduced me to many of the bands and sound worlds discussed in this book. At Navajo Technical University, the Roastingear and Bebo families were unswervingly supportive and engaged with my project, and they helped to make Crownpoint an inviting and engaging place to live. At Chaco Canyon, Russ Bodnar, G. B. Cornucopia, Ramona Begay, Carol Shattuck, Don Whyte, and Terry Jaquez supported not only the bands I played with—including hosting a Native Country dance (a first) at the Visitor Center—but also provided a beautiful home base from which I could explore issues of cultural patrimony, Diné creation narratives, and connections to ancestral Puebloan stories, as well as the unique realities of the Navajo checkerboard.

In Crownpoint, Shirley Bowman, Lester, David Thompson, McGarrett Pablo, Patrick Sandoval, Derek Begay, and Peggy Willetto-West created a welcoming and rich place from which to start my fieldwork. Shirley Bowman in particular mentored me in the Navajo language and in Diné cultural competencies both big and small; she also provided critical feedback and served as language consultant on multiple versions of the book manuscript.

In Chinle, Agatha Spencer, Cathy Bahe, and Tamara Sloan at Diné College provided me with some of the richest teaching experiences I have had to date. My deep thanks to Diné College students Wileen Bahe, Irene Littleben, Shirley Watchman, Aaron Begay, Demeshia Claushchee, LeAndra Desiderio-Bia, and Bonnie Yazzie, among many, many others, who shared windows into their worlds at crucial stages in fieldwork and writing.

My mentors Orin Starn and Louise Meintjes at Duke were guiding lights in all ways, and they continue to be role models both in their scholarship and as human beings. Valerie Lambert, Ajantha Subramanian, and Aaron Fox also all provided insightful comments and feedback. My introduction to Merle Haggard by Aaron Fox at a crucial stage influenced not only my research but my own aesthetic in country music in ways that continue to unfold in both my scholarship and my own performance, including in my five-piece, all-girl honky-tonk band, the Merlettes. Valerie Lambert's class on American Indian societies at the University of North Carolina (UNC) and the wonderful scholars working in critical Indigenous studies I was introduced to in the class were an invaluable part of my early graduate training in thinking through relationships between critical Indigenous studies and anthropology. At UNC, Courtney Lewis, Julie Reed, Dana Powell, Jean Dennison, Jenny Tone-Pah-Hote, and Malinda Maynor Lowery offered feedback and critique of my work at crucial stages. At Duke, Kevin Sobel-Read, Spencer Orey, Louisa Lombard, June-Hee Kwon, and Katya Wesolowski provided feedback, ongoing dialogue, and camaraderie in the beautiful North Carolina Piedmont.

At Arizona State University, Richard Haefer, Ted Solís, and Kay Norton were wonderful and supportive, and Christina Burbano-Jeffrey and Shauna Catania were delightful and engaging colleagues. At Columbia University, where this project had its infancy, Victoria McKenzie, Matt Sakakeeny, Ryan Skinner, Rosemary Hicks, and Lisa Uparesa all influenced its early formulations. Ana María Ochoa's classes on cultural politics and *nueva canción* particularly influenced my own approach to cultural politics in this text, and they led me to consider the stakes involved in how culture is used strategically. At New York University, Fred Myers's course, "Fourth World Peoples," and his support from my project's infancy were particularly appreciated and influential.

While teaching at Northern Arizona University, my colleagues Mary Roaf, Kerry Thompson, Chad Hamill, and Miguel Vasquez offered insight into my project, pushing me to bridge my research and teaching in border-town worlds and classrooms in ways for which I continue to be grateful.

I have been graced at the University of New Mexico with a collegial work environment across the Music, Anthropology, and Native American Studies Departments. David Bashwiner, Erin Debenport, Lindsay Smith, Ronda Brulotte, Cristóbal Valencia, Lloyd Lee, and Tiffany Lee have all engaged with portions of the manuscript at various stages. Jennifer Denetdale also offered important feedback and critiques of the project, and Raquel Z. Rivera offered collegiality and support at a critical stage. Steven Feld, Les Field, Steve Block, Regina Carlow, and Patricia Repar have offered unconditional support for the book, my research, my performing, and my teaching. My teaching assistant, April Goltz, provided invaluable help with final copyediting, and graduate students Regan Homeyer, Peter Njagi, and Caitlin Grann also offered helpful feedback on the book's introduction. Students Sandra Yellowhair, Renata Yazzie, Latasha James, Paulene Shebala, and Chad Abeyta have helped me stay connected with the Navajo Nation from the sometimes-distant space of Albuquerque, sharing with me not only tamales, mutton stew, Navajo tea, songs, phrases, and pictures from home but also their own profound perspectives on navigating their lives as University of New Mexico students, parents, Diné citizens, veterans, performing musicians, Diné language learners, and aspiring doctors, legal scholars, nutritionists and academics in Albuquerque and beyond. David Samuels, Jessica Cattelino, Alexander Dent, Anthony Webster, Michelle Bigenho, and Tom Guthrie have also offered long-term mentoring and support for which I am most appreciative.

At the UNC Press, Mark Simpson-Vos generously and enthusiastically shepherded this project forward from its pre-fieldwork days, pushing me to develop the connections between sound, critical Indigenous studies, and the politics of authenticity in contemporary Native worlds. Lucas Church, Jessica Newman, and Jay Mazzocchi also assisted in the final stages of manuscript preparation. The Critical Indigeneities series editors, J. Kēhaulani Kauanui and Jean M. O'Brien, have enthusiastically supported the book: their stewardship of this project and their own scholarship have been inspiring and motivating to a junior scholar.

Research for this project has been supported by many sources for which I am extremely grateful, among them: a Wenner-Gren Dissertation Fieldwork grant, the Jacob's Research Fund, a Duke Graduate School Summer Research Fellowship, and the Lynn Reyer Award in Tribal Community Development.

The songwriting and performance communities in which I sing and play lapsteel and acoustic guitar in Albuquerque, Chicago, Denmark, and beyond have also worked their way into these pages in ways both explicit and implicit. I am grateful to Gregg Daigle, John Feldman, Meredith Wilder, Alex McMahon, Steve Doyle, Keith Baumann, Cory Atkinson, Mette Lethan, Brett Perkins, as well as to cowriters and Merlettes band members Steff Chanat, Dair Obenshain, Laura Leach, and Sharon Eldridge. I feel blessed to lead a double life, actively performing and writing songs while also pursuing my passion as an ethnographer, teacher, and scholar.

Finally, to my mom, Helen Moorefield; my father, Kenneth Jacobsen; my late paternal grandmother, Jacqueline Clark Jacobsen; Douglas MacDonald, Maria Rosa and Luciano Passamani; Leslie Davidson; and my elementary and high school teachers Julia Núñez, Jane Laning, and John Beacco—thank you all for nurturing in me the desire to travel, learn new languages, connect with others, and deeply explore the world around me sonically, linguistically, and politically. Ayóo baah ahéé' nisin!

All author proceeds from the sale of this book will be donated to the Navajo Nation Museum.

Note on Orthographic and Linguistic Conventions

Writing in Navajo is primarily the domain of elite, educated Diné speakers and thus is not widely used in reservation contexts. Perhaps for this reason, very little standardization of the written language exists and one encounters a wide variety of written registers of Navajo on a daily basis: formal classroom Navajo, Anglicized versions, code-mixed English-Navajo versions, text-message versions without diacritics, and local signage indicating ceremonial events are just a few examples.

In the interest of internal consistency, I have chosen to use the orthography associated with Young and Morgan's monumental work, *The Navajo Language: A Grammar and Colloquial Dictionary* (1980) for Navajo words throughout the book. For words not found in that dictionary, I relied on the expert knowledge of my Navajo language teachers, Shirley Bowman and Lorraine Begay Manavi.

Pronunciation Key

1. There are four basic vowels in Navajo:

   a as in *art*
   e as in *met*
   i as in *sit*
   o as in *note*

2. Vowels may be short or long, and length is indicated by a doubling of the letter. The quality of the vowel is not affected by length, except that the long "i" is pronounced as in *seen* or *machine*.

3. Vowels may also be nasalized. The nasalized pronunciation is indicated by a hook underneath the affected vowel, as in *mąʼii* [coyote].

4. There are three tone levels in Navajo: low, middle, and high. A low tone is indicated by double vowels with no high tones, as in *hooghan* (house/home). A middle tone is indicated by a single vowel, also with no high tones, as in *tin* (ice). A high tone is indicated by a diacritic or a tone marker over a vowel, as in *tó*

(water) or *Dine'é* (the people). A high tone followed by a vowel with no diacritic indicates a falling tone and falling intonation, as in *bíighah* (good/sufficient/ enough). A vowel with no diacritic followed by a high tone indicates a rising tone, as in *hágoónee'* (goodbye). As in English, proper nouns are capitalized in Navajo.

5. Navajo has the following diphthongs, which require special attention:

ai as in *kite*
ei as in *day*
oi as in *buoy*

6. There are twenty-seven letters in the Navajo alphabet, including trigraphs such as ch', tp', and ts'. Most consonants in Navajo are more aspirated than are their English equivalents, and there are also two characters that do not appear in the standard English alphabet. They include the glottal stop ('), as in *mą'ii* or *adą́ą́dą́ą́'* (yesterday), and the voiceless glide (ł), as in *nííłch'i* (wind). The glottal stop is pronounced like the break between the vowels in the English expression, "uh, oh." The voiceless glide is pronounced by unvoicing the "l" familiar to English speakers, placing the tongue directly behind the front teeth, and blowing air out both sides of the tongue.

All translations in this book into English, unless otherwise noted, are my own.

Note: The pronunciation guide is taken from Paul Zolbrod's "Pronunciation Key" in *Diné Bahane': The Navajo Creation Story*. Additional reference guides for help with pronunciation and spelling include Navajo Rosetta Stone; Irvy Goossen's *Diné Bizaad: Read, Speak, Write Navajo*; and the web page http://navajonow.com /navajo-programs-books/. In order to ground discussions of language and song discussed throughout the book, readers are encouraged to access the songs and video clips provided through the author's website, www.kristina-jacobsen.com.

The Sound of Navajo Country

What's more cowboy than my Stetson hat
And my wing-tipped Tony Lama boots?
There's my nylon rope, we can't forget that
And I also gotta tell you about the shoes.

[Chorus] I don't know how it happened
But I'm really kind of glad
I'm an Indian cowboy
And being both [full stop]: can't be so bad.

I travel around to reservations everywhere
Relied on friends I've met along the way
Roping and riding at all the Indian Fairs
I've done a lot of winning in my day.

[Chorus] I don't know how it happened
But I'm really kind of glad
I'm an Indian cowboy
And being both [full stop]: can't be so bad.
—Written and performed by Apache Spirit
   (White Mountain Apache)

The Intimate Nostalgia
of Diné Country Music

An older Navajo woman stands in line in front of me at the Mustang gas station in the central reservation town of Chinle, Arizona. In Navajo, she asks the teenage Navajo cashier for kerosene.[1] Not understanding her and distracted by the heavy metal music he is playing behind the counter, the cashier shrugs his shoulders in embarrassment. A middle-aged woman standing between us intervenes, translating the older woman's request for the cashier. The older woman, finally realizing that the cashier doesn't understand Navajo, complains with obvious irritation: "Yáadi lá Diné shį́į́!" ("What kind of Navajo are you?").[2]

In this gas station scene, Navajo authenticity, difference, and belonging all surface. Diné citizens continually negotiate points of friction about who is perceived as being more or less Indigenous through linguistic performance, practice, and related conversation. In speech communities where English is increasingly the dominant and normative language for younger Navajos, what anxieties about language loss and, by extension, Navajo traditional culture and social authenticity might underlie a charge like the one leveled by the elder? And beyond language, what of its underlying sound? The clash of an elder's voice and a youth's hard rock raise the question: how do Navajos strategically use sound, and speech and song in particular, in their social spaces?

The right sounds can perform authenticity, or innovation, or a blending of the two. This is also true for the central subject of this book: Diné musicians performing country music. Navajo musicians are typical of Navajo citizenry at large in that social authenticity and affective senses of belonging are routinely top of mind, fueling many friendly conversations and even public debate. Tradition and authenticity coarticulate and affect tribal citizens' own senses of belonging, or what I call social citizenship. In the context of social citizenship, innovation and musical experimentation are often viewed with suspicion, and carving out spaces for new sounds—linguistic and musical—requires significant labor, dedication, and cultural capital. Building on what Audra Simpson terms "membership talk" (2014, 9), I believe these extralegal forms of belonging are often less inclusive than the broader, political identity of being an "enrolled" Navajo citizen, where criteria are based on a quarter minimum Navajo "blood quantum" and having at least one enrolled parent on the Navajo tribal rolls (Spruhan 2008, 11).[3] In the context of the Navajo Nation, language, aesthetics, and physical appearance and phenotype are sometimes used as seemingly clear-cut litmus tests for what is actually the inchoate, shifting, and difficult-to-pinpoint thing that is Navajo social citizenship. Thus the skill with which one does or doesn't speak Navajo and the way in which one does or doesn't appear phenotypically Diné—such as having black or brown hair, dark eyes, and brown skin—often determine one's social authenticity and "right" to belong within a broader community of Navajos, or Dine'é.

I wrote this book to explore how Navajo musicians today navigate this treacherous terrain, specifically in the context of Navajo country-western music. After almost two decades of studying the Navajo language, and two and a half years of ethnographic fieldwork,[4] singing and playing the lap-steel guitar with three Navajo country-western bands,[5] I wanted to examine the pitfalls of essentializing expressive culture in a social space where country music and "Indian cowboys" remain central to aesthetics and daily conversation.

While this conflation of "cowboys" and "Indians" might feel problematic or anomalous for non-Native performers and fans of country music, Indian cowboys, and Indians playing country music, are embraced by many Indigenous peoples as natural, logical, and even traditional (Witmer 1973; Downs 1972; McAllester 1979; Samuels 2004). While it might be surprising to some, in fact, two different songs actively circulating in the reservation country band canon are both titled "Indian Cowboy": one by the White Mountain Apache band, Apache Spirit, and the other by a band from New Mexico's Isleta Pueblo, the Isleta Poor Boys. Playing a version of one of these songs is a de facto requirement for Navajo country musicians, including the bands with which I performed on the Navajo Nation. What does it mean, then, that country music—broadly assumed to be a white genre—can so profoundly hail Navajo identity? The connection troubles our understandings not only of music genre but also of race and place. If country music is rooted in place-based expressions of southern working-class experience, how does its sound speak deeply to a group of Indigenous peoples hailing from the American Southwest?

Answers to these questions play out against a backdrop of structural forces that also shape difference and belonging: economics, the government-to-government relationship between the Navajo Nation and the United States, and the broader, if sometimes precarious, social fact of political and social sovereignty among Indigenous nations. Defined as a "bundle of inherent rights," sovereignty is also something that is "continually negotiated" (Lambert 2007, 18, 210). In letters to the editor of the *Navajo Times*, the main weekly Navajo national newspaper, sovereignty clearly influences tribal citizens, who differentiate between Indigenous land and U.S. land and refer to leaving the reservation as "going stateside" (André Leonard in *Navajo Times*, June 3, 2010). The keen awareness of being a distinctive nation within a nation informs Navajo ways of viewing the world and influences relations between tribal, state, and federal governments. But this sense of distinction also becomes expressed through musical and linguistic performance, and the frequent use of the term "stateside" is informed by the disproportionately high number of Navajos who volunteer in the U.S. military (currently more than 10 percent of enrolled Diné citizens). This is but one example of the way art and politics are linked in Diné spaces. Indeed, many of the male musicians who perform country music in this book are also veterans, and all of them have family members who have served, linking military service to sovereignty, senses of place, and rural expressive culture.

Structural forces also play out in relation to politics and place, for example, whether musicians live and perform on-reservation or off-reservation. There is a long, ongoing history of racial friction and discrimination against Native residents (including Navajos) in border towns,[6] or in off-reservation towns neighboring the Navajo Nation, such as Page and Winslow, Arizona; Gallup, Albuquerque, and Farmington, New Mexico; and Cortez, Colorado. Since many "Native bands"—the local term used to describe these musical groups—play gigs off reservation in these border towns, I observed tensions and "foreign relations" between Navajos and their border-town neighbors—citizens of other Native nations in the region, as well as the racially dominant majority known as "Anglos" living in these and other towns. As one response to ongoing injustices perpetuated in border towns, the Navajo Nation has recently spearheaded the Navajo Nation Human Rights Commission (or NNHRC) to investigate past and current conditions for Indians who reside or conduct business in border towns.[7]

Musicians negotiate these and similar tensions through specific decisions: where to perform; what repertoire to play; and whether to feature stage-banter in Navajo, English, or (sometimes) Spanish. For example, when playing the all-white

Elk's Club in the border town of Cortez, Colorado, one evening, the main band I played with, Native Country, received a lukewarm reception from the management (the club didn't know they had booked a Native band). Onstage, lead singer Tommy Bia went out of his way to introduce songs using a monoglot standard English pronunciation, avoided all use of Navajo, and insisted that I, as the Anglo singer, perform the majority of the songs.[8] Finally, he invited an Anglo fiddler and audience member onto the stage to sit in with us for an entire set. Suffice it to say that we left the Elk's Club immediately after the show.

Diné musicians confront these external prejudices and presumptions while retaining their own senses of cultural and political distinction over and above these other stylistic and linguistic choices they make in performance. Through a dual ethnographic focus on music and language, I consider in this book how some expressions of Navajo identity are flexible and negotiated, while others — for example, an affective attachment to place and the lived experience of being from what the Supreme Court chief justice John Marshall called a "domestic dependent nation" — are private, nonnegotiable, and often not shared in public contexts such as bars and chapter houses at all.[9] Thus musical and linguistic performances of Navajoness — also sometimes locally parsed in the broader frames of being Native, Indian and, less often, as Indigenous — are publicly celebrated. Other expressions of identity — for example, the culturally intimate use of the Navajo term for a working-class rube from the "sticks" known as a *jaan* — are elided or hidden from an outsider's gaze.

This is ultimately a generational story of language and belonging, told through the lens of a genre of music — and the weight of the nostalgia that it bears — popular among Navajo citizens middle-aged and older. Most of the musicians whose experiences inform my book are also fluent in Navajo, and they share key common experiences of time, place, and culture (Mannheim 1923), spanning about two generations (ages 40–55 and 55–65). If the distinct formation of a generation is defined by the rapidity of the social change it collectively experiences (Manheim 1923; Pilcher 1994), these cohorts are no different, as the Navajo Nation underwent significant social, economic, and linguistic shifts following Diné participation in World War II. In particular, compulsory English-language education became more common and was a widespread shared experience across the Nation by the early 1970s, so depending on when someone was born, musicians demonstrate a variety of proficiency levels in English, but almost all speak Diné bizaad, or Navajo.

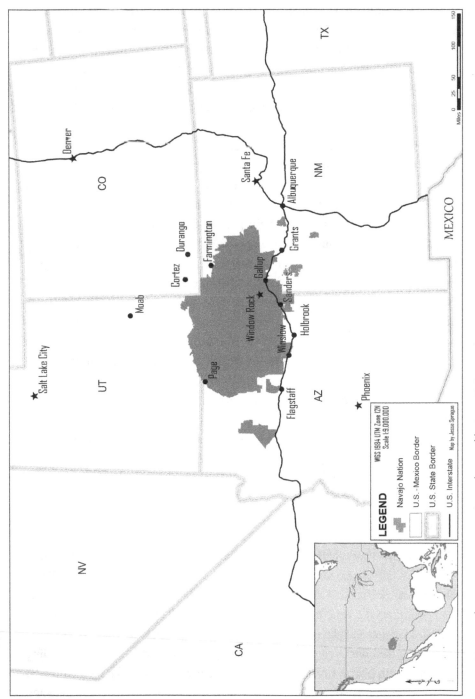

MAP 1. Contextual Map, Navajo Nation (Map designed by Jesse E. Sprague)

For many of these performers and heritage language speakers, country is the preferred genre of popular music. I argue that Navajo country music as a genre is inextricably tied to the daily politics of heritage language use, and the two can only be understood conjointly: loss of the love and appreciation for country music on the reservation is often implicitly tied to perceptions of Navajo language and cultural loss. Methodologically, this means that I learned by playing and focusing on country music, yet also by speaking and listening to language in everyday life.

Navajo country bands focus on the performance of country music from the 1960s to the 1980s. Country musicians and bandleaders are primarily Navajo men in their forties and older, along with their younger immediate family and clan members. Native, "rez" or "rez country" bands, as they are called in the vernacular, are dance bands, and, while playing predominantly country and rock songs, they perform exclusively up-tempo songs to which dancers can do the two-step, a partner dance that goes in a counterclockwise direction. This scene is particularly active on the Arizona side of the Navajo reservation, where well-known bands such as Aces Wild and Stateline perform regularly every weekend inside packed gymnasiums, community centers, chapter houses, converted airplane hangers, under rodeo bleachers, and in a multitude of other make-do structures.

But the present book also tells the story of younger generations, as I chronicle how younger Diné citizens seek to find their own voices—musically and linguistically—in a polarized aesthetic field built on the seemingly fixed but actually constantly shifting sands of "authenticity" and "tradition." So, whether they love it or hate it, country music—as the music of their parents' and grandparents' generation—is something that many younger Dine'é contend with and continually position themselves either for or against.[10]

Methodologies

During my fieldwork, I played regularly with three different bands: Native Country (Many Farms, Arizona), Re-Coil (Fort Defiance, Arizona), and the Wranglers (Crownpoint, New Mexico). I also sat in with other bands,[11] although I was never considered a band member in these groups. The first part of my research included singing and playing the lap steel guitar with bands in live performances throughout the Four Corners region, attending weekly band rehearsals, recording an album with Native Country, and procuring gigs and creating a social media presence for that band. I also participated in radio appearances and conducted semistructured interviews with my fellow band members. Ethnographic research included performing at open mics with individual band members, document-ing recordings of rehearsals and radio interviews and the conversation that sur-rounded playback, and, in the case of Native Country and the Wranglers, I also spent extensive time with band members participating in extramusical activities such as planting corn, shearing sheep, hauling wood and coal, and attending family dinners and celebrations.

The second part of my fieldwork entailed intensive Navajo language study, including classes taken at the tribal college (Diné College) in Crownpoint and Tsaile, at the University of New Mexico, and private study with my Navajo lan-guage teacher, Shirley Bowman. Language study also included a Navajo-language immersion home stay, which consisted of three months living in a traditional Na-vajo female *hooghan* in Rough Rock, Arizona, where I cared for an older couple, herded sheep, and participated in daily family life.[12] My ethnographic experi-ences were also informed by the many other roles I played in Diné communities as a late teen and into my twenties, including as a park ranger, high school social studies teacher, volleyball coach, country radio station intern at KTNN (AM 660) and language student at the Diné College flagship campus in Tsaile.

As per Jane Hill's discussion on the fixation with enumeration (2002) in en-dangered language settings, I want to resist the tendency, here and throughout the book, to discuss fluency in black and white terms (O'Brien 2010). To do so would constitute yet another example of what Anishinaabe scholar Jean O'Brien has termed "lasting," where the "last" of each category connected to perceived indexes of Indigenous cultural continuity—speakers, singers, medicine people, dancers, storytellers—is lamented as part of the passing of the last Indians à la Ishi, the Yahi citizen who was the "last of the his tribe" (O'Brien in Davis 2014, 110; Starn 2004).

Throughout my fieldwork I spoke and used Navajo consistently in daily situ-ational contexts, including in public settings when I was at the Basha's grocery store or at the dialysis clinic with my Navajo language teacher; with other class-mates in my Navajo language classes both on reservation and off; at various flea markets around the reservation; spending time with band members' extended families (mending fences, helping with family livestock branding); herding sheep and hauling water with my host sister and her auntie;[13] making purchases at reser-vation trading posts such as the one in Rough Rock, Arizona; and doing errands in Chinle at the tribal utility company, the tribal veterinary clinic, the chapter house, and the tribal college. Performative spaces where I also consistently spoke Navajo included onstage with band members when performing on reservation—

usually in the form of introducing my European "clans" in Navajo—and doing promotional spots for the band on local Navajo-language radio stations.[14]

I spoke Navajo much less when I was addressing Navajos forty years and younger—for example, with younger store clerks (such as at the Mustang gas station), older college-educated Navajos (they usually preferred to speak to me in English), older Navajos who attended Bureau of Indian Affairs (BIA) boarding schools and therefore were habituated to addressing Anglos in English, and during band rehearsals, which were usually code-mixed Navajo, English and, often for humorous effect, "Navadlish." Situations in which my Navajo sometimes failed me—or where I didn't have the comprehension and speaking ability I would have liked—included in ceremonial contexts, community chapter-house meetings, interacting with older speakers (usually male) when they were teasing me, and listening to political debates in Navajo.

My bandmates' own speaking abilities in Navajo varied, depending on factors such as age, where they were raised, their role as public figures, and their type of employment (a number are politicians or work for the tribe or the federal government's Department of the Interior). Each group I played with also had a slightly different opinion and understanding of my being an anthropologist and writing about my experiences. Some band members chose to speak to me in English only, while addressing each other primarily in Navajo. Most musicians asked that I use their real names, as they are proud to be identified with their artistic work, and each musician that I write about signed an informed consent form. The Wranglers' Carson Craig (of the Bit'ahnii, or Folded Arms People), for example, liked the idea of his daughter's band "going down in history," or at least in my book. Re-Coil's Steve Etsitty (of the Áshįįhí, or Salt Clan), who headed the Navajo Nation Environmental Protection Agency (NNEPA) and holds a graduate degree from Stanford, was supportive of the project but also somewhat wary about anthropology, explaining in detail to band members what participant-observation was and how it worked. On occasion, he would also sometimes out me onstage to fans between songs as "the cultural anthropologist studying everyone in the room." I read this as a sort of leveling maneuver, a way of not allowing me to get too comfortable in my role as either anthropologist or band member.

Native Country, and bandleader Tommy Bia (of the Naakaii Dine'é, or Mexican People Clan) in particular, seemed to accept my anthropological role as a non-negotiable part of the package, a quid pro quo for my musicianship. For me to play with Native Country, they understood that I would eventually need to have permission to write about their band. Tommy informed me early on that he had a younger brother with a Ph.D. in education, who worked as a high-level administrator at Pima Community College in Tucson. His brother had also done interviews and research on the reservation to gather data for his dissertation. At the same time, Tommy remained disinterested in the specifics of my research. Always direct, he told me, on reading my 2009 article about Native bands,[15] that he only has a high school education and that it all looked like gibberish to him. When I gave him a chapter draft focusing on Native Country, he responded again by saying he was too busy with his alfalfa farm and cattle ranch to sit down and read it, but followed this statement with "I trust you, Kris." While he supports what I'm doing educationally (he attended my graduation from Duke University with his family), he's also not especially interested in the particulars.

Historically, relations between anthropologists and Indians have been precarious at best, often fraught with tension, misunderstanding, and distrust. As I found, anthropology remains a politicized domain of knowledge production, and among a large number of my interlocutors, many of whom also have college degrees, I encountered varied and sometimes skeptical views of my role as someone "doing anthropology." I discovered, not unsurprisingly, how savvy many Navajos are, not only about anthropological method but also about the disciplinary politics of knowledge dissemination and the ramifications of research. After all, there is a reason that a widely circulating reservation joke about what a "typical" Navajo family looks like includes the punch line: "Mom, dad, son, daughter, and an anthropologist." For example, members of Re-Coil insisted on providing fairly minimal feedback on manuscript drafts with the explicit mandate that I "hurry up and publish the book." These discussions—ones which, I argue, wouldn't have occurred in this same fashion even fifty years ago—profoundly influenced the direction my research took; they speak to a relationship of equals and intellectual peers, in sharp contrast to the earlier perceived dynamic between the all-knowing anthropologist and the less formally educated research "subject." Consequently, the needs, desires, and intellectual interests of my Navajo interlocutors shaped much of my research and the writing of this book. And yet, at the same time, there is no denying my own racial privilege as a non-Navajo, amplified by my level of education, class positioning, and geographic mobility. These changing dynamics, I'm convinced, have profound ramifications not only for the nature of the shifting relationship between anthropology and Native North America (Deloria 1969; Starn 2011) but also for the ways we as anthropologists think about the field and the relevance of our scholarly interests for Indigenous communities when doing research.[16]

Each group of musicians I played with also expressed its understanding of anthropology as a politicized domain of knowledge production, albeit in slightly different ways. Overall, my fieldwork morphed from initial concern about whether I'd be accepted into a band to becoming, at times, a kind of low-level commodity because of my ability to play the lap steel guitar. My whiteness in particular became, for better and for worse, a trademark that identified a band and made it memorable, since an all-male Navajo band with a white female musician was considered a novelty. The bands I played with also regarded my whiteness and ability to speak some Navajo as an entertaining stage gimmick. In fact, I was frequently the only band member asked by the bandleader to introduce myself onstage in Navajo. For example, at the Albuquerque Centennial celebration in Old Town, Re-Coil's bassist Alfred Jim (A. J.) introduced me to the crowd as "the Navajo-speaking *Bilagáana* from Crownpoint [New Mexico]" and then asked me to introduce my "clans" — in this case, my four primary European ethnicities — in Navajo.[17]

Following a kinship system that Navajos often use to identify themselves to one another, throughout the book I include the names and primary (mother's) clans of those who knew and specified them to me on their informed consent forms (disclosing clan affiliation was optional). Although the mother's clan is the clan one is "born to" and is thought of as one's most important clan, Navajos with four Navajo grandparents will have four Navajo clans.

There are currently around sixty-six active Navajo clans,[18] and these groups are used to determine not only who one can and cannot marry but also allegiances, social status,[19] and structures of social reciprocity more broadly. In addition, there are a number of adopted clans that reflect not only early Navajo contact with other southwestern tribes but also Spanish (1539–1821) and Mexican (1821–48) occupations of what is now the southwestern United States (Thompson 2009).[20] Within the band context, clan relationships turned out to be important in band formation and in internal dynamics and loyalties,[21] often preventing bandleaders from outright firing other band members if they were related to one another by clan.

Yet there were also risks associated with having a voice onstage; my whiteness and my ability to speak Navajo sometimes proved a liability, especially in playing with a band named "Native" Country. By featuring a younger, Anglo female vocalist and steel player, Native Country opened itself up to critiques about how "authentic," "rez," or "Navajo" we sounded and looked. Oftentimes, this critique focused on the band name.

It's 8:00 A.M., and I am setting up for a show with Native Country. We are outside under a large, white tent in the small town of Chinle, Navajo Nation, Arizona. It's customer-appreciation day for the Navajo Tribal Utility Authority (NTUA), the tribally owned electric utility company, which has hired Native Country to entertain customers who show up at the event for free hotdogs, T-shirts, and key chains. It's windy, and red silt settles in our ears, covers our instruments, and blows into the black mesh of the public-address system and on top of the speaker cones, leaving a fine, dusty film over our entire setup. Gear ready to go and mic levels checked ("mic check, one, two, three, bíighah" [good/sufficient]), lead singer Tommy Bia and I begin looking over our set list, rehearsing last-minute changes to the duet "I've Got You" by Waylon Jennings and Anita Carter. Unplugged, our lead guitar player, LeAnder (of the Tó 'áheedlíinii, or Water Flows Together Clan), begins playing the chords to the song on his Fender Telecaster, as Arlondo (of the Tódích'íi'nii, or Bitter Water Clan), our drummer, is checking his bass-drum levels on his Ludwig drum set. We begin playing to a small crowd of middle-aged NTUA employees, customers, and the small fan base we've built over the last year and a half of playing together on and off the Navajo reservation.

Some couples begin to do the two-step, while others stand toward the back of the tent, "wallflowers" there to listen and observe. At the end of our first set, a middle-aged man yells out from the back of the tent, "You guys should call yourselves 'Native Country and Bilagáana Band!'" ["Native Country and the White Girl Band"]. Or, he adds in an animated voice, "Bilagáana and the Natives!" Some onlookers chuckle at the comment, and, as we begin our second set and Tommy introduces the band members, I am the only one asked to "introduce my clans" in Navajo.

Twenty minutes later, Tommy's vocal microphone makes a searing squawk mid-song and quits, as do our PA, our rainbow-colored strobe lights, and, in turn, the rest of the equipment. The irony isn't lost on anyone: the electricity is out at a celebratory event put on by the main supplier of electricity on the Navajo reservation. As we quickly pack up, we have a brief conversation about "dirty" power on the reservation, and then regroup at the A & W fast food joint around the corner to debrief. Responding to our fan's earlier comment, Tommy suggests that I add an eagle feather to my cowboy hat when I play to signal Native origins, or at least to buttress band-name credibility as Native Country. Arlondo chimes in: "Maybe you could say you're Lumbee or Cherokee?"

In our fan's suggestion that we change our band name to Native Country and *Bilagáana* Band, we see how Native bands in reservation spaces are expected to be both all-Navajo and all-male, because that's overwhelmingly the case and because deviance from that norm is called out as precisely that—deviant. In many ways, this marks a profound reversal of country music's perception nationwide: the genre is often described as "sounding white" and, in the Nashville version of country, often features female vocalists (but rarely female instrumentalists). On the other hand, *"Bilagáana* and the Natives" reverses this language, employing for ironic effect the othering language of early non-Native administrators and anthropologists who did sometimes refer to Navajo people as simply "the Natives." These power relations were always present, and as an Anglo woman, singer, and lapsteel player, my identity at this performance in particular was marked by virtue of my race, my gender, my class positioning, and the fact that I played a "male" lead instrument (the guitar).

In this case, my Anglo, female body and the fact that I would speak Navajo onstage sometimes posed a risk not only to the band but also to other Navajo listeners vis-à-vis their own authenticity and the racialization of the Diné language. This critique also extended to music genre and the perception that Native Country was bucking common musical practice on the reservation by covering the songs of female country artists such as Loretta Lynn, Linda Ronstadt, and Kitty Wells, in addition to performing the male "rez country" canon of Waylon Jennings, Merle Haggard, Johnny Horton, Gary Stewart, and at least one version of the song "Indian Cowboy." At the same time, fans also remembered and recognized us by virtue of these same social and sonic transgressions.

Perhaps the attempted policing of language, ethnicity, and gender erupts because of other ambient but pressing frustrations: infrastructural challenges tend to surround Native band performances, where access to a reliable power source isn't always a given and gas-powered generators are commonplace, even at an event hosted by a power company, and many bands have limited access to high-quality musical instruments, public-address systems, and recording equipment. The linguistic anthropologist David Samuels has referred to this phenomenon as the political economy of musical sound, where material constraints "enter into the imagination and production of cultural aesthetics" (2004, 203). Relationships to technology are thus under continual negotiation, and the technology in use directly impacts the sound of a band, its ability to produce its desired sound, and, consequentially, its perception in the community. This joining of infrastructure and social hierarchy to social citizenship and aesthetics also manifests itself in discussions of fluency, even among young Diné children.

> I am seated at the table with the daughter of a close friend from Many Farms, a small town within the Navajo Nation. In my sunny kitchen in Durham, North Carolina, a space far away from the reservation, seven-year-old Ashley relates her insights as a primary-school student with a Navajo mom and a Korean and French dad. As she carefully slices tomatoes for dinner, she tells how she one-upped a classmate from her rural reservation elementary school who was teasing her about her non-Navajo sounding last name during recess. Self-conscious about her French surname and the fact that she doesn't speak Navajo, Ashley went to her maternal grandmother for advice. Her *másání*, a Navajo speaker, told Ashley to address the male student by the Navajo version of his last name, Blacksheep—Dibélizhiní—to throw him off. Returning to school the next day, Ashley tried this tactic, appending a throaty "bah bah" for added effect at the end of the punch line. "And guess what?" she now announces, her eyes bright and animated: "It worked!" Her classmate got mad because he didn't understand what she was saying in Navajo, and eventually he stopped teasing her altogether. Triumphantly, she ends her story with the appraisal: ". . . and Kris: he's a full-blood Navajo, too!"

An analysis situated around voice reveals multilayered, generation-specific insights into cultural hierarchy, social citizenship, and belonging. Thus, while Ashley's "full-blood" classmate teased her about her non-Navajo sounding name, it turned out that he neither spoke nor understood Navajo himself. Once Ashley pulled the curtain back on this sociolinguistic disjuncture (Meek 2010), the two children became equals on a level playing field: he could no longer comfortably tease her as before. These voicing structures also include a strong emphasis on being locatably Navajo. Location here includes place of geographic origin and place-related dialectal distinctions so salient in Navajo spaces, but also the place of the tongue in the mouth when speaking, the linguistic sounds one can or cannot produce, the subtle habitual wrinkles of facial muscles as a by-product of these speaking abilities, and "how much Indian" one is considered to be (Barker 2011, 2), as measured bureaucratically by one's Certificate Degree of Indian Blood (CDIB).[22] Thus, while many younger children today have excellent passive fluency in Navajo, it's often difficult for them to confidently reproduce these same idiosyncratic Navajo sounds, such as ł; high nasal tones such as ą́, ę́, į́; glottal stops ('); and trigraphs (tl', ch', ts'). (Please refer to the "Note on Orthographic and Linguistic Conventions.")

Voiced another way, location in the linguistic sense is about the successful manipulation of breath or wind (*nítch'i*) in the body (McNeley 1981), the way in which glottal stops and air are first produced in the diaphragm, voiced in the throat, and constricted and then released in the epiglottis. But location is also about proper language use and knowing the cultural contexts where using one's heritage language is most appropriate, such as when to perform one's clan introduction—the same introduction I as an Anglo was asked to perform many times onstage throughout my fieldwork. Being locatably Navajo, therefore, is marked by place of origin and linguistic knowledge, but also by an overall heightened sensitivity to sound, identity, and to the politics of daily language use (Nevins 2013).

If we understand voice both in song and everyday speech as the instrument through which a politics of authenticity is expressed, we then see how voice and vocality not only join terms of linguistic approval and disapproval but also wed ideas of inclusion to exclusion, soul to spirit, head to chest, and metal to wood, to use some metaphors often employed to describe contrasting vocal sounds and ideologies. If words are the "sign" of the voice (Frith 1988, 121), voice is also the sign or signature of a person and therefore of a particular identity. As something that is "culturally inscribed" (Reed 1998, 526), voice is a primary sign of group social difference—this is often brought home over the telephone when we "identify" a speaker's region, race, education, and economic status through his or her voice alone.

At the same time, voice is also uniquely idiosyncratic and idiolectal, where individual ways of speaking and singing are brought to bear. Voice—this incredibly private, vulnerable instrument controlling our ability to speak and to sing—acts as the most official, representational part of our selves, the public sound of the self. Indeed, this is why something like vocal grain—often glossed as timbre or tone color, although it's also much more than that—is so deeply personal; to criticize someone's voice is akin to attacking (and often silencing) a person's core identity (Barthes 1985; Harkness 2013), and to lose one's vocal apparatus is often experienced as a fundamental loss of the self. This is evident in discussions, for example, surrounding the current critique of female news anchors and radio commentators where the phenomenon of both upspeak and vocal fry—what linguists refer to as "creaky voice"—are pathologized by older listeners as both "unhealthy" and "annoying" and are effectively used as mechanisms for silencing these same voices on air (Eckert 2003).

In another instance of voice and identity, the drummer of Native Country inadvertently criticized the voice of another Native band's lead singer during a recording session by telling him to "sing normal," and their relationship has never been quite the same since. In this case, this lead singer was deeply influenced by the vibrato-heavy singing style of hard country icon Gary Stewart (1944–2003), and incorporated a very fast, dramatically wide vibrato when singing most country songs. Some listeners hear this sound, a part of this Diné singer's vocal fingerprint, as reminiscent of Gary Stewart's singing and appreciate the trip down memory lane; others hear it as contrived and out of place and this, in turn, has affected his reception and fan base when playing in on-reservation venues. Our voices are so deeply naturalized and unconscious, so unique to our sense of self and so specific to our individual bodies—chest size, vocal cavity, position of the larynx, diction and dialect—that there's often nothing we can do to change the foundational elements of our voices, even if we were determined to (accent-reduction therapy notwithstanding). Looking at voice in Indigenous contexts therefore offers us a window not only into identity, authenticity, and cultural politics but also provides insight into perceptions of social difference, civic estrangement, and the role aesthetics plays in senses of belonging.

Navajo Country

Understanding Navajo expressive culture begins with understanding who Diné peoples are geographically, that is, who Dine'é are with respect to where they live. Thus, grasping Navajo country music begins with knowing Navajo territory or country. *Country* is a word that does triple work. It can refer to a genre of music, a nation-state, and also a specific type of place within a nation ("the country"), most often rural.[23] The country often represents everything that the city is not: the idea of a natural way of life and associations of "peace, innocence, and simple virtue" (Williams 1973, 1), but perceptions of backwardness and anti-cosmopolitanism also often gather around all things "country." Cities, by contrast, are associated with centers of learning, achievement, communication, and upward mobility, but also social disconnection, anomie, and aggressive self-aggrandizement. Thus, country and city stand in for the perceived crises of global modernity, existing in continual opposition and relation to one another, a type of "boundary contestation" (Dent 2009) where country and city define each other as much by what they are as by what they are not (Williams 1973, 7, 290–91).

If the word *country* is an ideologically charged, multivalent term, so too is the musical genre that often becomes synonymous with rurality, rusticity, simplicity, and the various ideologies, both idealized and pejorative, that accompany a "country" lifestyle (Darling 2009; Gibson and Davidson 2004; Malone 2006; Peterson 1997; Strom 2013; Willman 2005). Indeed, the thematic content of many American country songs is profoundly place-based, emphasizing tropes of the nation, the hometown, rural upbringing, and nostalgia for times, places, and kinship now disappeared.[24]

Like the country itself, country music is highly contested, a genre criticized for its reputed whiteness, its clichés, its obsessive narrational style, its "twang" (Samuels in Duranti 2004; Mann 2008),[25] and the perception that it gratuitously wears its heart on its sleeve. Country music is also notorious for its emphasis on heteronormative romantic love and class-inflected thematics of upwardly mobile, blue-blooded women and their rural-identified, redneck men (Fox 2004a, 244–45). On the other hand, there is something very rigid about the coinciding expectation that one live the lifestyle one sings about.[26] If an entertainer does not come off as "true country," the authenticity of his or her performance itself comes into question (Peterson 1997); to defy this expectation leaves a performer open to the charge of being a "hat act" (Lewis 1997, 164; Peterson 2004, 98). Understanding Diné expressive culture and Indian country music therefore means looking not only at musical performance but also at other spheres of speech, place, and performance where authenticity and belonging are at stake.

Country music's fixation on authenticity and its performance constructs a straightjacket imposed on many Indigenous peoples, including Navajos. As we see in country, the rigid demarcations of supposedly authentic Native identity enforced by both non-Natives and, in some cases, Native peoples themselves, demand that Indigenous peoples follow a certain kind of lifestyle—living in a traditional dwelling place such as a teepee, speaking one's heritage language or speaking English with a "rez" accent, or being knowledgeable about one's "culture"—in a certain kind of place, most often a rural one such as a reservation, reserve, or Indigenous homeland.[27] And, as in country performance, if these expectations aren't met, sometimes the performance itself—of one's identity, of one's authenticity, of one's right to claim and celebrate one's Native identity—becomes open to question and critique. Dialect, rurality, and performance are expected to coincide, and when they don't, one risks being labeled as inauthentic or even charged with "playing Indian" (Deloria 1998; Green 1998; Hitt 2005; Sturm 2011). In Navajo parlance, these charges sometimes take the form of one citizen referring to another as an "apple," or someone who is "red" on the outside but "white" on the inside, or even as an "urban Navajo."

From a less charitable perspective, country is also sometimes associated with a defensive articulation of whiteness, where racist or racialist ideologies prevail (Fox 2004a, 25). From this vantage point, southern, white-identified, working-class men are ostensibly the main fans and performers of country music. However, as Jerry Wever (forthcoming and 2011) and others have convincingly argued,[28] country is by no means exclusively enjoyed or performed by white people, and probably never was (Malone 1985). Indeed, the genre's origins are inseparable from rural African American music including the blues, country blues, and string band traditions, and iconic country instruments such as the banjo are widely acknowledged to be Afro-diasporic in origin (Epstein 1975; Coolen 1984). As Aaron Fox suggests, country's main demographic in the United States may now be suburban, Midwestern moms, and not, as one might be led to believe, southern white men.[29]

In fact, since its first widespread commercial dissemination in the 1930s, country music has been consumed and produced by Indigenous communities as far-reaching as Alaska, Canada, Brazil, Australia, Hawai'i and Kenya, to name but a few. If the genre sometimes calls people to their whiteness, a process Mann refers to as "musical interpellation" (2008, 87), country music calls people with equal force to working-class Indigenous identities too. This Indigenous connection to country music is often heightened by the lyrical content and country's iconic crying vocal style,[30] where songs about heartache, pain, civic disenfranchisement, and land dispossession map directly onto contemporary Indigenous experiences of settler colonialism and intergenerational trauma. This holds especially true for rural Indigenous communities such as the Navajo who ranch, and where country music and rodeos have gone hand in hand since the early 1940s. Because of the marked, class-based identities shared by many working-class whites and working-class Indigenous peoples, country music can and does powerfully call people to their Navajoness too, traveling and transforming itself in the process.

Country music travels because its themes map onto working-class consciousness, and thus it is transposed and recalibrated—musically, linguistically and geographically—in the process. An analysis of expressive culture in this context is therefore not just about music or the arts, but it also centrally includes the everyday speech that, together with country performance, reveals the politics

MAP 2. The Navajo Nation (Based on a map first published in Peter Iverson, *Diné: A History of the Navajos* [2002].)

of authenticity and belonging for today's Diné citizens. It is incumbent on us, to now turn our attention to this place known as the Navajo Nation or *Diné Bikéyah*.

Located in the region of the American Southwest known as the Four Corners, the Navajo Nation spans 27,000 square miles, roughly the size of West Virginia, and the main reservation covers portions of Arizona, New Mexico, and Utah.[31] While about 288,000 Diné citizens live on the reservation per the 2010 census, an additional 44,398 individuals live off reservation in more urban areas such as Phoenix, Albuquerque, Denver, and Los Angeles,[32] making the total number of enrolled Diné citizens about 332,000. In comparison to many other Indigenous nations in the United States, the Navajo language is actively spoken by approximately three-quarters of tribal citizens, or 73 percent of on-reservation Diné. However, the ratio of older to younger speakers is uneven and, bringing to mind country music's generational divide referenced earlier, most self-identified fluent speakers are predominantly over the age of forty; more specifically and due to differential educational policies, individuals aged forty to fifty-five are usually fully bilingual in English and Navajo, and folks sixty-five and older speak English, also, but are often Navajo-dominant. Many individuals under forty, including some of the band members with whom I played, are passively fluent, or can understand what is said to them, but aren't comfortable speaking Navajo themselves.

Understanding Key Terms

Fluency, of course, exists along a continuum, and being designated as such is as much about social status, cultural knowledge, gender, senses of belonging, and the right to speak as it is about a speaker's actual linguistic competence (Debenport 2015, 19; Nevins 2013). Expanding on the ways in which fluency, language ideologies, and aesthetics intersect and are used strategically to assay social citizenship, therefore, is one of the major aims of this book.

Very few Diné speakers read and write their heritage language, including the majority of musicians I chronicle in *The Sound of Navajo Country*. However, in contrast to the secrecy and concerns regarding the circulation of written texts that we see at San Ramon Pueblo (Debenport 2015, 6) and among other New Mexico Pueblos,[33] written forms of Navajo—including dictionaries, grammars, curricular materials, phone apps, and even the new Navajo Rosetta Stone program[34]—are encouraged by the Navajo tribe, and basic language literacy is taught in many reservation schools. In fact, Navajo citizens often discuss Navajo in its written form as not only demonstrating the continued vitality of the language, for outsiders in particular, but they also see written Navajo as a contemporary expression of tribal sovereignty and diplomacy, where Navajo achieves the status of a "global language" (Vice President Rex Lee Jim, July 2013, Navajo Language Institute).[35]

Navajos are also known as a largely endogamous tribal nation, with most Navajos marrying other Navajos. This results in a citizenry with a fairly high percentage of "Navajo blood," such that 86 percent (286,000) of Navajo citizens self-reported being "full-blooded" or "full Navajo," as it is sometimes termed locally, in the 2010 Census (Yurth 2012). The majority of these individuals also reported living on one of the four Navajo reservations, which perpetuates the perception within Diné communities that living on the reservation, having Navajo "blood," and speaking Navajo are linked.

Like other performative categories of identity, however, *blood* is a constructed social category that is contingent and negotiated, playing a crucial role in the politics of authenticity and belonging. Because it is naturalized in conversation as concerning biology, however, blood as a category often goes unmarked, both in Diné-based local discourse and sometimes within U.S. news media and earlier anthropological scholarship. While scholarly attention in critical Indigenous studies has focused on the ways that blood, like race, constitutes a social construct, newer works have shown us (Bond, Brough, and Cox 2014) that blood and "blood talk" prove socially meaningful for Diné citizens who employ these terms. Blood signifies broadly and deeply, functioning as an index for a host of authenticity markers. Thus this book seeks to balance two perspectives: the socially constructed nature of blood, on the one hand, and the ways in which this category is socially real across generational divides for many of my Diné interlocutors, on the other.

Throughout *The Sound of Navajo Country*, I distinguish between blood quantum as it is discussed in biomedical terms via percentages and fractions, and "blood talk" (Bond, Brough, and Cox 2014) or "blood quantum logic" (Kauanui 208, 2) as a discourse for community, belonging, and connections to Diné cultural tradition (Allen 2002). In both cases, blood is often used conversationally as a placeholder to refer to phenotype, where the more "blood" one has, the more "Navajo" one looks. To be clear: blood quantum is never an actual measurement of one's Navajo or Native blood, nor does a genetic test exist that distinguishes Indigenous blood from other blood types. Similarly, despite many attempts within and outside Navajo country to observe and verify Native blood via skin color (Bond, Brough, and Cox 2014, 6), there is no direct corollary between having Navajo ancestry and one's physical appearance. Rather, blood quantum as it appears on a CDIB card reflects what has been passed down in the administrative record on a given citizen based on a combination of happenstance and history: "Blood quantum is a fractionalizing measurement—a calculation of 'distance' in relation to some supposed purity to mark one's generational proximity to a 'full-blood' forebear" (Kauanui 2008, 2). "Looking Navajo," by contrast, locally constitutes a complicated mix of biology, lifestyle, body language, outsider and insider expectations, and self-identification. As in the Aboriginal Australian context, blood talk in Diné contexts casts a wide net, where "to talk about blood is to talk about temperament, kinship, ancestry, ethnicity and spirituality, as well as human body functions and physiology" (Bond, Brough, and Cox 2014, 2). This conflation of blood quantum with language and authenticity, or what Barker terms "biological-as-cultural difference" (2011, 6), undergirds the micropolitics of difference that I interrogate in this book. Registers of authenticity are indexed within the Navajo Nation through a set of widely shared, commonly used terms referencing blood quantum, heritage-language abilities, place of residence, and taste. These terms can be parsed as designations of linguistic approval traced throughout this study—*full blood, full Navajo, traditional, deep rez, real rez, mono, Diné*, and *old Navajo*—and go along in discursive frequency and intensity with terms of linguistic disapproval, including *jaan, apple, generic, urban Navajo*, and even *New Mexico Navajo*. Both sets of terms speak to the privileged currency of cultural distinction and affiliation that permeates many layers of Navajo discourse, private and public. These denotations also demonstrate beyond a doubt how varying identities become attached to different Navajo-speaker types, often in essentializing ways.

With this book, I make two broad interventions. First, I argue that, rather than being one all-encompassing category, authenticity takes multiple shapes, forming in response to differing expectations and performing various kinds of cultural work (Bigenho 2002). By looking at sound—in other words, country music yet also spoken everyday language—as it relates to the politics of difference n the Navajo Nation, we can understand these ideologies of authenticity more deeply and with a fuller appreciation for the promises and pitfalls of realness as they apply to Indigenous peoples. My second intervention is to argue that sound itself is directly linked to politics, where associations between identity, nation, belonging, and the utterances a person makes together form, building on Mauss (1966), a "total sonorous fact" of contemporary Diné identity. I draw attention to ideologies that accord sound prominence to make this linkage explicit and self-evident, showing how some sounds are connected with cultural, political, and financial capital, while others are associated with civic estrangement.

In this study of contemporary identity politics and an aesthetics of cultural intimacy, a more specific application of *expressive culture*,[36] one centered around singing and speaking—vocal timbre, singing style, vocal register, dialect, idiolect, personal dialect, and speaking voice—takes center stage. I analyze sound in its broader musical and linguistic sense, including everyday speech, stage patter, casual conversation, personal interviews, political speeches, response cries, jokes, dialect, humorous burlesque, AM radio airplay, and musically organized sound in the form of jam sessions and band performances. Here, I understand the speaking voice as being equally central as the singing voice in illuminating the nuance of Diné politics of authenticity and belonging. This is because all these vocal qualities feed into an understanding of Diné country music and the unique social space it occupies on Navajo land. For example, volume, speech style, and vocal tone color (timbre) come to implicitly code upbringing, place of origin, and cultural orientation, where women raised in traditional reservation families often speak more softly than men and rarely sing in public, and men from similar families may employ a more forced or pharyngealized speaking and singing register as a marker of their masculinity. Men who employ unusual vocal timbres and tessituras or vocal ranges—for example, by speaking or singing in a higher register or using a smoother speaking voice with less pharyngealization (rougher-sounding vocal quality)—are sometimes deemed to sound "less Navajo," "like a lady" or even "like a *bilagáana*."

Cultural intimacy has long been overlooked as a site of analysis within Indigenous communities,[37] in part because outsider expectations—many of them influenced by anthropology's own disciplinary origins and focus—were placed on Native peoples to perform their authenticity in prescriptive ways signaling cultural continuity. Yet part of taking tribal sovereignty and Indigenous nationhood seriously means examining such intimate, national practices as they are perceived and received *within* the boundaries of Indigenous territories. Thus I foreground the internal differences and aesthetic shifts that characterize all human communities but that, in the case of Native North America, anthropologists have often depicted as monolithic and unchanging. Cultural intimacy was first defined by Herzfeld as the embarrassing aspects of cultural identity that "nevertheless provide insiders with their assurance of common sociality" (1997, 3) and has also been described as "the rueful self-recognition that comes with certain practices thought to be crucial to national identity, but which are nonetheless somewhat embarrassing" (Dent 2009, 12). I emphasize the socially constructed boundaries of cultural intimacy, erected specifically through locally inflected speech and music genre, where the embarrassment often cleaves along on-reservation/off-reservation lines. Cultural intimacy in a study of Navajo country bands offers us a unique window into a musical genre rarely performed for—or intended to be heard by—outsiders beyond the boundaries of the Nation and where, as a result, embarrassment surrounding these sounds abounds.

Native or *rez band* music is sometimes deemed by insiders as being "not very good," "all rezzed out," or even as "bad" music (Washburne and Derno 2004). I argue that this is in part because many Navajo performances of country music don't "wink" (Dent 2009, 105), that is, they don't signal an ironic distance from the music genre and generational nostalgia they are performing and reenacting. For example, when sharing that I studied, played, and hung out with rez bands with other Navajo citizens during my fieldwork, I often fielded responses of amusement, embarrassment, discomfort, and even incredulity, sometimes followed by suggestions that I study a more "authentically Navajo" genre of music. Suggestions included song and dance,[38] "peyote songs,"[39] Native American flute music, or other music genres deemed traditional by non-Natives and that, through no coincidence, are mostly off limits to scholars as mandated by the Navajo Nation Institutional Review Board (NNIRB) and Navajo Nation Historic Preservation Department (NNHPD). Such responses were particularly vociferous from citizens living off the reservation and by those who identified with a higher socioeconomic status, including politicians, educators, and tribal college administrators. Native band music isn't made for outsider ears such as my own, and when outsiders do listen, there is some embarrassment associated with it. Thus the terms I discuss ethnographically throughout the book—*jaan*, rez, "redskin," the chapter-house beat, and comedian Vincent Craig's use of "Navadlish"[40]—cohere through a focus on how culturally intimate forms circulate within the Nation and how these genres are transformed, hidden, or elided when circulating beyond Diné borders.

Generational nostalgia is a term I use to describe the heightened affection many older Diné have for older country music and its associated worlds. If nostalgia is defined as "an essential, narrative function of language that orders events temporally and dramatizes them" (Stewart 1988, 227) around themes of pleasure and sadness, then the pleasure and sadness associated with listening to rez bands is as much about heritage language and cultural continuity as it is about music. This generational nostalgia also remembers a Navajo Nation that, in the 1950s, was becoming financially self-sufficient with the discovery of uranium (*łéétso*) and uranium mining, however bittersweet that legacy may seem today (Brugge, Benally, and Yazzie-Lewis 2007; Powell 2017). Rez bands and rez band music summon this total sonorous fact, transporting older listeners to a longed-for place, time, and emotional space in ways that, arguably, only sound and the sensorium can do. This generational aesthetic, in turn, holds weight among on-reservation Diné young and old where, as fluent Navajo speakers and culturally knowledgeable elders, older generations possess a cultural capital in the current climate of language revitalization and renewed attention given to Navajo culture and tradition.

Country Music That Doesn't Wink:
Nostalgia, Nationalism, and Social Class

Generational nostalgia and cultural intimacy have been persistent themes in the history of country music, with the common refrain that country music "isn't what it used to be." The embarrassment associated with country's early hillbilly image, for example, acted as the catalyst for major changes in the sound of country music, including the development of the slicker so-called Nashville sound in the late 1950s, an attempt to legitimize country in the eyes of commercial music moguls and upwardly mobile listeners and performers (Pecknold 2007). The embarrassment surrounding country music as a national U.S. practice thus marks a partial rejection of a working-class identity and also forms part of what I argue makes people either love or hate country music, with very little room in between these polarized camps. In some ways, however, Navajos have embraced country music more completely and with less seeming embarrassment than the U.S. population at large, due perhaps in part to the large percentage of on-reservation Dine'é who identify solidly—and unapologetically—as blue-collar and working-class.

Although many Navajos know that country is often heard as sounding white to non-Native ears, this plays out differently within the boundaries of the Navajo Nation, where musicians and fans often explicitly frame country as a traditional genre of Diné music. In fact, country music has long been the popular music genre of choice on the Navajo Nation, and since the 1950s, Navajo bands have been performing covers of well-known country songs, and sometimes writing originals as well. Indeed, the local versions of these cover songs are so well known that, when listeners called in during a request and dedication hour on the tribal radio station when I worked there,[41] requestors would typically identify the desired cover song and then specify the Native band version they wanted to hear, such as a request for "'Picking White Gold' performed by the Navajo Sundowners,[42] rather than by the original recording artist, Waylon Jennings (Jacobsen 2009).[43] Certain cover songs thus come to act as signature tunes for specific bands, often "so closely associated with particular singers in the community to act almost like fingerprints" (Samuels 2004b, 338; see also Samuels 2009).

Today, Native bands continue to perform songs from a selective canon of hard country tunes, including covers by artists such as Gary Stewart, Johnny Horton, Merle Haggard, and Waylon Jennings. (The late Waylon Jennings in particular enjoys almost cult-like status on the reservation, and Waylon is a common first and middle name for middle-aged Navajo men.)[44] Building on country music as Navajo music, country is sometimes referred to as a traditional Navajo music genre and sometimes, as I found ethnographically, referred to as the "national" musical style of the Navajo Nation. Thus Navajo identity, tradition, nation, and cultural intimacy are often fused in Diné country music, and bands that choose to perform country frequently extol and defend it as a bona fide Diné aesthetic, one that speaks to and about Navajo lives in profound and even uncanny ways. Examining country music in this and other Indigenous contexts can therefore afford us deeper conceptions of Native tradition, modernity, and how Indigenous peoples navigate their self-representation in the contemporary moment.

Singing style and voice also feature prominently in discussions about country music performance. Most Navajo traditional healer-singers (hataałii) are men. Similarly, Native band vocalists are typically male, and they often sing and speak with a rougher, or more pharyngealized, tone. The signification is reflexive, with these characteristics in turn becoming important expressive resources for enacting contemporary forms of Navajo masculinity through country performance. In reading gendered identities out of country performance and mapping them onto a broader Diné politics of difference, I find that musicians who venture beyond these expected parameters—female vocalists who sing in a lower, supposedly manly range, male musicians who harmonize and sing the "girl" part, musicians who play blues instead of country, vocalists who don't speak their heritage language or sing the "wrong" kind of country music such as pop country[45]—often face exclusion from the reservation music community and encounter difficulty getting on-reservation gigs.

Within that ethnographically discerned framework of authenticity, I build on political identity and citizenship within the Navajo Nation—a given for most of the musicians and Navajo speakers I worked with—to examine social citizenship and civic belonging. As I found, political and social citizenship are not interchangeable, and the painful gap between them is but one example of the ways in which settler colonialism—ongoing forms of colonial occupation focused on the appropriation of Indigenous land by colonizing settler powers—weaves its way into everyday Diné lives.[46] As a category, social citizenship is less inclusive than the broader, political identity of being an enrolled Navajo. Building on Rosaldo's idea of "cultural citizenship" (1994), defined as the everyday cultural practices used by citizens to "claim space and their right to be full members of society,"[47] social citizenship emphasizes the sometimes exclusive and difficult-to-pinpoint thing that is belonging and the ways this ground can shift from moment to moment in various social settings. The stakes of such civic estrangement (Tillet 2009, 125), however, are high, and their effects are keenly felt by all (Dennison 2012, 67). As Audra Simpson notes about belonging for Mohawk nationals from the Kahnawake Reserve, "The ongoing conditions of settler colonialism have forced Kahnaawa'kehron:non to take an offensive position not just against the settler nation, but in some ways *against themselves*. This position then manifests . . . in vexed determinations of 'membership' and belonging in that state" (2014, 12). Navajo musicians are attentive to these distinctions; the desire for inclusion influences a band's target audience, the type of PA it might use, the thickness of a singer's reservation accent when singing on-reservation or in a border town, the radio stations a band seeks to receive airplay on (or, as I show, sometimes refuses), and whether vocalists insert Navajo words into English-language songs.

In the United States, as elsewhere, class is crucial to deeming certain forms of culture palatable and others less so. Standardized monoglot speech forms (Silverstein 1996) and more esoteric musical genres such as opera and jazz are often associated with upward mobility and cultural capital. The Navajo Nation is hardly immune to class-based music genre and speech-style distinctions, but they take on locally nuanced meanings and are often more generation-, gender- and place-specific. Sounding "like a rez band," for example, may feel embarrassing to some, but rez bands are also assigned a covert prestige, which in turn has important ramifications for how Navajo a band sounds—or is perceived to sound—on the reservation. Moreover, where a band chooses to play and the songs a band opts to perform (for instance, playing in bars versus in "dry" reservation venues) target different age groups of fans and signal a band's stance about its own relation to place.

My particular interest in linking cultural geography to a politics of difference also stems from the internal divisions I observed within Navajo communities, where there is always a "deeper rez" somewhere beyond the horizon.[48] These discourses are often parsed along the lines of Arizona Navajos—who live on contiguous reservation land and often have larger landholdings—as being more authentic and living on the "real" or "deep" rez. In contrast, New Mexico Navajos often see themselves (and sometimes are seen by their Arizona counterparts) as being less Navajo because they live on a noncontiguous, checkerboarded land base,[49] and because they (allegedly) have fewer fluent Navajo speakers, particularly among youth. It was helpful to explore class-based cultural tension and cleavage through the lenses of geographic and linguistic distinction that tend to fall along these territorial lines.

Physical appearance, or phenotype, doesn't sift out in the same ways, but it also plays a role in a Navajo politics of authenticity. Particularly in the case of Navajos who hold public office or are in the public eye for other reasons, the criteria for assessing Navajo identity become increasingly narrow and prescriptive and sometimes echo dominant U.S. racial ideologies based on phenotype. The "one-drop rule," or law of hypodescent (Harris 1964, 56; Kauanui 2008, 14), where one drop of African American blood makes one black, is undeniably operative, but it contrasts with the more malleable, non–race-based criteria historically used by Dine'é to determine cultural affiliation and belonging (Denetdale 2006; Lee 2012). Kinship, matrilineal clan, clan adoption, and place affiliations have held sway in the past, and scholars have shown that such measures preceded scientific reckonings of racial belonging within Navajo and many other Native communities in the United States.[50] For example, it was common for Diné communities to adopt Hispanic and other Native war captives—mostly women and children—and then fully incorporate them into Diné society, where they were given equal social status as other Diné community members (Thompson 2009, 134). Today, however, "blood" comes to be understood differentially; that is, so-called white blood, black blood, and Indian blood take on contrasted social meanings: according to a one-drop logic, black admixture is understood to "pollute" and overshadow one's Indianness, but white admixture is understood to merely "dilute" or become subsumed into one's Indian blood.[51] White blood is also linked to a social mobility in ways that black blood often is not. Thus cultural constructions of blood are strategically linked to systems of power and privilege where, crucially, "the 'inauthentic' status of Natives is a condition for sovereign dispossession in the service of settler colonialism" (Kauanui 2008, 25).

Yet playing country music and speaking Navajo often replace phenotype as key "ethnic tropes" (Fast 2002) employed by Navajos in assessing the Indigenous authenticity of compatriots. Thus one essentialism of Navajo identity—that of the fluent heritage language speaker or rez band musician—replaces or builds on another, a racialized one based on phenotype. As a result, race and looking phenotypically Navajo are often equated with Navajo language fluency.

My interrogation of language also builds on the assumption that musically organized sound is inseparable from social practice and cultural politics.[52] For anthropologists of music and language, this means that the study of music and the human voice can enable us to track social experiences and relations in sometimes unexpected ways.[53] Through an emphasis on the voice as a site of both public performativity and a poetics of intimacy, this research builds on scholarship coming from the ethnography of communication,[54] as well as the politics of Indigeneity, bloodedness, and belonging.[55] It becomes clear that the Navajo singing and speaking voice joins aesthetics to politics (Jacobsen-Bia 2014; Meintjes 2004).

Recent scholarship within Native American and Indigenous studies has often focused on the larger-scale meanings of tribal sovereignty: global Indigenous politics, legal status, recognition, and relations between Native nations, counties, states, and the nation-states that surround these nations. By contrast, the present book takes an ethnographic, ethnomusicological, and sociolinguistic approach to foreground the everyday aesthetics of Indigenous cultural politics. To put it another way, while larger political structures undeniably impact lived experience and affect daily senses of self in relation to community, focusing on aesthetics gives us a window into the culturally intimate and negotiated aspects of this lived experience. So it is productive to join an aesthetics of the speaking and singing voice to a broader politics of voice and Indigenous identity.[56] Analyzing voice marks an entry point into Indigenous identity politics and social hierarchy as seen, for example, in who has the authority to sing or speak for whom (Dinwoodie 1998; Moore 1988) and which contexts—musical, geographic, or otherwise—give one more or less leeway to do so.

Arizona Navajo experience often stands in for all Diné experience, with the perspectives of New Mexico and Utah Navajos often hidden from view, particularly in regards to the representativeness of expressive cultural forms including weaving, silversmithing, language, and music. From this perspective, it is significant that all Navajo Nation chairmen and presidents, from 1923 to the present, have hailed from the Arizona side of the reservation, with the exception of two recent officeholders (the current president, Russell Begaye, and the former president, Ben Shelly) who both hail from the New Mexico (no candidate from Utah has ever won).[57] Therefore this study begins by looking at country music through the lens of geography (in particular through discussions of difference between the Arizona and New Mexico portions of the rez), focusing on the use of the culturally intimate term *jaan*, or "john," to describe rural, "hick," or hillbilly reservation identities. I then turn to country vocalist, drummer, and bandleader Candice Craig (of the *Kinyaa'áanii*, or Towering House Clan), analyzing how class, place-based, and *jaan* identities are reflected and parodied in her own performances of Merle Haggard's "Okie from Muskogee" and Gretchen Wilson's "Redneck Woman." Here, I analyze Craig's embrace of a working-class "rezneck" sociophonetic identity as a refusal to adhere to race- and place-based definitions of Diné identity, stretching the boundaries of what it means for a Navajo female performer to sound and be Diné.

After establishing the centrality of place and social class in Navajo country music, I then examine language and social authenticity as it relates to Diné expressive culture through the lens of musical and linguistic genre. Here I focus on the speaking voice in the context of intimate, everyday discourse such as band rehearsals, on-stage patter, and recurring references to *jaan* identities as they relate to nostalgia in musical performance. I interrogate ethnographically the expectation that full Navajos should speak Navajo or need merely activate the Navajo language gene that resides within them. In these ways, the perception of speaking the Navajo language shifts from being an index of Navajo identity to an icon of Navajoness itself.

But what about those Navajo singers whose ability to pass the blood-quantum litmus test isn't quite as secure? To examine this question, I turn next to the story of the first biracial, Navajo–African American Miss Navajo Nation, Radmilla Cody (born to Tł'ááschí'í, or Red Cheek People Clan). Fluent in Navajo and raised by her maternal grandmother on the Navajo Nation, I show how Radmilla's singing voice, by performing traditional yet R&B–inflected songs in the Navajo language, signals both inclusion and exclusion within Navajo communities. Here, sounding other than Navajo indicates a way of refusing to adhere to the ascribed status of Diné identity, including phenotype. Radmilla's voice signifies the intricacies of Diné social difference and a meeting point of the singular and the social: as something innate and idiosyncratic to each singer and speaker, voice is also something learned, socially acquired, and culturally inscribed.

Following this discussion of how sound becomes racialized and quantified, I then interrogate what is defined as "sounding Navajo" and what happens when someone refuses to adhere to these expectations. Looking at how gender, nation, and the idea of a prescriptive Navajo sound intertwine, I show ethnographically how Navajo blues and rock bands are often told they don't sound Navajo by local radio station deejays who refuse to play them on air. Instead, these deejays insist that sounding Navajo is defined as a male vocalist singing either Anglo-affiliated genres such as country music, or genres historically associated with Navajo tradition, such as social dance and ceremonial songs. Tracing why Navajo identity came to be aligned with country music, the rez accent, and the male singing voice through the work of the late singer and comedian Vincent Craig, it becomes clear how Navajo musical taste is inflected by class, generation, and gender ideologies.

I conclude by reflecting on how Diné citizens negotiate a politics of difference and belonging — and the idea of Indigenous social authenticity more broadly. Focusing on the language fluency controversy in the most recent Navajo presidential election (Thompson and Jacobsen, forthcoming), I address what the stakes might be in reifying social difference through the lenses of linguistic knowledge and performance, place of residence, musical taste, and phenotype. Bringing together ethnomusicology, linguistic anthropology, and critical Indigenous studies, I examine the parts of Navajo identity that are either publicly celebrated or hidden from view, and I interrogate what these categories of difference mean for those who utilize — or refuse — them today.

CHAPTER ONE

Keeping up with the Yazzies

The Authenticity of Class and Geographic Boundaries

"Do you guys know any songs?" I asked the Aleuts.

"I know all of Hank Williams," the elder Aleut said.

"How about Indian songs?"

"Hank Williams is Indian."

"How about sacred songs?"

"Hank Williams is sacred."

— Sherman Alexie (Spokane/Coeur d'Alene,

"What You Pawn I Will Redeem," *New Yorker*, 2003)

I am talking with Kornell Johns, the lead guitarist for Dennis Yazzie and the Night Breeze Band, a well-loved group from Eastern Navajo Agency, a portion of the reservation on the New Mexico side. They're about to play a show in Navajo Technical College's multipurpose room for students living on campus.[1] Johns is talking about the Navajo reservation battle-of-the-bands competitions he's participated in with Night Breeze, and his perception that the judges care as much about geography as they do about music. "If we play a Battle of the Bands in New Mexico," he says, "there's a chance we'll win. If we play in Arizona, the prize almost always goes to an 'Arizona' band. Where you're from matters."

Indeed, in playing at and attending numerous Native band competitions, mostly on the Arizona side of the reservation, I noticed that prizes did often go to Arizona bands. Moreover, the Arizona side of the reservation has access to more infrastructure and resources — such as Window Rock's Naakai Hall — than the New Mexico side of the rez. These state discrepancies are also reflected in tribal politics where, until the most recent presidential election, all Navajo Nation presidents hailed from the Arizona side of the reservation and all vice presidents came from the New Mexico side (there has yet to be a president or vice president from Utah).

Johns's commentary invokes discourses of east and west: state boundary lines demarcate differing perceptions of Navajo identity. While numerous dialectal differences exist for speakers from the Arizona and New Mexico portions of the reservation—for instance, *gohwééh* (Arizona) versus *ahwééh* (New Mexico) for "coffee" or *yás* (Arizona) versus *zás* (New Mexico) for "snow"—these linguistic divisions also speak to a larger sense of perceived cultural difference and the internal social hierarchies of Navajo authenticity. The Chuska Mountains, running north-south along the Arizona–New Mexico border, act as the symbolic dividing line between east and west, and between supposedly traditional and assimilated identities, with the western part of the reservation often fixed as more authentic and the locus of Navajo traditionality. While a Navajo homeland and Navajo sovereignty long preceded the demarcation of state boundaries and the birth of the United States, these constructed categories offer insight into larger debates about place, authenticity, and belonging in the Indigenous Americas and beyond. Here I highlight these themes through an analysis of origin narratives, language ideologies, the Navajo "hick" or *jaan*, and rural, class-based identities as they surface in the evocative songs of the country singer Candice Craig, based in Crownpoint, New Mexico.

In his provocatively titled article, "Why Does Country Music Sound White?" (2008), Geoff Mann attempts to denaturalize the supposed linkage between whiteness and country music, arguing that whiteness is not *reflected* in country music so much as self-consciously produced and reinstantiated by it (75). Using country music as a way to explain how race can be overdetermined through the idea of musical genre, Mann shows how country music, through its use of linguistic and instrumental twang, acts as a narrative cultural practice, something people tell themselves *about* themselves, where supposed racial authenticity is created through the genre's reiterative performances. Here I argue that, given the long and deep history of Navajos performing country music in reservation spaces, it is not just whiteness but also a generation-specific, class-based Indigenous identity that is produced and affirmed through the genre of country music. Country, for many Navajos in their forties and older, indexes a twentieth-century version of Navajo tradition—it offers us a window into a contemporary Navajo politics of difference.

Recently returned from the Grand Canyon in Arizona, a college-aged family friend from Eastern Agency related her experience visiting a Navajo vendor at the canyon's edge with a male friend, also from New Mexico's Eastern Agency. The Navajo vendor asks where they are from. "Crownpoint," my friend says. "That's funny," the vendor responds, adding, "You guys don't *look* Navajo." She proceeds to offer my friend a discount on her jewelry, and they move on to discuss other topics at hand. What does it mean to "look" Navajo, and how does "Eastern" become marked as the non-normative space, as Navajo matter out of place? We see Navajos differentiating among themselves through language about music, culture, and Navajo identity—emerging in conversations about dialect, place of origin, and social class. "Culture," a term imported onto the Navajo reservation by early anthropologists invested in the continuity of traditional expressive practices including ceremonial music and speaking Navajo, has now taken on a similarly rigid meaning within Navajo communities and is often a fraught concept. In contrast to the broader definition given by cultural anthropologists today, culture for many Diné specifically signifies historical continuity with the past, including traditional singing, ceremonial practices, social dancing, and the use of one's heritage language. When used in reservation spaces, the phrase "knowing one's culture" is often synonymous with a traditional, reservation-based lifestyle and excludes so-called urban Navajos, non-Navajo speakers, and anyone who wasn't reared in a traditional manner, however that might be conceived.

Specific places on the Navajo Nation are central to understanding the politics of culture as it relates to Navajo country-western performance. Placemaking becomes a mechanism for forging cultural intimacy and tribal sovereignty—but it also becomes a vehicle for political and social exclusion. Social class, in the way I use it here, intersects directly with a reservation-based Indigenous authenticity, or a perceived lack thereof. Possessing a working-class reservation identity, implied by such things as living on the reservation, hauling water,[2] owning livestock, or having a home-site lease or grazing permit, is a coveted form of Diné cultural capital, particularly for those, such as urban Navajos, who may not possess that symbolic currency.[3] By contrast, living off reservation, being more upwardly mobile, not speaking Navajo, or performing music that's not traditionally Navajo signals a different form of class- and culture-based identity. While at least 13 percent of Navajos now live off reservation (Yurth 2012), on-reservation Navajos sometimes frame this second, more middle-class orientation as being less traditional and, by extension, less authentically Diné.

At the same time, urban and rural reservation spaces aren't necessarily class exclusive: we also find working-class Diné living in urban areas and middle-class Diné living on the reservation. And, in fact, "keeping up with the Joneses, the

Yazzies, and the Begays,"[4] as one father at a recent high school graduation dinner put it, is as important to Navajo Nation citizens on the reservation as it is for those living off rez throughout the United States. This is to say that upward mobility and performances of middle-class cultural capital as a national pastime—"the white picket fence and all that," as one of my interlocuturs put it—is as important to Diné citizens as it is to many other Americans. However, in keeping with Raymond Williams's (1973 [1985]) theorization of the "country" and the "city" as opposite ends of a mutually constitutive spectrum, Diné citizens often reference working-class urbanites and middle-class reservation dwellers as anomalies bucking "typical" Navajo experience. In this framework, city dwellers are associated with wealth and prosperity, and reservation dwellers are associated with poverty and more primitive lifestyles. Associating poverty with Indigeneity has deep roots in federal Indian policy (Merriam 1928), and working-poor reservation identities and deprivation are thus framed as the norm, so that in local usage, terms such as "tradition," "authenticity," and even "Navajo" signal specific socioeconomic affiliations and understandings of Navajo culture.

With few exceptions, anthropological scholarship about Navajos has historically focused on communities living on the Arizona side of the reservation.[5] This may seem unimportant, given that a Navajo homeland—*Diné Bikéyah*—long predates the creation of the U.S. nation or individual U.S. states. Yet because of the ideologies of authenticity attached to each state today, this omission unwittingly reifies these state-based ideologies that germinated, at least partially, off the reservation. In addition, the original reservation boundaries of the Navajo reservation, created on the return from *Hwéeldi* or Fort Sumner by executive order in 1868, were initially primarily in Arizona, and only later were larger portions of present-day New Mexico and Utah added to the existing Navajo reservation, also known as Naabehó Bináhásdzo.[6] Due to the historical privileging of Arizona Navajo experience as representative of all authentic Navajo experience, I write this chapter from the vantage of Navajo New Mexico—the place where I lived for the first eighteen months of my fieldwork.

Anthropologists do mark Navajo New Mexican identities as Other, but Navajo New Mexicans position themselves that way, too, consistently foregrounding their difference from Arizona Navajos not just in terms of where they reside but also in their phenotype, their cultural practices, and distinct ways of speaking. From a New Mexico perspective, Arizona often stands as the unmarked portion of the reservation, the normative contingent. This politics of difference plays out particularly vibrantly on the ground in one Eastern Agency chapter[7] and town[8]

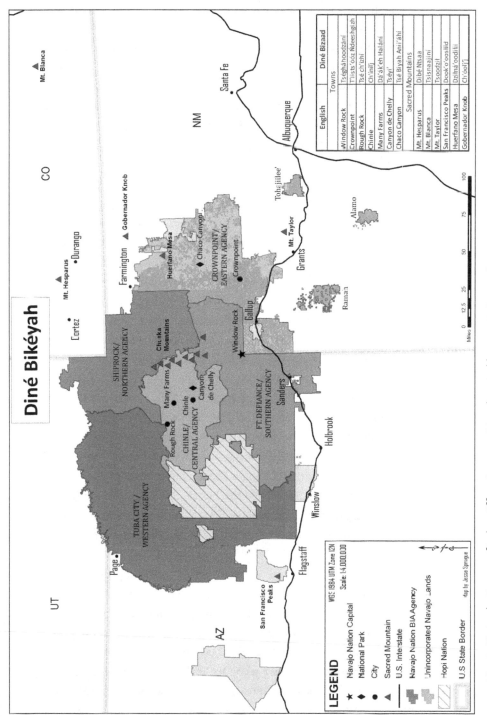

Diné Bikéyah

English	Diné Bizaad
Towns	
Window Rock	Tségháhoodzáni
Crownpoint	Tlʼistsʼóóz Ndeeshgiizh
Rough Rock	Tsé chʼízhí
Chinle	Chʼínílį́
Many Farms	Daʼákʼeh Halání
Canyon de Chelly	Tséyiʼ
Chaco Canyon	Tsé Biyah Anííʼáhí
Sacred Mountains	
Mt. Hesparus	Dibé Ntsaa
Mt. Blanca	Tsisnaajiní
Mt. Taylor	Tsoodził
San Francisco Peaks	Dookʼoʼoosłííd
Huerfano Mesa	Dziłháʼoodiłii
Gobernador Knob	Chʼóolʼį́ʼí

LEGEND

WGS: 1984 UTM Zone 12N Scale: 1:4,000,000

★ Navajo Nation Capital
◆ National Park
● City
▲ Sacred Mountain
  U.S. Interstate
  Navajo Nation BIA Agency
  Unincorporated Navajo Lands
  Hopi Nation
  U.S State Border

Map by Jesse Sprague

0 12.5 25 50 75 100
Miles

MAP 3: Navajo Nation by Bureau of Indian Affairs Agencies (Map designed by Jesse E. Sprague)

called Crownpoint, and in the lives of community members from this marginalized reservation space.

Navajos are, and perhaps have always been, highly mobile. Since the arrival
of the Spanish in 1539 and the subsequent introduction of horses and *churro*
sheep to the Southwest, sheepherding and range management has required Navajo people to move around.[9] In sharp contrast to more fixed Pueblo villages that
are inhabited year-round, Navajos from the Dinétah phase (1550–1700) onward
traditionally had at least two sheep camps (a summer camp, *keeshį́*, and a winter
camp, *keehai*). Pegged as "nomadic" by early anthropologists who didn't have
the vocabulary to conceptualize a people living in two semipermanent homes,
Navajos moved seasonally between their summer and winter camps. Thus, while
the number of sheepherders has decreased in recent years, movement as a central
tenet of Navajo identity is still highly valued. Today, for men in particular, this
mobility — as for many Americans — is associated with cultural capital, where
the ability to travel either for one's job, hobby, or for pleasure is a coveted form of
upward mobility. Playing in country bands allows for a similar kind of mobility,
and participation in country performance increases this movement — social, economic, and geographic — for male musicians. And Navajos are still going "where
the resources are at" (Don Whyte, personal interview, 23 July 2010): many Diné
today work urban construction in Phoenix, Las Vegas, and elsewhere across the
United States. Navajos are also known for their state-of-the-art welding, iron-
work, silversmithing, and their high enlistment rate in military service, jobs that
all require considerable ability to travel. Those in country bands can work the
Navajo Nation rodeo circuit, itself a status marker for rural Diné men in particular. The reputation for moving around and cosmopolitan identity grounded in
working-class experience led my Navajo teacher to joke: "Navajos are like beer
cans . . . they're everywhere!" The 2000 decennial census statistically supports
this statement: 5.6 percent of Navajos live in a U.S. state other than Arizona, New
Mexico, or Utah (Begay 2011, 16).

Place also figures prominently in origin stories of the Diné people, and, like
Navajo identities, places are often highly contested. While some traditional creation stories tell of ancestral Diné communities emerging into this world — the
fifth or "glittering world" — through a reed near Dinétah (present-day Huer-
fano Mesa,[10] New Mexico), others trace Diné origins to a place near Canyon de
Chelly (*Tségi'*),[11] Arizona. Still other accounts, including those most commonly
espoused by archeologists and other, mostly non-Native scholars,[12] hold that Diné
peoples migrated from Siberia across the Bering Land Bridge into present-day

Alaska and then southward to the American Southwest and northern Mexico.[13] From this perspective, Navajos are known as a relatively recent arrival to the Southwest.

More recently, Navajo archeologists and historians have begun to tell a different story, informed by Navajo oral histories, ceremonial knowledge, and ethnoarchaeology.[14] In these accounts, southern Athabaskan speakers migrated into the Southwest in the sixteenth century but merged with other Indigenous groups already living in the region (Thompson 2009, 94) to form what later became known as the Diné people. Thus, although the first Navajo *hooghan* is dated to 1541 in Dinétah, this should not necessarily be understood as an indicator of Diné ethnogenesis in the Southwest. The Diné archeologist Kerry Thompson (Ashįįhí), for example, criticizes the use of linguistic evidence alone to tell the story of Diné origins (e.g., Reed et al. 2000, 65) and critiques anthropological reliance on only language as "the defining characteristic of anthropological discourse about Navajo people" (Reed et al. 2000, 240). Instead, Thompson proposes models for Navajo ethnogenesis that are more amenable to—and actively incorporate—Diné journey narratives and creation scripture as part of the evidence used to tell a place- and language-based history of Diné peoples (Thompson 2009, 241).

Language and place continue to play a central role in Diné worlds and senses of self. Indeed, dialectal preferences and language ideologies undergird the formation of Diné society, including the convergence of clans. For example, some Diné scholars now posit that Navajo, a southern Athabaskan language, was consciously adopted by "leaders of different people who shared similar lifeways but spoke different languages" (Thompson 2009, 64); Navajo became a lingua franca once a southern Athabaskan convergence in the Southwest took place. Even more specifically, Navajo journey narratives relate that *Diné Bizaad* was introduced by a specific clan from the west, the Tábąąhí or Water's Edge Clan (Matthews 1897 [1994], 143; Zolbrod 1984, 301), a clan name indicating possible coastal connections with present-day California.[15] Thus, even from Navajo inception as a cultural and self-governing political entity, Navajo peoples made strategic, synecdochic, and self-conscious language decisions, in which often a part—the language of one clan among many, the Tábąąhí—comes to stand in for or represent the whole, the Diné people. In each case, these origin stories matter because they have repercussions for current language ideologies, land-use practices, and legitimizing claims to sacred sites (e.g., Brugge and Missaghian 2006). As a result, these stories are often used to correlate or contradict larger narratives of place- and language-based authenticity.

If we understand Kornell Johns's earlier comment about the role of place in battle-of-the-bands competitions — "where you're from matters" — as a key to social citizenship more broadly, we see that social citizenship is defined differently for Navajo tribal members based on location of residence. Reservation residents on the Arizona side, for example, often leverage tribal citizenship to claim access to resources; their Eastern Agency counterparts frequently assert their rights as New Mexico and U.S. citizens rather than as tribal citizens per se. As a result, New Mexico residents often focus on a transcendent idea of Navajo culture, while Arizona residents use territorial authority, cultural knowledge, and access to a tribal elite in Window Rock to assert their Navajo identity.

Perceptions of geographic and cultural difference stem in part from the divergent histories of land allocation in the Arizona and New Mexico portions of the reservation. While parts of the reservation that lie west of the Chuskas in Arizona and the so-called Utah Strip are contiguous and bounded — that is, with the exception of the Hopi Nation and the San Juan Southern Paiute, they are not divided or partitioned by non-Navajo lands — the New Mexico portion of the reservation comprises a patchwork of multiple land owners, resulting in a checkered map (map 4), and in Eastern Agency residents often framing themselves as "matter out of place" (Douglas 1966) vis-à-vis the larger Navajo Nation and the tribal capital of Window Rock, Arizona. Defined as substance that defies existing social categories or an extant social order, "matter out of place" is used here to refer to the ways in which "checkerboard" residents often feel as if they, and by extension their language and cultural practices, are not wholly a part of the political and social entity known as the Navajo Nation. This stigmatized identity has been exacerbated by the fact that the single-largest release of radioactive materials in U.S. history, the 1979 Churchrock Uranium Mine spill, occurred in Eastern Agency, contaminating the Rio Puerco and affecting local ranchers' ability to graze, water, and own livestock in the area to this day. This sense of being apart also leads to not only political but also civic estrangement from the larger Navajo Nation, exemplified in a Crownpoint Chapter official's comment that Eastern Agency is the "minority to the minority of the Navajo Nation."

The Eastern Navajo checkerboard is technically not reservation land[16] — instead, before and after the General Allotment Act of 1887, Eastern Navajo Agency was partitioned as square tracts of land given to separate and often competing entities (Deloria and Lytle 1985, 10). Tracts of 160 acres were allotted to individual Navajo families, non-Navajo ranchers or "stockmen," the Navajo tribe, the Bureau of

Indian Affairs, the National Forest Service, the Bureau of Land Management, and the National Park Service. Current land ownership in the Casamero Lake Chapter illustrates the partitioning that happened in Eastern Agency at large, seen in map 4.

Map 4 shows the interspersion of Navajo tribal fee land (light gray), Indian allotment land (medium gray), remaining private land (black), privately leased land (white), BLM-leased land (vertical crosshatch), and National Park Service land (crosshatch) in a section of Crownpoint Chapter. To assess who was eligible for land during allotment (1887–1934), the Office of Indian Affairs (now the Bureau of Indian Affairs) instituted the first Navajo tribal rolls, using blood quantum as the criteria to assess eligibility. By the end of allotment (1934), individual and collective tribal landholdings in the checkerboard had been reduced by more than half. In addition, many private Navajo landowners found that the land they had been given was unfarmable or, worse yet, sold their land for a fraction of what it was worth and lost it. Attesting to the scarcity of eastern Navajos who still retain rights to their original allotment, a former chapter-house official from Thoreau Chapter proudly mentioned to me that she is one of few people in her chapter to still live on her family's original allotment land.

Following the Dawes Act, individuals passed their allotted land down equally, generation to generation, usually to their male heirs, creating a complicated network of present-day owners possessing small fractions of the original 160-acre allotted tracts (160 acres = one section). Thus "a parcel of land that at the time of allotment had one clear owner may now have more than 100 owners who hold the land as tenants in common" (Shepelwich and Zalneraitis 2000, 104–5). This collective tenancy has had a negative effect on the economic value of checkerboarded land, since large-scale land-use planning, such as installing electrical lines, building businesses, or paving roads, becomes extremely difficult due to the number of parties to be consulted. As a case in point, in the town of Crownpoint, land is under the control of the Bureau of Land Management, the Bureau of Land Reclamation, the Department of Defense, the U.S. Postal Service, the National Park Service, the State of New Mexico, the Navajo Nation, individual Navajos, and private, non-Native land owners (Shepelwich and Zalneraitis 2000, 104).

The net effect of checkerboarding today results in a much greater non-Navajo population living in Eastern Agency (surpassing 10 percent) than on other parts of the reservation. As a result, towns such as Crownpoint feel minimally like Navajo social spaces for its three thousand or so residents.[17] Because tribal sovereignty is often most effectively exercised over people, events, and infrastructure

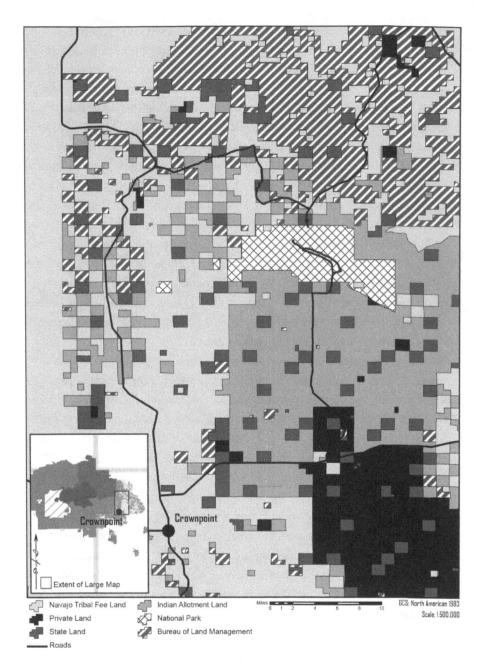

Navajo Tribal Fee Land   Indian Allotment Land

Private Land   National Park

State Land   Bureau of Land Management

Roads

Extent of Large Map

Miles
0 1 2   4   6   8   10

GCS: North American 1983
Scale: 1:500.000

MAP 4. Checkerboarded Navajo Land in Eastern Agency: Crownpoint, New Mexico
(Map designed by Jesse E. Sprague)

located on tribal trust land, checkerboarding has also severely curtailed tribal authority, cultural cohesion, and tribal economic development in the region.

Having a noncontiguous tribal land base also has less tangible effects on issues relating to Navajo cultural continuity, senses of community, social citizenship, and togetherness. A fragmented land base leads to a more fragmented sense of community. My Navajo teacher sometimes expressed this fact thus: "Crownpoint is not really a 'together' community." What I take her to mean is that checkerboarding affects the ability to create Navajo cultural spaces where Navajoness is practiced and reinstantiated, be it through shared language, music making, ceremonies, or community celebrations. Thus, while territory or land held in common isn't the only basis for cultural collectivity, for many contemporary Diné, it is a central tenet of that collectivity.

From the perspective of many Eastern Agency residents, Arizona reservation landholding and communities appear much more "together." This extends not only to perceptions of access to resources but also to Diné linguistic and cultural continuity, perceived to be more alive in Arizona reservation communities. For example, in Navajo language classes I took at Diné College in Crownpoint and at the University of New Mexico, students from New Mexico often deferred to Navajo speakers from the Arizona side of the reservation and recommended I do the same. This perception of cultural and linguistic continuity, however, can prove a double-edged sword, and not all perceptions of Arizona reservation land or Arizona Navajos are quite so laudatory. The local term "john" or *jaan* is one salient example.

Matter out of Place: The Cultural Figure of the *Jaan*

Glossed as "hick" or "rezneck" by Diné citizens, *jaan* is a Navajo lexeme denoting someone who lives close to the land and leads a traditional, reservation-based lifestyle. *Jaan* is a set of cultural practices indicating rural origins and a Diné working-class or working-poor worldview, but it also references a specific musical sound, a sound often associated with older country music. The linguist Robert Young (1948, 86–89) traces Navajo usage of *jaan* to the late 1940s, where rural Navajos leaving the reservation for work rarely had last names that were pronounceable or legible to their Anglo employers. Adapted from the Anglo name *John* and similar to other catchall addresses used for strangers such as *Bub* or *Mac*, *jaan* became the default term Anglos used to refer to Navajo men with unknown last and first names. *Jaan* was thus a term anonymizing the identities of off-reservation Navajos who spoke primarily Navajo. *Jaan* was quickly adopted into Navajo as both a noun, such as *Naabeejaan* (combining it with *Naabeehó*, for "Navajo"), an adjective such as "ayóo bijaan" ("he/she is really *jaan*") and a verb, such as "nléidi ła' dah 'oojaan" ("there's a Navajo standing over there"). According to the Diné language scholar Tiffany Lee, *jaan* "stems from the indoctrination of Western education, worldviews, and ways of life during colonization, carried through the boarding school era, and continues now" (2009, 22).

Thus, from its first emergence, *jaan* is a term reflecting a non-Navajo gaze, the internalization of that gaze by Navajo people, and a class-specific association with "unacculturated" (Young 1948, 87) and non-English-speaking Diné peoples. Being labeled a *jaan* can function as an "object of shame" for many that are assigned this identity, linked to "something that is premodern, backwards, and associated with reservation poverty" (Webster 2015, 26). Today, in its everyday usage, you might hear someone say that another person either *acts* really *jaan* or has a really *jaan* name; someone simply *is* a *jaan* or, at its most pejorative, is a *jaaner*. *Jaan* might also be used to mean simply "Navajo," as opposed to another racial identification; once, while sitting with my friend and speaking in Navajo at the Many Farms laundromat, I was questioned as to whether I was a *jaan Bilagáana*, or "white Navajo" / "white Native?" (I am not.)

Used to denote rural Navajos from many parts of the reservation, *jaan* seems to occur more often when referring to Arizona Navajos. As both a noun and an adjective, the secondary implications for a *jaan* are of an uneducated individual, the rural rube or "backwoods Navajo" who lives in the "deep rez" and is really "rezneck." A *jaan* is what my Navajo teacher, Shirley Bowman, refers to in jest as "prehistoric Navajos." This typology denotes those whose mother tongue is Navajo and, if they speak English, employ a thick Navajo English or "Navadlish" accent. Like the pejoratives "redneck," "hick," or "white trash" in dominant U.S. sociolinguistic practice, *jaan* connotes someone lacking savvy about technology or navigating non-Navajo, more cosmopolitan milieus but, crucially from the perspective of those who use the term to refer to others, without the cultural capital to notice or be self-conscious about this lack of savvy. As one Crownpoint resident articulated it, acting *jaan* connotes someone who isn't playing with a full deck and who, furthermore, "doesn't know any better" (Candice Craig, personal correspondence, June 4, 2015). *Jaan* is the wrong sort of rural, a speaker type that can't be easily romanticized, where constructions of identity, geography, and place converge in what Eliza Darling has termed the "space-hick conflation" (Darling 2009, 4).

But *jaan* is also a conveniently malleable identity. Paralleling insider/outsider terms such as redneck, *jaan* can also be used in an affectionate way between Diné peoples, reflecting a sort of cultural intimacy where people humorously, and sometimes lovingly, are on the lookout to catch each other when, to use the singer Candice Craig's phrase, they are "slippin'" back into practices deemed overtly *jaan*. As Candice describes it, having a *"jaan* moment" is like having a "blond moment," where momentarily you forget your bearings and lapse into rez-based behavioral patterns—speaking English with a thick reservation accent, patching your broken window with duct tape—that you might not intend to reveal in certain places. As Candice notes, "You can take the *jaan* out of the rez, but you can't take the rez out of the *jaan*. It's like no matter what you do or how you do it, someone out there will still find a way to make fun of each other, and call each other a *jaan*" (Personal correspondence, June 4, 2015).

Jaan identities reveal the slippages, or cracks, between worlds, and are fundamentally tied into Diné negotiations with modernity, social class, and Anglo cultural worlds. The "backwoods Navajo" implies that, instead of riding a tractor or making moonshine, a *jaan* lives off the land through ranching and herding sheep, hauling water, conserving resources, and growing traditional foods through dry farming. Thus, a *jaan's* working-class identity comes from working the land—in that sense, sharing linguistic origins with the term *redneck*—rather than through holding a blue-collar job or participating in a modern wage economy. In this way, the *jaan* who communes with nature is an internalized stereotype of Native peoples as tree huggers, first environmentalists, or even as the marginalized noble savage.

Conversely, the flip side of the *jaan* stereotype, and one that historically goes hand in hand with the noble savage, is that of the "bloodthirsty savage," or unsuccessful modern, often gendered as a man. In these depictions of the *jaan*, we see the tension and ambivalence in how tradition is defined, who has it, and who doesn't. On the one hand, the *jaan* is considered the pure touchstone of authentic Navajo culture and tradition. On the other hand, the *jaan*, whether man or woman, is shunned and criticized for this same cultural purity, portrayed as behind the times, backward, and less than fully modern. Both stereotypes, that of the noble savage and the bloodthirsty savage, feed off a larger American narrative about Native communities, in which "Indian people, corralled on isolated and impoverished reservations, missed out on modernity—indeed, almost dropped out of history itself" (Deloria 2004, 6).

The late Diné comedian and singer Vincent Craig plays with the *jaan*-as-historical-holdover trope in his Navajo stock characters such as Ch'ízhii ("person with the rough skin"), Mutton Man (a radioactive man who has superpowers as a result of the Churchrock Mine Spill), and Rita(hhhhhhh) (aspirated by Craig to emphasize final aspirated vowels occurring in Navajo and its translation into the Navadlish accent). Craig, the key public figure to establish the *jaan* and the Navajo accent as cultural typologies in the 1980s, was a comedian and musician from Eastern Agency who made fun, more often than not, of Western, or Arizona, Navajos.[18] It is as if, speaking and singing from the margins of New Mexico, satirizing Arizona Navajos and *jaans* allowed Craig to leverage some cultural capital in a political landscape skewed in other ways toward Arizona residents. As a youth, Craig left the reservation to go on the Mormon Placement Program, found religion, served in Vietnam, and later came back to Crownpoint with a more critical outsider's perspective on his hometown and the cultural politics surrounding his Native nation. Craig's songs, which largely focus on making fun of Navajo speaker types and are designed to evoke a nostalgia for the 1960s and 1970s, especially for older listeners, provide ironic distance from the New Mexico Diné space in which he grew up: Craig's humor gives him the ability to wink about *jaans*, and in so doing, he makes the culturally intimate public. It is perhaps for this reason that Craig is deeply loved by some and strongly disliked and disavowed by others. Craig's interpretation of the *jaan* foregrounds the meeting of music and language through humor, while also positioning himself as higher status and more cosmopolitan than the *jaans* he is ridiculing.

Building on Craig's early routines, an entire body of self-deprecating humor has been built around the *jaan*. Navajo comedians James June and Ernest Tsosie III ("James and Ernie") regularly include impersonations of *jaans* in their comedic routines, replete with heavily aspirated, thick Navadlish accents. In a performance in Newcomb, New Mexico, James and Ernie ended their routine by asking the audience, "So, what do you call a tribal councilman?" Punning on *jaan*, the bad guys of the *Transformers* action franchise, and poking fun at tribal politics in Window Rock, the punch line was: a "DECEPTI-*Jaan*!!"

James and Ernie's joke does the work of distancing the comedians from both *jaans* and Window Rock politics, but others embrace this identity. At the Basha's parking lot in Crownpoint one afternoon, a friend from Denmark and I were approached by a local artist selling "long hairs," Zuni Pueblo katsinas (kachinas) intricately carved out of single pieces of cottonwood. Assuming that my friend, obviously a tourist, was looking for something specifically Navajo, he said to her: "It's called a Zuni Longhair," listing the different prices. With a knowing smile he then looked at me, the anthropologist, and added reassuringly, "but it's *made* by a *jaan*." Here, *jaan* is used as a racial identity, an insider's term denoting Navajo affiliation and rural authenticity that, the seller hopes, will make his artwork more marketable to tourists on the reservation.

Place-based authenticity and cultural continuity are also assigned through terms such as "deep" and "real," where remote portions of the reservation are denoted as being deeper and more real than places closer to border towns. Like Diné understandings of identity, however, these places and their meanings are constantly shifting in relation to a speaker's class status, life experience, and sociolinguistic positioning. One morning in the border town of Gallup, New Mexico, I was filling up my one-hundred-pound propane tank for the long drive back to Many Farms. I chatted with a young Diné employee as he filled my tank, and, noticing the mud on my truck, he asked me to which part of the rez I was headed. "Many Farms . . . " he repeated in response to my answer, trailing off. Then, with a mix of admiration and what sounded like sympathy, he rejoined, "The *deep* rez, huh?" He proceeded to tell me about how he was raised in Gallup and only knew the "big" reservation towns such as Chinle, but had not ever been to communities "way out there" such as Rough Rock and Many Farms.

From the vantage point of many Diné citizens living in the so-called deep rez, however, there are places that are more rural still, places where you're "really in the sticks." Enjoying dinner with Native Country bandleader Tommy Bia and his family one evening in Many Farms, we discussed the recent heavy snowfalls and their impact on small, rural communities located on the top of Black Mesa mountain, including chapters such as Hard Rock. Tommy mentioned that he would like to drive some supplies over for community members in need, opining: "Now those communities like Hard Rock, they're really in the sticks. They don't have *anything*—they're what you call the deep rez!"

Internal perceptions of reservation-based authenticity can also overlap with Navajo forms of colourism, defined as "system of privilege and discrimination based on the degree of lightness in the colour of a person's skin" (Gabriel 2007, 11). Eating lunch with the band at a food stand by the Indian Health Services hospital in Chinle one day, we were joined by a middle-aged hospital employee and began to chat. She animatedly told me about her two adult daughters. One of them, she said, was a doctor and was really light-skinned, while the other had dark, *ch'ízhii* (rough) skin and "looks really *jaan*." Continuing, she talked about her family's sheep camp, located on an isolated peninsula (Black Rock) between Canyon de Chelly and Canyon del Muerto close to the town of Tsaile. She explained how she lives and works in Chinle during the week, noting that Chinle was "way too city" for her. She'd rather be in

Black Rock any day. "Now Black Rock, *that's* what you call the *deep* rez!" Here, Black Rock is figured as the desirable ur-text or "real" reservation, the place in the sticks where she'd really like to be. At the same time, her daughter with lighter skin, whom she described as having phenotypically whiter facial features, is also figured in more favorable terms as more "beautiful," thereby reinforcing the values of colorism where lighter skin/approximate whiteness is associated with being more attractive, more desirable and, in this case, having heightened intelligence and social status (Tate 2016).

But Arizona isn't the only state to have a purchase on authentically rural Navajo places. Chatting with my line-dancing teacher, a Pima citizen from Scottsdale, Arizona, one afternoon in Crownpoint, I mentioned to him that I would be driving to Albuquerque, New Mexico, via a paved, two-lane road that passes Chaco Canyon and the communities of Torreon, Pueblo Pintado, and Ojo Encino. Noting that his wife hailed from Torreon, he responded: "Pueblo Pintado? Now you're going to the *real* rez!" Similarly, recounting her niece's recent preschool parade at Pueblo Pintado Head Start, a friend from Crownpoint started cracking up, describing how all the preschoolers were dressed up traditionally, wearing hair buns, dresses, moccasins, and jewelry, walking down the main street accompanied by fire trucks but completely "in the middle of nowhere," with no one to see them. "Now that," her older sister jokingly intervened for my benefit, "that's *jaan.*" This is how rural signifiers shift. Deep, real, and *jaan* are assessed relative to a speaker's own positioning. For people living in more urban spaces such as border towns, the entire reservation might be considered *jaan.* For residents of larger reservation towns, however, the deep rez is often understood to encompass places accessed only with difficulty, places that may not have running water and electricity. In all cases, these terms imply a certain literal and symbolic inaccessibility and inability to fully know the place — or person — so denoted.

Country music's detractors often treat country musicians as "matter out of place." This critique extends to some Navajo country musicians and their ability to use recording equipment, public-address systems, sing in "accent-free" English, and successfully perform popular music in off-reservation spaces (Jacobsen 2009). Consequentially, fans assign class-based terms such as "uptown" and "downtown" to a band's sound and cosmopolitanism based on their varying engagements with recording and performing equipment. It is this stereotype that many Navajo country musicians actively work against through their insistence, for example, that "Indians can play country music too" (Emmett "Toto" Bia Jr., July 2002).

"We Still Weave Our Rugs down at the Chapter House": Place, Mobility, and *Jaans*

The songs of Candice Craig, a female country singer, niece to Vincent Craig and drummer who fronts her dad's band, the Wranglers, incorporate the image of the *jaan* while simultaneously asserting her self-conscious, class-based identity. Candice hails from Crownpoint, but she lived in Albuquerque for twelve years, raised her first son there, and has traveled widely across the continental United States. As an upwardly mobile Navajo woman from Eastern Agency with a bachelor of science degree in engineering, place figures ironically and self-consciously in her word substitutions when performing Gretchen Wilson's "Redneck Woman" and the late Merle Haggard's "Okie from Muskogee."

During my fieldwork, I played and sang intermittently with Candice and her band, performing for a variety of community events, including a parade, an outdoor field day celebration, a political rally, and a veteran's building completion celebration. Candice started off her musical career singing along to the radio on the flatbed of her uncle's eighteen-wheeler diesel truck, using her hairbrush as a microphone. Later, due in part to the challenges of getting a male band to back her, she began performing as a karaoke singer in off-reservation towns like Grants, Laguna, and Albuquerque. A charismatic performer with a great stage presence and a husky voice resembling that of country icon Tammy Wynette, Candice has now gained a following beyond Crownpoint. When she sat in and sang with Native Country for a gig at the Class Act in Gallup, Tommy commented to his son afterward: "Asdzą́ą́ nizhónígo hataał lá" ("That lady really sings beautifully!") (She does.)

Candice is a songwriter and wordsmith in her own right. Although her public performances do not currently feature her original songs, they show her frequently rewording the lyrics of the classic country songs she covers. In this manipulation, one catches a glimpse of her own views on gender, class positioning, and her identity as a Navajo woman from the checkerboard. At the same time, her songs reference a sense of social and political marginalization from not only the U.S. nation but also from the greater Navajo Nation as well as from the tribal capital of Window Rock, Arizona.

Candice's own sense of civic estrangement stems in part from the fact that she is not a Navajo speaker, and therefore is often made to feel she isn't "Navajo enough." Like many speakers of her generation, Candice grew up listening to her parents speak Navajo but never learned to speak herself, and in fact often told me she is more comfortable speaking Spanish than Navajo. In her first conscious attempts to speak Navajo with her uncles in junior high school at the urging of her Navajo language teacher, Candice remembers mostly their guffaws and responses that "it didn't sound right" when she spoke. Always aware of language use, she strongly dislikes the term "American Indian" for its historical inaccuracy, and herself uses the terms "Original Americans" and "American Originals" to refer to her own people and to other U.S. Native tribes.

After high school, she decided to no longer attempt to become a fluent speaker, and, as she put it, "learned to express my Navajo identity in other ways." Crucially, and recalling that the word for healer and singer (*hataałii*) are synonymous in Navajo, Candice expresses her identification as Diné primarily through her singing, where she nuances lyrics to reflect her experience as a Diné woman from what is sometimes referred to as the forgotten agency. Here, as elsewhere, heritage-language politics, authenticity, cultural intimacy, and song are inextricably intertwined, with each a performance in its own right.

In the Merle Haggard, self-penned classic of politically conservative hardscrabble living "Okie from Muskogee," Candice changes the final chorus from "I'm proud to be an Okie from Muskogee / a place where even squares can have a ball" to "I'm proud to be a Navajo from New Mexico / A place where all you squaws can have a ball." In her lyrical substitution, Candice foregrounds her place-based political identity as a Navajo citizen, a "Navajo from New Mexico"— where the patriotism and small-town references, she brashly claims, apply to her own life as a Diné woman. As with Haggard's reference to Muskogee, Oklahoma, Candice's indirect reference to the town of Crownpoint, New Mexico, both here and later in the song, becomes a defensive stance, an in-your-face designation of small-town America on the margins.

Candice also plays with gender expectations: with the line "a place where all you squaws can have a ball," she inverts the gender of the singer by replacing "squares" with a sometimes derogatory term for Native women, "squaws." An English loanword from the Algonquian language in use as early as 1622, the meaning of "squaw"—and this is part of Candice's argument—didn't become explicitly derogatory until the twentieth century.

Candice toys with the meaning of "ball" in the song, as well; in her usage, she uses it to encourage her female listeners to loosen up and have fun, to hitch up that skirt and ride a bronc, to have, in her own words, a "Ball of Laughs, a Ball of Joy!" (C. Craig, personal communication, June 4, 2015). In one of our many conversations about this song, Candice explained that her use of "squaw" is both for convenience—it's a one-syllable word that effortlessly substitutes for "squares" and is easy to sing—and for political reasons as well. For Candice, "squaw" isn't really pejorative and it connotes any older woman—Native or non-Native—who wears a scarf and a skirt; but she is also trying to demonstrate how non-Natives historically understood and then interpellated Native female subjects such as herself through the use of pejoratives like "squaw." The word's appearance imbues the song with historical depth and weight, further emplacing its themes within Native North America and outside the purview of a small, Anglo-majority town in Oklahoma.

In more recent performances (April 2014, May 2015) of "Okie from Muskogee" at the University of New Mexico and at Navajo Technical University, Candice also changed the remaining lyric of the chorus from "We still wave Old Glory down at the courthouse / and white lightning's still the biggest thrill of all" to the more politically and historically specific lines, "We still weave our rugs down at the chapter house / and Garden DeLuxe is still the biggest thrill of all." Whereas the squaw manipulation was intended and performed for a primarily non-Native audience, these whole-line substitutions are directed internally, intended for Navajo listeners or, at a bare minimum, listeners familiar with the Navajo reservation and cultural practices such as weaving rugs. As Candice herself put it in a recent conversation, "those lines are intended for people from the area—Navajos and Anglos—that know something about Navajos, to make them laugh; it's sort of an inside joke" (C. Craig, interview by author, Crownpoint, New Mexico, May 19, 2015).

In these third and fourth lines of the chorus, Candice supplants a generic expression of American patriotism, waving Old Glory, with a more locally meaningful reference to the quintessential textile for which Navajos are known.[19] Navajo rugs are made of both handspun and store-bought wool, handwoven on upright looms, and sold at the Crownpoint Navajo Rug Auction, across the reservation, around the Southwest, and beyond. One of the only events attracting tourists to Crownpoint, the auction is an important source of income for Navajo weavers and artisans in a town with an unemployment rate of more than 60 percent (McCloskey 2007, 81; Shepelwich and Zalneraitis 2000, 103). Candice's reference to this storied craft acknowledges the economic importance of rug weaving for many Navajo families in Crownpoint.

At the same time, since rug weaving is also something that anthropologists have long deemed an "authentic" Diné cultural practice, Candice's allusion makes a strong case for the cultural continuity of Crownpoint residents, something that

Navajos from other parts of the Nation sometimes dispute. In fact, she explains that her inclusion of this line makes a direct reference to her late paternal grandmother, who worked with the elderly when Candice was in grade school, assisting them at the Crownpoint chapter house with their weaving and quilting as part of a program for senior citizens. So the small word "still" in the lyric is a particularly weighty one, reminding other Navajos that Crownpoint is still Navajo and still traditional, and rug weaving buttresses this point. As Candice's auntie mentioned one evening during a girl's puberty ceremony I attended, Arizona Navajos think that Eastern Agency residents "are all just Anglo and Hispanic" and that there are no "real" Navajos in Crownpoint.

Built environments and political institutions also take on additional meaning in Candice's transformation of the lyric from "down at the courthouse" to "down at the chapter house." Many Navajo towns don't have courthouses;[20] instead, they have Navajo-style town halls where meetings and public events are held for community members and elected officials; these are called chapter houses. The foregrounded image of Crownpoint residents selling rugs at the chapter house adds effect, emphasizing the sharp political differences in local governance — chapters instead of counties and chapter houses instead of courthouses — between a predominantly Anglo town in Dust Bowl, Oklahoma, and a majority Diné town such as Crownpoint, New Mexico. Because these rugs are actually sold at the elementary school where the auction takes place, not at the chapter house, the pairing of weaving with chapter houses has the effect of compounding the cultural and political distinction she experiences as a "Navajo from New Mexico."

The satire that Candice infuses into the final lyric, "Garden DeLuxe is still the biggest thrill of all," is generation-, gender- and family-specific, supplanting Haggard's reference to white lightning — (illegal) homemade, high-proof moonshine — with a nostalgic and ironic nod to the inexpensive fortified red wine known as Garden DeLuxe or "GD." A former reservation favorite from its inception in 1946 until its discontinuation in the late 1990s, Garden DeLuxe Tokay Wine is also referred to as *bik'os dilwolii* ("bottle with the bumpy neck," referencing the grapevine pattern on the shoulder of the bottle) and was infamously bottled and marketed by a well-known family at a plant in the "wet" border town of Gallup, New Mexico. Since the Navajo Tribal Council prohibits alcohol sales and consumption on the reservation, GD was instead aggressively marketed from Gallup and sold to primarily male Navajo patrons.[21] In this gloss, Candice maintains the anti-establishment, speaking-from-the-margins stance that Haggard promotes through his own reference to illicit production and consumption of moonshine. Here, Haggard's image is very much in keeping with the stereotypic Hollywood version of the rural, Anglo redneck or hillbilly as portrayed in popular films such as *Deliverance*. Her genius lies in lacing this line with Diné historical reference, nostalgia, family history and, in its larger commentary on predatory alcohol sales as part of settler colonialism's legacy, with anticolonialist critique.

During its heyday, GD was also colloquially referred to as "Grandpa's Drink," or, more pointedly, as "Gallup Disease" or even "Garden Death" (Brodeur 2006, 3). All three of these glosses are implicit in Candice's usage of the term. We see a self-recognition of the havoc that cheap alcohol and predatory border-town businesses have wrought on reservation communities, where GD is framed as a type of social disease, blight, and even a cause of death,[22] affecting the entire town of Gallup and, by extension, lives and families throughout the Navajo reservation. As a remnant of the colonial encounter and of settler colonialism's mark, alcohol and GD consumption constitute a "disease" that now has roots deep enough to be referenced in a retooled country song for historical, familial humorous effect.

Garden DeLuxe as "Grandpa's Drink" is a partly serious, partly playful reference to one of the target populations of the Gallup Bottling Company: older Navajo men with fixed incomes. In fact, by 1987, 5,500 gallon tankers of wine fortified with brandy (to increase the alcohol content to 19 percent) were being driven in from California twice monthly and sold in Gallup via a system where customers provided their own, refillable containers (Brodeur 2006, 3). These patrons purchased the drink because it was inexpensive; along with other Gallup residents, they also sometimes consumed it to excess in public spaces, because, as a friend of mine pointed out, unlike other local Anglo and Hispanic residents who lived in town and could return home after a night at the bar, most of these men were reservation residents, in town temporarily, and thus were at a distance from their homes (there are no bars on the Navajo reservation). This hypervisibility led to the increased surveillance of Navajo bodies in public, border-town spaces such as Gallup.

What is less audible when listening to this performance of "Okie from Muskogee" is that Candice inserted the line about Garden DeLuxe for her late *nálii*,[23] or paternal grandfather, a country music fan whose drink of choice was Garden DeLuxe, though always in moderation. Recalling how he would create a playful cadence with the name, pronouncing it "GARden DeLUXE," she retains this inflection in her own performance of the song. Candice's grandfather also related to her how, during the Gallup era of the 5,500-gallon tanker trucks, he would bring in his one-gallon jug to Gallup for his "GD refill." In the case of her *nálii* and his playful affection for Garden DeLuxe, Candice emphasizes his moderate consumption, his balanced lifestyle, and the small joy he took in an occasional sip of GD, where in her family the emphasis was on "down home, clean, healthy fun, where things are done or taken in moderation and not in excessive measures" (C. Craig, personal communication, June 4, 2015). Refusing to go along with the stereotypes associated with Gallup or GD, Candice offers another, more intimate perspective on GD. Moreover, for Candice this family reference to GD also calls to mind her paternal great-grandfather who, like Merle Haggard's Okie, also sometimes made his own moonshine on the reservation and was a respected *hataałii*. In all these ways, Candice's reference to GD is a culturally intimate and specific reference to a generationally and community-specific drink around whose memory structures of feeling have accrued. While she recognizes all the havoc, disintegration, and pain such consumption has caused in Diné lives, Candice refuses to let that be the last word on the public image of Diné people, including her late family members. In keeping with a long tradition of country songs commemorating connections with loved ones now deceased, Candice's GD reference is a deeply personal, playful, and ironic reference to and remembrance of her *nálii* and the good life he lived.

Suturing time and place in reservation country-music performance, Candice's reference to GD also places her Diné listeners in an earlier time, where GD becomes a chronotope in its own right. Since GD was discontinued in the late 1990s,[24] its references are time specific, indexing a time when GD consumption was commonplace, a time before heavier drugs such as crystal meth began to invade rural reservation lives, and a time when "hard country" music was the predominant sound track of many reservation towns.[25] In coupling the lines "We still weave our rugs down at the chapter house / And Garden DeLuxe is still the biggest thrill of all," Candice combines and then challenges two essentialized Indigenous identities: one relating to cultural continuity, the other to Indigenous deprivation.

In constructing an intimate composite image of her hometown as she knew it growing up in the 1970s and early 1980s, Candice's lyrical substitutions push back against these stereotypes by historicizing GD as the predatory practice that it was and refusing to portray Native alcohol dependency as "genetic" in the way academics and the press sometimes have (Beauvais 1998; Wall, Carr, and Ehlers 2003).[26] Instead, she insists on its structural, historical, social, and settler-colonial origins in the case of her hometown and its nearest border town, Gallup or *Na'nízhoozhí*. Similarly, as a Diné citizen descended from a long line of weavers and as someone who also weaves herself, Candice refuses to allow rug weaving be the end-all, be-all of her identity as a Navajo woman, either in a song or in her daily life. A successful engineer, singer, DIY-er, and "lady from the rez" who sometimes does things she herself would describe as *jaan* (and then laughing about it), Candice embraces all these identities forcefully and simultaneously in the space of her version of "Okie from Muskogee" as the "Navajo from New Mexico."

Candice's lyrical substitutions are also self-consciously ironic, as Garden DeLuxe, most Navajo citizens will tell you, is perceived as anything but deluxe. Thus, we can also read "Okie from Muskogee," or "Navajo from New Mexico," as layered with double meanings, a song full of ironic twists and turns exemplifying what Barbara Ching refers to as the "abject burlesque" (2003). Indeed, as Ching and others have intimated, Merle Haggard's performance of this song may also be partly satirical, creating a persona that "voices both sides of the dialogue of abjection" (2003, 41). This is evidenced in class-specific lines like "leather boots are still in style from manly footwear," where a working-class man from Muskogee, Oklahoma, would be unlikely to use the term "manly footwear" to reference a man's shoes, but those who were well off enough to stay in Muskogee and avoid the Dust Bowl migration in the 1930s very well might.

We can also hear the double entendre of the song in the semisneer Haggard uses on the word "college" when singing the line "the kids here still respect the college dean" at the end of the first verse. Singing in a voice that again might be heard as impersonating another class identity—for example, that of a middle-class college student—Haggard seems to imply that neither the "kids" nor Haggard himself respect the dean at all. In her invocation of the "squaw" and Garden DeLuxe, Candice may be employing a similarly ironic strategy emphasizing these images' abject and burlesque aspects. She incorporates unoriginal media images of Native peoples into her song to critique these stereotypes with their origins in the settler-colonial encounter from the vantage point of her present positioning as a college graduate from the Navajo reservation.

Candice refers to herself as a "Navajo from New Mexico" and, sometimes, as a "redskin woman." She has changed the lyrics to Gretchen Wilson's self-conscious articulation of working-class womanhood, "Redneck Woman," to "Red*skin* Woman." With the title switched, she sings the chorus as follows: "I'm a redskin woman / ain't no high-class broad / I'm just a product of my raisin' / And I say "hey y'all" and "yee haw" / And I keep my Christmas lights on, on my front porch all year long / And I know all the words to every Tanya Tucker song[27] / So here's to all my sisters out there keepin' it country/Let me get a big "Hell Yeah" from the redskin girls like me." Her crowds routinely respond with an enthusiastic "HELL YEAH." By renaming the subject of Gretchen Wilson's song "Redskin Woman" but leaving all other lines of the song intact, Candice cleverly shows the gender and class parallels between two regionalized caricatures of working-class womanhood: the "southern redneck woman" who loves Tanya Tucker has much in common with the "southwestern redskin woman" who also loves — and grew up listening to — Tucker. Underscoring how both depictions are, in their own ways, equally overdetermined and self-conscious, it seems almost incredible that, with a mere two-word substitution, the song absolutely and undeniably *works* — it is believable, it is top-notch songwriting and craft, and it is popular with Candice's (mostly female) fan-base.

But authenticity is also gendered; indeed, in country music, "gender structures the processes through which country's authenticity is renegotiated and revitalized over time" (Pecknold and McCusker 2016, xi). Constructions of masculinity and femininity in country music have long formed core thematics of the genre, and part of country music's playfulness often comes from the ways in which singers and songwriters challenge and play with heteronormative and cisgender expectations while also conforming to very strict formal and harmonic structures within the genre (Fox 2004a, 242). Thus, just as Candice and Gretchen Wilson do, here, in addition to tropes of masculine authenticity and feminized commercialism (Pecknold and McCusker 2016, xi), country allows a space for rural, working-class women to perform more masculine aspects of their identities in important ways (Hubbs 2014).

Candice identifies the character in "Redneck Woman" as closely paralleling the lives of many women on the Navajo reservation, including her own. Some (but not all) of these practices, she underscores, might also be considered *jaan*. When speaking to her about how she defines this term, she gave me the example of a lady who, like herself, is "found under her truck more often than she's found *in* it," that is, her vehicle is often in need of repair and is disabled more often than it runs. *Jaan* is an accent, but also, like hard country music, an ideological stance and a set of life practices, where you're "stuck in the past," can't really navigate the modern world but "don't even know it" or don't "know any better." Thus, a *jaan* identity is underscored not only by a lack of ironic distance from one's life — the ability to wink — but also by an idea of futility. Unlike Candice's songs, a *jaan* aesthetic points exclusively inward and thus communicates a fundamental lack of awareness of the settler-colonial gaze and of what lies beyond the reservation.

But there are white *jaans*, too. Defined by Candice as a "rezzed-out white person," white *jaans* are Anglos who don't have self-awareness about their own habitus and class positioning. Using Diné, place-based, and reservation-centered epistemologies—*jaans* and being "rezzed out"—to describe the dominant racial group in the Southwest from a Navajo perspective, Candice nuances the internal class differences among Anglos and also between Anglos and Navajos in the process. She shows that Anglos, too, can be marginalized, a view not often foregrounded in reservation discourse, as the majority of Anglos living on the reservation hold solidly middle- or upper middle-class jobs. Strongly opposed to what might be considered equivalent terms from an Anglo perspective—including pejoratives such as "trailer trash"—"white *jaan*" for Candice is a gentler, more culturally intimate and inclusive designation for many of the border-town Anglos she knows. It is a way of making space for Anglos in her own, Diné-centered worldview, all while viewing such individuals on Navajo terms and from the perspective of sovereign Navajo land. White *jaans*, for example, might well include Haggard's "Okie"—a pejorative term designating an Anglo from Oklahoma during the Dust Bowl migration to California, but later standing in for a much wider swath of southeastern working-class migrants to western states—a term that Haggard pridefully resignifies as a character trait pertaining to grit, endurance, and learning how to "make do" under difficult circumstances, something Okies and many reservation Navajos have in common.

Candice's use of "redskin," "squaw," "GD," and even "Navajo" work in a similar way as does Haggard's "Okie." When Candice voices these epithets, she rehistoricizes, winks, and makes herself at once distant from and intimate with these terms. Candice's aesthetic points inward and outward simultaneously, a tricky, liminal, and even transgressive place for a Diné female artist to inhabit for any length of time. Decidedly *not* a fan of rez bands but performing in what for all purposes might be labeled as such by many Diné listeners, Candice carves out a place-based, cosmopolitan worldview in her songs where she does "know better" and uses this knowledge mindfully, strategically, and skillfully in her own performances.

In recrafting the lyrics to "Okie from Muskogee," Candice underscores the shared history of economic and class marginalization—the sense of living on the border of something unattainable—for working-class Natives and small-town Anglos. In so doing, she poignantly emphasizes the truth of this same marginalization for Native-majority spaces such as Crownpoint, one of the places she calls home. In changing "Okie" to "Navajo from New Mexico," "rednecks" to "redskins," "squares" to "squaws," "courthouse" to "chapter house," and "white lightning" to "GD," Candice recalibrates songs about economically marginalized Anglo, small-town identities ("Okies" from Muskogee and "redneck" women from rural Illinois) to tell the story of a Navajo woman—from New Mexico—of a similar class background instead. In this way, she fundamentally questions what Geoff Mann has termed a racial-musical "coupling" (2008, 82)—the deeply held assumption that country music calls people exclusively to their whiteness.

Candice's singing style challenges all that: she foregrounds race- and class-based similarities between herself and her Anglo counterparts. In her recordings and live performances, Candice sings with a husky voice and a mid range typical of a contralto. Her singing style, timbre, and range capitalize on a type of crying country voice made most prominent by vocalists Tammy Wynette and Loretta Lynn, artists whose careers peaked in the early 1970s but whose voices continue to be iconic for fans of honky-tonk and hard country today. These influences are clearly heard in Candice's singing style and choice of repertoire, and in the words on which she chooses to perform so-called cry breaks when she covers their songs. This is intentional. As the daughter of a prominent Crownpoint musician who played in a chapter-house band until his bandmates left for Vietnam, Candice was reared listening to many country artists—Lynn, Wynette, Tucker, and Crystal Gayle among them—whose heyday occurred before she was born. These singers, along with Etta James, were and are her musical idols. Her dad raised her on his music and musical aesthetic, and as a Navajo woman singer, she embraces these influences while also distancing herself from her dad's rez-band aesthetic in her song choices, her drumming, and lyrical substitutions. For the hard country fans, both Anglo and Diné, who come to hear her sing, Candice's voice activates a powerful point of connection.

Candice's style also avoids many of the stylistic devices associated with Navajo female singing voices: using one's "head" voice, affecting a nasalized tone, employing little to no vibrato (diaphragmatic pulsing that makes a note waver or tremble), and, when singing with men, singing a full octave higher than the male voices. Instead, when Candice performs country, she sings primarily in her chest voice, employs subtle amounts of vibrato at the end of long notes, introduces cry breaks on nouns and verbs of sorrow, and sings with a fairly standardized New Mexico English dialectal inflection, one that doesn't specifically index her identity as a Navajo from a small reservation town. And unlike many Diné female performers and speakers, for whom modesty and relatively little eye contact on stage are encouraged, Candice is flamboyant, assertive, and gregarious in her stage persona. Although she strongly signals her Diné identity through her lyrical substitutions, her dress style (which often includes Concha belts and women's traditional moccasins), the venues in which she performs, her sound, and her voice don't mark her as Navajo. Her more outwardly oriented aesthetic reaches off rez and is infused with a self-conscious irony that her dad's band doesn't possess; it is geared toward other working-class listeners, people for whom Tammy Wynette, Crystal Gayle, and Loretta Lynn played meaningful roles. In contrast to her dad's earlier chapter-house band, however, Candice's singing voice gestures beyond Navajo country music's early history and reservation-centered aesthetic.

On the San Carlos Apache reservation in Arizona, we also see the class similarities between working-class Athabaskans and their Others, in this case Anglo residents of reservation border towns (Samuels 2004). In an effort to distance themselves from border-town whites in particular, David Samuels shows how certain Apache musicians often will not diphthongize their vowels when singing, such as when Marshall from the Pacers refuses to twang the final syllable in the word "Vietnam," pronouncing it "Viet-nahm" instead. It is what one might do, as Samuels humorously puts it, if you "love country music, but you cain't staind the sound" (Samuels 2004, 339).

But apparently Candice can and does "staind the sound." What accounts for her departure from the norms on other reservations? In contrast to San Carlos, her embracing of twang may be due in part to the relative cultural hegemony Navajos enjoy in the Southwest vis-à-vis other Indigenous nations. (Navajos are the largest Native nation in the Southwest and the second largest in the United States.) Native peoples even call the Gathering of Nations, the Albuquerque mega powwow, the "Gathering of Navajos and Other Indians." So while Navajo cultural capital is relatively low in the Southwest when compared to that of Anglo communities, Navajo visibility is high, especially in border towns. There is safety and potential power in such numbers, so the need to demarcate herself as different from working-class Anglos may feel less crucial for Candice than it does for citizens of San Carlos, a tribe with fewer than ten thousand enrolled members. Candice, as a Navajo woman, makes her presence heard by fusing Anglo linguistic practices such as twang with Diné-inflected, place-based, and make-do lyrics. In "Redneck Woman," by *continuing* to diphthongize and nasalize the name Tanya instead of lengthening the vowel to become "Tohn-ya," Candice embraces the performative and linguistic similarities between working-class Anglos and her own checkerboard community, then making these indices more regionally specific and idiosyncratic, solidifying their relevance to her and her listeners' life experiences. Secure in her own identity as an Eastern Agency Diné woman, Candice calls attention instead to the ways she relates to the patriotism, rural lifestyle, small-town mentality and dialectal self-distinctions of the "Redneck Woman" and the "Okie from Muskogee." These songs, and Candice's execution of them, can be understood as highly stylized, performative articulations of American working-class experience.

By incorporating "Okie from Muskogee" and "Redneck Woman" into more specifically embodied, gendered, and regionalized contexts, Candice answers the question why country music sounds white: she shows that it doesn't, necessarily. Indeed, it can also "sound Native." In an uncanny though perhaps not uncommon inversion, the Hank Williams songs referenced at the beginning of this chapter can sound "Indian," and Candice, when she wants to, can sound redneck. Like the Aleuts whom Alexie quotes, Candice embraces country music as a genre that forms a deeply meaningful, almost sacred, part of her life. In her own words, singing country music is her sanctuary. This is a genre, therefore, that effectively expresses her identity as a Navajo, her spirituality, and the ways in which she is connected to the spaces of Crownpoint, Albuquerque, and beyond.

We see both a rejection and an embrace of the *jaan* identity here. Weaving references to place, mobility, and various marginalized identities into her country songs, Candice muddies the waters of contemporary Diné identity, refusing to adhere to existing categories with a definitive statement of who she is, at least in the performances of her songs in public spaces. She embraces her own position as matter out of place, as a Navajo from the wrong part of the reservation, as a woman singing country music, and as a country artist singing older, sometimes out-of-date songs. Speaking strategically from the margins and refusing to be labeled as either simply traditional or assimilated, her voice holds power and force for her listeners. Coupled with "redness," country music can index Navajoness just as it has been presumed to index whiteness since the division of race and hillbilly music in the early 1920s.[28] For many Navajos living, dancing, and performing country music on the Navajo Nation today, country music describes their worlds; it is a narration, a place-based expressive genre, and a marker of what—for some, at least—it means to be Diné.

CHAPTER TWO

. . . .

Generic Navajo

The Language Politics of
Social Authenticity

Some have carried it, held it close, protected.
Others have pulled it along like a reluctant child.
Still others have waved it like a flag, a signal to others.
And some have filled it with rage
And dare others to come close.
And there are those who find their language
A burdensome shackle.
They continually pick at the lock.
— Ofelia Zepeda, "Walking with Language"

Flagstaff, Arizona: Three Diné contestants compete in the annual Miss Indian NAU Pageant in the Northern Arizona University Music Department's main recital hall. After introducing themselves and their Navajo clans from the elevated stage in Navajo and answering a series of "quiz bowl" questions, the contestants, all NAU students, perform the "traditional talent" portion of the competition. Before the crowd and a panel of judges, Contestant #1 demonstrates how to wash one's hair using yucca root, while Contestant #2 discusses the significance of the Navajo wedding basket, its color pattern and its sunwise (shádbik'egho) woven structure. Contestant #3, the strongest Navajo speaker and a classical pianist studying to become a doctor, gives a brief introduction in English to the set of classical piano pieces she will perform. Raised playing Diné gospel and country, and tired of "all the beat dropping," she associates these genres with amateur musicians on the reservation. She has actively sought out classical music instead, and recently returned from a successful master-class series with a prestigious pianist in Germany. Knowing that her selection for "traditional talent" will be questioned on the very grounds of its "traditionality"[1]—based in part on the perception within her own community that classical music is "hoity-toity Anglo music"—she begins by saying: "Some of you may be wondering what's traditional about the piano. For me, the piano is traditional because we are Indigenizing classical music; by playing it in spaces like these, we're making it our own." Seated at the piano, dressed in traditional moccasins, hair tied in the traditional Navajo women's hair bun, and wearing the *biil* (rug dress) her paternal grandmother made for her, she begins to play on the concert Steinway, wrists delicately arched, long fingers gently and expertly gracing the keys. Much to the crowd's surprise and delight, Contestant #3—urban-identified but with strong ties to the reservation—is crowned as the 2015–2016 Miss Indian NAU.

How do the performative modes of music and language intertwine in this story, and how does tradition get redefined by a young Diné pianist (and the judges who crown her) insisting that classical concert music on a Steinway *is* Indigenous music, if and when she wants it to be? In an Indigenous musical field so sonically and ideologically dominated by country that one has to play classical music to innovate, how can other music genres too become Indigenized? Finally, what story of language and tradition is told through the other "traditional talents" thus selected, and what is the relation between music genre (art music inspired by traditional Diné social dance songs), speech genre (Navajo language introductions, English explanations foregrounding "traditional" talent), and innovation enacted here?

In this chapter, I argue that Diné language politics give us greater insight into the broader story of country music, belonging, and generational nostalgia chronicled in this book. I trace ethnographically how language—often portrayed as a key index of culture—is linked to a Navajo politics of difference through specific registers of speech and song. After an overview of Diné language politics, I turn to how a culturally intimate speech genre referred to as *jaan* (john) or "*jaan* Navajo" is incorporated into Native band rehearsals and Navajo comedy, forming the bedrock onto which generational wordplay and humor are overlaid. In chapter 1, we saw that Navajo identities crystallize around social class and *jaan* identities. Similarly, in this chapter we will see that identities are also crafted around registers of speech (Bakhtin 1981), music genre, and generational nostalgia, where the Navajo language itself is often biologized as something that those with Navajo "blood" are expected to speak (Peile and Bindon 1997). We again see how Navajo identity is composed of multilayered, overlapping, sometimes contradictory markers, from the color of one's skin to the pitch, range, and timbre of one's voice.

In some cases, language legitimizes Navajo identity and social citizenship—as an analysis of Radmilla's Cody's experience in the limelight shows in the following chapter. But language can also be used to exclude, creating a sense of civic estrangement, or "legal citizenship that is complicatedly coupled with a persistent sense of . . . estrangement from the rights and privileges of the contemporary public sphere" (Tillet 2009, 124). Nowhere is this truer than in Native women's beauty pageants, where, as in the case of the Miss Indian NAU Pageant, introducing oneself in one's heritage language is often obligatory as a way to establish kinship or *k'é*. In these and similar cases, not speaking Navajo often prevents a contestant from either competing in or winning a pageant,[2] reflecting the idea that to publicly represent the Navajo Nation one must speak Navajo.

Civic estrangement also occurs for full-blooded Navajos who don't speak Navajo. It is a powerful rhetoric that occurred repeatedly throughout my fieldwork: for these "4/4" Navajos, it is as if having Navajo blood leaves them with the obligation to activate their Navajo language inheritance, regardless of mother tongue or the geographic location of a speaker's upbringing. Language is biologized as something latent that needs simply be drawn out in Diné who don't hold speaker status (Davis 2015). Heritage language serves to both incorporate and disenfranchise Navajos living on the reservation today, creating boundaries between those who speak and understand prestige varieties of Navajo (full fluency), those who speak and understand so-called *jaan* Navajo (a version of Navajo using fewer older words), those who understand but speak haltingly (semifluency), those who understand but don't speak (passive fluency), and those who don't—or can't—do either (Meek 2010, 130).

Such an approach builds on the "undiscussed yet highly visible linguistic and behavioral practices" that inform more unconscious language ideologies shared by many speech communities (House 2002, xvi; see also Kroskrity 2004 and Webster 2009, 2015), yet I also depart from this methodology by examining language ideology in the specific context of blood quantum, voice, and generational aesthetics. If language ideologies are "beliefs, or feelings, about languages as used in their social world" (Kroskrity 2004, 498), *how* one uses one's voice—who one is permitted to admonish in public, who has the vocal authority to speak for whom, and how one does so—points to internal class-, gender-, and blood-based hierarchies within Navajo culture. As an analytic concept, I use the idea of voice as a framing device to analyze and understand daily discourse and linguistic performance at a symbolic level.

Like voice, "blood" and "blood quantum" are extremely broad signifiers, and their usage in daily discourse includes metaphorical, symbolic, pseudobiological, and bureaucratic meanings, often interchangeably. And, as in many spaces in Native North America, many Diné speakers have naturalized the language of blood. In all cases, however, undergirding this analysis is an understanding of blood as a socially constructed phenomenon—but one that, like race, is also a lived social fact, where to be Indigenous and on the receiving end of this fiction can prove deeply dehumanizing and disenfranchising (Biolsi 2004, 400).

In reservation spaces, the genre of music one plays is often used strategically to buttress and reflect claims to both voice and blood. While the boundaries of both speech and music genres are messy, boundary contestation and turf wars are essential for the defining of each. Following Levi-Strauss (1964) and other theorists, what makes country "country," or reservation English "really rez" is often defined more by what they are not than by what they are. Thus the boundaries of genres are as much about a specific sound as they are about the identities attached to and affiliated with that sound. For example, singing a country song but refusing to diphthongize one's vowels runs the risk of the song no longer being labeled as country, just as a Navajo speaking English with midwestern monoglot standard pronunciation (Silverstein 1996)—the equivalent of "broadcast English"—on the reservation might also run the risk of the speaker no longer being identified as being "rez," or from the reservation. Such boundary contestation also holds true for other speech genres spoken on the reservation, including Navajo, Navajo English (English spoken with a reservation dialectal inflection), and "Navadlish,"[3] or code-mixed English and Navajo (Webster 2015, 17–23). This slipperiness notwithstanding, musical and linguistic genre distinctions—and their corresponding socioeconomic, cultural, and identitarian worlds—are extremely meaningful for their adherents, including Diné peoples.

While scholars have spilled much ink discussing the problems around defining both speech and music genres and questioning whether "genre" as a category may indeed have outlived its usefulness (Bauman and Briggs 1992, 2003; Fox 2005; Novak 2013), little has been written about how musical and linguistic genres might coarticulate in ways essential to understanding both more deeply from a social scientific perspective. Preferences for musical genre and the speech style in which one speaks are not coincidental, and both act as key markers of how identity is performed and refracted through the social worlds we inhabit.

For example, it is no coincidence that the bandleader for Native Country loved to do dialectal impersonations of the late Diné comedian Vincent Craig while we jammed out to honky-tonk music of the 1970s and 1980s, and that he continually interlaced this humor with our band rehearsals at his son's ranch. By contrast, he maintained a fairly standard midwestern dialect of English during live performances when announcing songs and introducing the band. Displays of cultural intimacy are performed in select, private spaces, and rarely in public.

Moreover, affective connections to genre—to both music and speech—are often generationally defined, where listening to a certain genre of music or speaking in a certain way can instantly mark not only place of origin but age and generational outlook. Generational nostalgia, and a corresponding felt attachment to genre—what Webster terms intimate grammars, or "emotionally saturated uses of language that run the risk of negative evaluation by outsiders or nonoutsiders but are deeply and expressively feelingful for individuals" (2015, 7)—help us more deeply understand the source of these affective connections to country music and language politics in Diné lives.

In the larger U.S. context, links between music and speech genre might take the form of adults in their fifties and above feeling a strong affective tie to folk music of the 1960s and 1970s and a corresponding speech style and habitus connected to that genre, or folks in their thirties and forties feeling a strong connection to 1980s classic rock and employing, at least nostalgically, a "rocker" speech genre associated with this style of music. As we know from the example of the folk revival (Cantwell 1996, 2003; Rosenberg 1993), these linguistic and musical worlds do not form ex nihilo and are sometimes actively cultivated by music moguls, industry professionals, and cultural brokers. Nonetheless, they remain extremely meaningful to fans and participants and powerfully structure senses of self vis-à-vis generational cohorts. These musics, then, are generationally defined and defining for a specific age group, tightly corresponding to a linguistic habitus as well.

Similarly, on the Navajo Nation, loving and playing hard country often remains the domain of those aged forty and over, folks who likely speak Navajo as their first language and may also speak Navajo English and Navadlish; by contrast, loving hip-hop or R&B corresponds to those in their teens, twenties, and early thirties, a demographic defined by the ability to understand Navajo but not necessarily speak it (with some notable exceptions). The latter group of music listeners may also speak "Navajo English" and/or another variation of American English, including monoglot standard. Genre preference and speech genres correspond, often with a high degree of isomorphism, and genre and social class correspond as well.

On the Nation, nostalgia and affection for country music is linked to a post–World War II Navajo Nation, a time when the reservation underwent rapid and significant social, political, and economic changes: uranium was booming, jobs were plentiful, cosmopolitan Diné veterans and Code-Talkers had recently returned from fighting in the Pacific, Diné had finally gained the de facto right to vote (in 1948),[4] and American popular culture was powerfully taking hold in rural reservation spaces.

Most notably, beginning in the 1950s, larger numbers of Navajo teenagers began attending high school off reservation at vocational schools, and schools such as the Intermountain Indian School (1950–1984) in Brigham City, Utah, served exclusively Navajo students (Opsahl 2013; Campbell and Brainard 2003; Pegarero 2015; Shirley Bowman, personal communication, February 6, 2016). Other students, such as the comedian Vincent Craig, began living off reservation with Anglo, Mormon families in Utah and in neighboring states through a program known as the "Lamanite" or Mormon Placement Program (1947–2000) (Allen 1998; Garrett 2010).[5] At these schools, students began playing electric instruments and even forming their own bands, playing classic country, swamp pop, Tex-Mex, Cajun country, and rock-and-roll cover tunes of the era. Some bands, like the Navajo Sundowners who met at Intermountain, stayed intact and returned to the reservation to gain fame there and beyond. And almost immediately on their return, early Navajo bands such as the Fenders and the Valley Boys began modifying these same cover songs—lyrically, dialectically, and in terms of tempo—to reflect reservation lives, aesthetic preferences, and Indigenous worldviews.

According to many of my interlocutors, the distinction between those who left the reservation for high school and those who did not also began to create new and more sharply defined internal divisions in the Nation. Those who left and returned often acquired a new prestige and sense of perceived worldliness, sometimes seeing themselves and their newfound facility with the English language, popular music, and Anglo cultural and religious practices as higher status. Those who stayed behind, on the other hand, were increasingly denoted as lower status, unacculturated, and "backward" by those who left and then returned, reflecting Anglo ideologies absorbed off reservation. These educational and class distinctions—and the larger ideologies of settler colonialism, assimilation, and internal politics of difference they reflect—form the bedrock for many of the contemporary Diné aesthetics and politics of difference examined in this book.[6]

Professional rodeo—a previously Anglo-dominated sport—also made inroads on the Nation during the 1950s, with the All Indian Rodeo Cowboys Association (AIRCA) forming in the late 1950s and the Indian National Finals Rodeo and Navajo Nation Rodeo Association forming soon thereafter, around 1975 (Penrose 2003; Burgess 1993; Denzin 2002). In addition, in 1959, the Navajo Nation was the first American Indian tribal nation to form its own court system regulating all criminal and civil matters within Navajo territorial jurisdiction. Music, rodeo, education, and tribal politics reflected a larger move toward self-determination not only for Diné peoples but for American Indian nations throughout the United States. At the same time, during this "golden age," most reservation Navajos still spoke Navajo, and the imminent danger of language and culture loss associated with Anglo cultural hegemony was yet a few decades away. So, when older Navajos today listen to the first Navajo country western bands such as the Wingate Valley Boys or the Fenders, or to Vincent Craig reminiscing about and making fun of these bands by impersonating the speech styles of on-reservation Navajos, fans remember not just the music but a period when Diné people spoke Diné as a lingua franca, and when their tribe was mobilizing and transforming, politically and financially. Music is chronotopic—it sutures space and time—and can transport us almost instantaneously to other space-times (Bakhtin 1981), allowing us to access and dwell deeply, however momentarily, in those hard-to-reach affective spaces. Listening to hard country on the rez and on the radio—and to Navajo country western bands—creates a socially intimate space for a generation of Diné to not only relive their youth but also to ponder the present moment and potential futures, including the future of the Navajo language.

Navajo Language and Diné Language Politics

Compared to most American Indian nations, Navajos have a high percentage of heritage language speakers, with 73 percent of on-reservation Diné self- reporting as speaking a language other than English (presumably Navajo) in the home (Yurth 2012). However, these numbers reflect predominantly older speakers, and speakers thirty and younger overwhelmingly speak English as their first language. Blood quantum among Diné people is also collectively higher than among most U.S. tribes, with 286,000, or 86.3 percent of Diné citizens, self-reporting as full-blooded in the 2010 census (U.S. Census Brief 2010, 18). Having a higher Navajo blood quantum or, in local parlance, having more Navajo blood, is often linked to phenotype, observed via skin color, facial features, and having dark hair and dark eyes. Having many full-blooded tribal members is also often offered up — on the reservation and on other reservations throughout the country — as an explanation for why so many Navajos continue to speak Navajo relative to other Native American tribes. Here, the supposedly innate characteristics of biology, place of residence, and phenotype link powerfully with the learned, namely, language ideologies of heritage-language purity versus its contamination. While this latter discourse is often coupled with the perception of Navajos as a more rural tribe who are also the second-largest tribe in the United States (such that having more speakers reinforces a more vital Diné speech community), the idea that blood lends itself to fluency forms a central part of Diné-based blood talk and thus proves essential to the story of language, generational nostalgia, and belonging I document in this book.

Navajo is an agglutinative, southern Athabaskan language. As in most Athabaskan languages, the verb is central to *Diné bizaad*, and verbs are categorized by modes rather than tenses. The Navajo sound system features several sounds not found in Indo-European languages, including velar fricatives (aspiration), the lateral or "slash l," glottal stops, and glottalized consonants. Navajo is also a tonal language, featuring three tone levels, which makes it ripe for punning and double entendre, linguistic skills that Navajo speakers adeptly use in a variety of contexts (please refer to the "Note on Orthographic and Linguistic Conventions"). Crucially, tonal and nasal distinctions are often not heard by semispeakers and passive users, so grasping the full meaning of jokes and puns can be challenging even for those who generally understand the language but don't speak it with ease.

The Navajo language is highly onomatopoetic and often quite literal in its creation of neologisms. For example, words like *chidí* (car), *hashtł'ish* (mud), *Gáamalii* or *Máamalii* (Mormons) and *Éé' Neishoodii Daachaaígíí/Nidaamaasígíí* (Pentecostals) come directly from the perceived sounds and actions of these objects and people (Young and Morgan 1987). *Chidí* and *hashtł'ish* are onomatopoeias for the noises of a car (allegedly from the sound of the Model T Ford when it came to the reservation in the 1930s) and the sound one makes walking in mud (*tł'ish tł'ish* or "squish, squash"), respectively. Similarly, Christian denominations on the reservation are distinguished from one another by their speech acts, the way they dress, and how they comport themselves during religious worship. According to my Navajo language teacher, Navajos perceived Mormon missionaries, for example, to be mumbling all the time in their sermons and door-to-door proselytizing. These utterances were sometimes described as *ghálí ghálí ghálí* ("bla bla bla"), so Mormons were given a Navajo name, *Gáamaliis*. Similarly, since Pentecostals are known to be very emotional, sometimes even crying during their services, they are called "the ones with the long robes [religious persons] who cry" (*Éé' neishodii daachaaígíí*), or sometimes "the ones with the long robes [religious persons] who roll around on the ground" (*Éé' neishodii nidaamaasígíí*) (Shirley Bowman, personal communication, January 25, 2011).

The descriptive qualities of *Diné bizaad* also make it particularly apt for describing new cultural phenomena from a Navajo perspective, and Navajo speakers often enjoy playing with contact between languages—for example, between English and Navajo. This is something that David Samuels (2004) notes about linguistic puns in other southern Athabaskan and western Apache contexts. As Anthony Webster notes, "English is ripe for punning opportunities in Navajo" (2009, 10). We can hear the remarkable amount of detail in the Navajo language in Diné compound nouns,[7] including Navajo place names. Popular restaurants in the border town of Gallup such as Furr's Cafeteria and Golden Corral have titles that simply describe the manner in which food is obtained at these establishments. Thus the Navajo name for Furr's Cafeteria is Hazhdiisho'ídi, or "at the place where you scoot your tray along," referring to its self-serve buffet, and the name for Golden Corral is Dziits'ílídi, or "at the place where you eat 'til you pop," referring to its all-you-can-eat policy (Shirley Bowman, personal communication, October 1, 2009). The name for Furr's is even more specific and socially descriptive, as it also implies that you are "scooting your tray along" with someone else, out on a date at Furr's.

Similarly, Wal-Mart lends itself to a variety of Navajo names. The most common one, Naalyéhé bá hooghan hótsaaídi, "(at) the large trading post," uses the earlier term for trading posts and then adds *hótsaaí*, or "large," to distinguish it from other stores and trading posts. Speaking to its popularity with many surrounding Native communities, Wal-Mart is also humorously referred to in English as the "Gathering of Nations," or even "The Gathering of Navajos and other Indians." These names are inspired by the famous annual intertribal ceremonial that takes place in Albuquerque each April and which many Dine'é attend. In fact, the Gallup Wal-Mart Supercenter is rumored to be among the highest-grossing Wal-Marts in the country (Wilkins 2013, 189).

Yet another name for Wal-Mart from a male perspective is Hastóí dach'ilídi, or "at the place where the men get roasted." This moniker, according to Tommy Bia, describes a weekly ritual: when families go to border-town Wal-Marts (a.k.a. "town") on Saturdays to do their shopping, the men often wait in their vehicles out in the paved parking lot, getting hotter by the minute and "roasting." Meanwhile, the women are inside, laboring over purchasing decisions or perhaps visiting with acquaintances (Tommy Bia, November 5, 2010). Making this roasting moniker even more apropos for its users, the Gallup Wal-Mart in particular has become popular for offering the free roasting of Anaheim green chilies, a New Mexico culinary specialty, bought there in the late summer months.

Because so much of Navajo humor revolves around wordplay and artful punning, many Diné speakers show a heightened sensitivity to language, genre, and proper language use. Perhaps because of this, Navajo citizens who are non-speakers of Navajo often feel the need to prove they belong through other, extra-linguistic means. Language for many Navajos is much "more than a grammatical system"; it is also "something that people inhabit and that inhabits them as well" (Webster 2009, 11). Language, then, is one outlet for the expression of the felt attachment to aesthetic forms, including music, or what has elsewhere been called "feelingful iconicity," where the feeling and connection to the past remains the same over time, but the form—speech styles or the genre of music one plays or listens to—itself changes (Samuels 2004a, 11).

One example of responses to changing linguistic forms can be seen in the "What kind of Navajo are you?" exchange that begins this book, in which an older speaker admonishes a younger one for not understanding her use of an older Navajo word for kerosene. The conversation reveals the linguistic and cultural generation gap often experienced among Navajos. It also exemplifies a language ideology in which Navajo language is being activated as a trope indexing Navajo identity, a process linguists have called "iconization" (Irvine and Gal 2000; Meek 2010, 132) that "denies the ubiquity of English and any corresponding bilingualism, multilingualism, or dialect differences" within a sociolinguistic landscape (Meek 2010, 132). For example, one commonly hears community elders and politicians link Navajo identity to the ability to speak and understand Navajo. This proves especially problematic in Native North American speech communities where, more often than not, English has become the hegemonic language. One of the social ramifications of iconization is that it "renders invisible the fair speakers, the poor speakers, and the nonspeakers by excluding them from the linguistically essentialized 'we' of aboriginal identity" (Meek 2010, 133). Following Phyllis Ann Fast's discussion of ethnic tropes in northern Athabaskan communities, language can be "another trope that is used as a weapon," where "those who were not known to speak, understand, or read an Athabascan language were deemed less Athabascan than others" (2002, 23). Iconization in effect often excludes non-speakers from social citizenship within Indigenous nations.

Also missed in the process of iconization are the felt attachments many Diné have to speech genres such as Navajo English. As a genre, Navajo English is often stigmatized and marginalized by both Diné and non-Diné. Here, it is important to recognize that speaking in "what some Navajos sometimes call *Diné'kehjí yátti'* (he/she is talking the Diné way) does not presuppose speaking something called 'Navajo'" (Webster 2015, 65). This holds especially true for younger Diné, who may not speak Navajo but identify strongly as Diné in myriad ways, including through their use of Navajo English. As Webster shows in the case of Navajo poets, Navajo English—defined by the regularization of irregular mainstream English forms such as sheep/sheeps and phonetic carryovers from Navajo, including the aspiration of final vowels—is used expressively, affectively, and with deep attunement to artful language use.

The older Diné woman referenced at the beginning of this book, Irene Bilagody, and her comment—"Yáadi lá Diné" or "what kind of Navajo are you?"—also provide insight into a Navajo sociolinguistic hierarchy that often divides Diné speech communities. Here, older heritage language speakers are marked as core members of an Indigenous community, while younger non-speakers are marginalized as not fully belonging, either culturally or politically (Meek 2010, xxiii). This is the distinction Chickasaw linguist Jenny Davis makes between citizenship in its strict legal sense and centralized community membership, with the latter inhering to heritage language speakers and "language affiliates," or community members who have either familial relationships to speakers, some level of Chickasaw language learning or activism, or a familial relationship to language learners or activists (Davis 2015, 103, 106). Thus, embedded in the Diné exchange we hear at least two levels of "sociolinguistic disjuncture" (Meek 2010, xxiii; Shirley Bowman personal correspondence, July 30, 2016). Defined as "the breakdown between and across theories and practices" of language use (Meek 2010, xxiii), the first disjuncture we see is that the cashier doesn't understand Irene's request, and, responding to her in English (a language Irene may or may not understand), tells her that the gas pump is already on. The second disjuncture is a generational one. It is quite possible that the young cashier actually *does* speak or at least understands Navajo; even so, the word Irene used for kerosene—*ak'ah kǫ' bitoo'* ("fat, fire, its juice/liquid")—is an older, descriptive word. So, *ak'ah kǫ' bitoo'* is associated with a world and a lifestyle that the teenage cashier, depending on where he was reared, may not know. Implied in Irene's request for kerosene is a lifestyle typical of some older Navajos, and it specifically references her own possibly limited access to electricity and the need (or preference) for kerosene to light her lamps. Assuming that the cashier lives in the more urban environment of Chinle, where the exchange took place, he also may never have had the opportunity or need to use kerosene or learn the specific Navajo word for it.

These practical disjunctures reflect the larger theoretical disconnections undergirding the exchange, as well as the "linguistic double bind" that characterizes language politics in Indian country today (Davis 2015, 100). On the one hand, we see a language ideology that demands the use of dominant languages such as English to be considered local, national, and global citizens; on the other hand, Indigenous citizens are expected to maintain "the use of their heritage languages in order to be deemed authentically indigenous" (Davis 2015, 100). Irene's "Yáadi lá Diné" is certainly a stinging accusation to direct at another Navajo. When I shared this encounter with other Diné, individuals often expressed discomfort or sadness with this speech act, especially since it was directed at a teenager. But they also weren't surprised, explaining that they had witnessed similar scenes in other contexts. It is the sort of exchange you might hear, as Shirley Bowman suggested, when older heritage speakers become impatient with younger speakers —or perhaps even with themselves and their own inability to communicate in English. In frustration, older speakers occasionally lash out to show their own unease with these sociolinguistic disjunctures and with the larger processes of language shift now occurring on the reservation (House 2002; Lee 2014; Webster 2009). After all, as my interlocutors pointed out, this occasion probably marked just one of many moments of linguistic disconnection that Irene has experienced.

Moreover, monolingual Navajo speakers are perceived as being predominantly women, and the majority of Navajo language educators are also women. Irene's gendered identity, therefore, also plays a role in this exchange, where an older Navajo matriarch chastises a younger Navajo man for not knowing his culture. Women are often charged with teaching and transmitting Navajo language and culture to their children. And because of the spiritual associations between language and culture, women as language teachers are by extension associated with the spiritual side of Navajo identity. For example, during the 2014 Navajo Nation presidential debate in Tuba City, Arizona, Carrie Lynn Martin, the only female candidate, told the crowd that her identity as a woman would help connect the Navajo Nation back to its roots "in the home and with its spiritual side" (Martin 6/23/14, Tuba City, Arizona). Moreover, although male puberty ceremonies (tachééh) are conducted only infrequently, the female puberty ceremony known as the kinaaldá is still frequently performed for young women after their first menses, and it is seen as a key moment in a young woman's life when cultural and linguistic knowledge is transmitted (Frisbie 1967; Lee 2012).

Older women ("grandmas") are also associated with a "prestige variety of spoken Navajo" (Peterson 2006, 123), often referred to as "real" Navajo or "old" Navajo. It is less plausible—although certainly possible—to imagine an older Navajo man chastising a teenaged Navajo girl in public for not speaking or understanding Navajo. If anything, a similar linguistic disjuncture might be highlighted through extended teasing, especially if the girl were related to the joshing older man in question. Thus, similar to de la Cadena's observation about Quechua women's roles as Indigenous "culture bearers" in rural Peru, older Navajo women are in some ways expected to act "more Indian"—or, in local Navajo parlance, to act more traditional—than their male counterparts (de la Cadena 1997).

Ideologies of social authenticity and of who has the ability to speak for whom are also foregrounded in everyday language use. For example, those who regularly speak Navajo in public spaces—politicians, rodeo MCs, medicine men, Miss Navajos, bureaucrats, and professors—are often portrayed by other Navajos as being "more Navajo" than non-speakers. This holds particularly true for those running for public office, because although Navajo proficiency is only officially required for the offices of Navajo Nation president, vice president, council delegates, and tribal judges, speaking and understanding Navajo is nonetheless hoped for and expected in all public offices (Thompson and Jacobsen, forthcoming).[8] When living in Crownpoint, I often heard the Crownpoint chapter president, a vocal and proactive community leader, criticized for not speaking Navajo. In fact, in a conversation that frequently repeated itself, community members would compare my Navajo to his and to other Navajos learning their language. Blood and language are so linked that my Anglo heritage and relative facility with the Navajo language were sometimes used to shame people with Navajo blood who "should" speak Navajo but did not.

Perhaps in an attempt to assuage similar criticisms and to sound more Navajo, this chapter official would often add the nominalizer *igíí* ("the one") to English words when he had the floor at meetings, effectively code-mixing terms such as chapter house to become *chapterhouseigíí* ("the one that is the chapter house"). This practice, however, was heard as redundant because he was nominalizing words that were already nouns, thus leading to a further critique of his language abilities. These censoring discourses marginalized the official, to some extent diminishing his ability to have an effective voice in the public sphere. Thus, although legal and cultural requirements for Navajo public office sometimes contradict each other, social expectations for fluency carry symbolic weight.

The unofficial expectation that a chapter president be fluent in Navajo also reveals the changing set of criteria required of those who, as community leaders, represent the public face of Navajoness. As Sturm (2002) shows in her research, expectations for political leaders—how phenotypically Indian they look, how fluent they are in their heritage language—often don't match the actual demographics of the tribe they publicly represent, projecting instead what she calls the "imagined" or idealized center of the tribe (2002, 107). In this case, the chapter official's age (mid-forties), high level of English proficiency, and his lacking fluency in Navajo gave a fairly accurate linguistic representation of many Navajos in this age range from Crownpoint and throughout the reservation. However, the expectations placed on him also speak to the performative aspects of Indigenous language use.

At a political rally in the fall of 2010, the Navajo Nation vice presidential hopeful Earl Tulley noted the expectation that political leaders would campaign in the Diné language, as he so eloquently did. Tulley then courageously went on to apologize, in English, to younger generations for the disjuncture wrought by Navajo parents of the boarding-school era: "We didn't teach you our language." He ended this observation very movingly, by admitting: "and it's our fault." Somewhat perplexingly, however, after making this public apology, he went back to speaking only in Navajo, effectively excluding non-Navajo speakers from the rest of his stump speech and from the important conversation about language loss he had played a part in beginning (Earl Tulley, Newlands Chapter House, fall 2010). This brief address in Navajo was made all the more poignant because it was being broadcast over the Armed Forces Network for younger Navajo military personnel overseas, many of whom are English dominant. With public oratory in particular, then, we see the expectation that Navajo officials deliver their message either in Navajo or that they code-switch between Navajo and English (as is most often the case). Tulley's switch back to Navajo revealed that, at that moment, his primary emphasis lay in the symbolic performance, or in what Jakobson would call the poetic function of Indigenous language use, where "the focus [is] on the message for its own sake" (Jakobson 1960, 356).

Earl Tulley's apology about language loss reflects a key shift in Navajo and U.S. government attitudes toward Native languages. While Native language use was actively discouraged in Bureau of Indian Affairs boarding schools until at least the 1980s (Lomawaima 1995; Reyhner 1993; Archuleta, Child, and Lomawaima 2000), today Navajo is taught both in Bureau of Indian Education (BIE) and in public and grant schools on the reservation, and also in some neighboring border town schools. Moreover, losing one's language is now talked about as something to actively work against, and language loss has become intrinsically linked to loss of Diné culture and identity.

Those who speak nonstandard varieties of Navajo and English often find themselves linguistically and socially marginalized. This holds true for speakers of Navajo, Navajo English, and Navadlish. For example, my Navajo language teacher often referred, albeit with a twinkle in her eye, to newer Navajo as "slangy" or "lazy-tongue" Navajo, indicating it was grammatically incorrect. Such slang was pointed out to me in words where the Navajo gerund *go*, as in *hazhǫ́'ǫ́go*, is elided to become *hazhǫ́'ǫ́*, or in code-mixed expressions such as "Háʼátʼíísh baa nanDOing?"[9] ("What are you doing/up to?") or "Tʼóó shił déez" ("I'm just out of it/in a 'daze'/possibly intoxicated"). For instance, I sometimes would hear middle-aged and younger Navajos refer admiringly and defer to certain (often older) Navajos as individuals who speak "the old Navajo" or *Saadsání* (old words /old language). According to this language ideology, older Navajos were considered people of "few words." Language was considered sacred and not to be used casually or with needless repetition (Shirley Bowman, personal communication, October 16 ,2011).

At the same time, since the median age of Navajo citizens is twenty-four years and many younger speakers aren't fluent,[10] code-mixed versions of English and Navajo are quickly becoming the standard. The standardization of newer Navajo, and the playfulness created from the spaces between the two languages, is best exemplified in certain terms now used by radio announcers in their broadcast speech. Younger deejays heard on the Four Corners' Navajo-language radio stations (KNDN, KGAK, KTNN, and KYAT) will mark their speech on air through the repetitive use of filler words such as *yáʼ*, *éiyá*, and *ałdóʼ* (also). They will often refer to days of the week and numbers in English rather than in Navajo. These same deejays, representing a younger generation of speakers, also sometimes will omit nasalizations altogether, opting to pronounce vowels as non-nasalized sounds instead. Older speakers tend to single out these terms as features marking these announcers as younger, less fluent speakers. For example, the affective particle, *yáʼ*, meaning "you know what I mean?," is used more frequently by speakers aged forty and below. After attending a chapter meeting where I heard a middle-aged chapter official say, "I heard it through the grapevine, *yáʼ*," I relayed this humorous quip to my Navajo teacher in New Mexico (in her fifties) and to my host parents (in their early seventies) in Arizona. They all found this code-mixed sentence humorous but also nonsensical, as they understood it as a self-directed rhetorical question, translating as, "I heard it through the grapevine, didn't I?" From the perspective of older speakers, these terms are used gratuitously and make it hard to take the speaker seriously.

As the linguist Michelle Kiser points out, however, no standardized entity exists that can simply be called "old Navajo" (Navajo Language Academy, Tsaile, Arizona, July 17, 2013). Like all language systems, Navajo is a living and constantly changing entity. For example, during the Spanish colonial period (1535–1821), the Navajo language changed significantly, incorporating a large number of Spanish loan words such as *bilasáana* for *manzana* or "apple" and *mandagíiya* for *mantequilla* or "butter," and Navajo vocabulary continues to significantly change every twenty years or so. Old Navajo is more of an ideal type than an actual linguistic phenomenon, but it's an ideal continually assigned tremendous power.

Fluency is also defined differently by various speakers, and is often determined by the prestige level associated with one's speech. Thus a speaker of *jaan* Navajo, while technically fluent, might not be considered proficient because of the low-prestige variety of Navajo she or he speaks. I often observed Navajo speakers whom I considered quite fluent comparing themselves and their Navajo against old Navajo or other varieties of prestige Navajo they didn't themselves speak. These comparisons were then followed by confessions, often offered in a hushed voice, that they "weren't really fluent." Similarly, many speakers who have excellent passive fluency, and understand everything that is said to them in Navajo, are the first to claim that they don't know their language. Not being fluent is also sometimes offered as an explanation for why speakers, in turn, don't speak to their kids in Navajo, since they are concerned about proper language use and the ramifications of teaching incorrect Navajo to future generations.

These perceived shortcomings for some speakers are based on the traditional belief that language is sentient, accordingly insisting that there are proper and improper ways to use *Diné bizaad*. This idea is something Navajo speakers take very seriously. At the 2013 Navajo Language Academy held in Tsaile, a lively conversation occurred about the use of the term "dissection" in reference to analyzing Navajo morphology and verb structures in a classroom setting, since, as one participant noted, one only dissects something that's already dead. Many Navajo speakers and teachers advocated, instead, to replace "dissect" with a more life-affirming verb such as "illuminate," or *saad bik'i'diyildlaad* (shedding light on words). Similarly, at this same conference, second-language learners expressed some frustration with their inability to ask for new words to be repeated, recalling that they were told repeating a new word (especially on the fourth time, a sacred number in the Navajo cosmology) showed disrespect to the language and to Navajo culture.

Speakers of nonstandard varieties of Navajo often self-silence—or render themselves invisible. Building on this, we could say that linguistic invisibility is rendered between the poles of two linguistic ideal types, those of "mono-glot" Standard American English, on the one hand, and *Saadsání*, or old Navajo, on the other. Thus, although multiple speech communities exist on the Navajo Nation—among them those who speak English, Navajo English, *jaan* Navajo, and what Peterson refers to as Grandparents' or old Navajo Navajo (Peterson 2006, 75–78)—those who speak Navajo English and *jaan* Navajo are often stig-matized and silenced compared to those deemed to speak more standardized, prestige varieties of English or Navajo. Speaking, for many Navajos, "is a tension-filled site, where they always run the risk of negative evaluation for their choices and uses of linguistic forms that are always the subject of scrutiny" (Webster 2015, 12).

Ramifications of linguistic othering, of course, reach far beyond linguistic realms into the political, the cultural, and the social (Feld et al. 2004; Jenks 2014, 9; T. S. Lee 2009). Those who speak "bad language" are often considered to be "bad citizens" (Battistella 2012). Language stigmatization speaks to a larger Navajo politics of difference and authenticity, where Diné citizens struggle with the question of whom to include and to whom to give a voice based on linguistic abilities alone. Language becomes one strategic choice utilized to index belong-ing and social authenticity for Diné individuals. Music is yet another.

As mentioned previously, one of the most stigmatized forms of newer Navajo speech is referred to as *jaan* Navajo. Often labeled as incorrect or "improper" Navajo (Peterson 2006, 76), *jaan* Navajo refers to Navajo language use that com-municates the gist of the message—Jakobson's phatic function—but isn't deliv-ered in an elegant, humorous, or kinship-oriented manner. *Jaan* Navajo lacks a self-awareness about language use and its poetic function highly valued among many Diné speakers, because the impetus for speech isn't based in Diné teach-ings but in the mundanity of the speech act itself. *Jaan* Navajo is betwixt and between, neither old Navajo nor a prestige variety of English, falling somewhere in the cracks between the two and thus accruing the status of neither. *Jaan* Navajo is matter out of place.

Jxaan Navajo, or *jaan* with an added *x* or velar fricative, constitutes an even more stigmatized version of nonstandard Navajo. As an expressive feature in-dicating a pejorative affective stance (Webster 2013, 117), the velar fricative in Navajo serves as an intensifier, for example changing the color yellow (*łitso*) to orange (*łitsxo*). In addition, the velar fricative, always added after consonantal clusters, is optional, such that words can stand on their own without it. As Reich-ard (1948) noted, the velar fricative constitutes an augmentative form, amplifying and intensifying extant meaning. Here, the velar fricative amplifies the already stigmatized and abjected status of the *jaan* speaker type.

Jaans also often speak English, but their English is as stigmatized as their Navajo. The comedian Vincent Craig's routines of Navajo-English are one example of what might be considered *jaan* or even *jxáán* English. In his routines, Craig reassigns meaning to the code-mixed "Oh *shí* heart" ("Oh my heart," similar to saying "Be still, my heart") in a Navajo context, exhibiting both an affection for and distance from these terms in the process of satirizing them. Craig's use of Navadlish and a *jxáán* accent in his many live recordings has deeply influenced reservation humor and attentiveness to humor and language use in public spaces, including billboards.

Craig also resignifies English words such as the word "somehow" for a Diné-specific audience in his comedic routines. In story vignettes such as "Are Indian Men Romantic?," recorded live at Many Farms High School in 1995, Craig riffs on the inhibition some Navajo men feel about expressing their feelings toward women. In this vignette, a Navajo teenager and his girlfriend sit in his truck on a mesa overlooking Many Farms. The moon is full, they're looking at each other by the lights of the dashboard, KTNN (the local country music station) is playing on the radio, and the mood is perfect. In the apotheosis of his desire to tell her how he truly feels, the guy says in a Navajo-inflected accent: "Oh honey, yer eyes are . . . jus' *some*how." Similar uses of "just *some*how" are often heard in daily English discourse on the reservation, in a form of reported speech that most folks know is an impersonation of Craig in particular; it's funny and uniformly elicits laughs because "*some*how" is a nonspecific euphemism used to describe something very specific, so it acts as a completely *inadequate* substitute for these feelings. Its inarticulateness, and the user's recognition of this inadequacy while continuing to use it, is what makes "yer jus' *some*how" so funny. The speaker is literally at a loss for words. Many Navajos—and Diné men in particular—love to create their own riffs using this expression and others like it as the punch line.

During band practices on Carson Mesa in Many Farms, Native Country's Tommy Bia and his son Arlondo also frequently used "jus' somehow" when riffing on the Navajo accent. As two men who specifically reject a *jaan* identity— both are middle-class government employees, livestock owners, and ranchers from a high-status reservation family—these jokes both embrace and distance themselves from *jxaan* speech styles and identities. After a long night of recording and finalizing the fourth song for our album at the family sheep camp,[11], we all felt particularly pleased and satisfied with the end product. As Tommy and I exited the sound booth, Arlondo, referring to the song, quipped in an animated voice, "it's just *some*how!" Tommy started to chuckle, responding to Arlondo's reference by adding another layer of multivocality. Changing the English adjective "good" into a comparative ("gooders"), in the style of Vincent Craig's non-standard, code-mixed Navajo-English, Tommy then appended the particle *yá'*, exclaiming in an animated, falsetto voice also imitating Craig: "It's really gooders, *yá'.*" Riffing on another element of Navajo English in which singular nouns are often pluralized, Arlondo concluded the exchange by one-upping his father's response with a signature phrase: "BIG times!"

Craig's pervasive influence on public discourse about Navajo authenticity and *jaan* identities can most clearly be seen in a spoof application circulated a few years ago, ostensibly from the Navajo Housing Authority (NHA). A series of questions designed to humorously determine one's eligibility as an authentic rural reservation Navajo are listed: "Occupation (check one): Spring sheepherder, Summer sheepherder, Fall Sheepherder"; "Model and year of your pickup: 194__ (fill in the blank)"; and so forth. The final two questions on the questionnaire read as follows:

Do you listen to Vincent Craig while traveling? ( ) Yes ( ) No
Are you just somehow? ( ) Yes ( ) No ( ) Sometimes ( ) All the time

Since his passing in 2010, Vincent Craig's vibrant legacy continues in current musical practice in much the same way that he, too, continued the legacy of the chapter-house bands in his own songs and humor. He is referenced on reservation billboards, such as the one between Gallup and Window Rock, which read "Oh, *Shí* Heart! Buckle Up Navajo Nation," in male-centered wordplay and humor, and in musical styles and sounds that some bands seek to emulate and others explicitly distance themselves from. For example, we hear Craig's influence on musical style in the classic "chapter-house band mic check," performed and re-enacted by bands throughout the reservation by histrionically blowing three times, open-mouthed, into the microphone when checking the channel of a public-address system. This is the sort of performance that might be referred to, either jokingly or disparagingly, by listeners as being "very *jaan*." Here, yet another stereotype of Native peoples and of *jaans*—that of being technologically "primitive" (Deloria 2004)—is addressed head-on through one of its most effective tools: humor.

Speaking Navajo also marks one's identity *as* a Navajo among other Diné, while losing that marker leaves one open to other charges, for instance, of being a Navajo tabula rasa whose identity is a floating signifier and up for grabs. One day I took my friend's bicycle in for a tune-up at the Navajo Cycle Shop out-side of Window Rock. The Cycle Shop is located at the turnoff to the Chevron Coal Mine on the northeast side of town. Naively thinking that "cycle" refers to bicycles — a rarity on the reservation given the terrain — I was surprised to find the Cycle Shop was an independently owned business that repairs Harleys. Nonetheless Rick Wilson, the co-owner, graciously offered to repair the bicycle just the same. Finding out that I'm a student of the Navajo language and an an-thropologist, he started to chat about his experiences living on the reservation and the hardships of running a small business on the rez, when everyone was programmed to get their motorcycle repairs done in border towns like Gallup and Farmington. His mom, he said, was Taos Pueblo and his dad Diné, but he and his brothers were raised in Taos. He recalled the challenges of relocating to the Navajo reservation as an adult, something he did because his dad owned land on the Nation. He found the move particularly difficult because he didn't really speak or understand the Navajo language, and didn't know much about Navajo ceremonial life. "They call me — what do you call it? — a 'generic' Navajo."

The use of the term "generic" and the expression "Yáadi lá Diné!" share sig-nificant similarities in the social work they perform. Calling him generic ref-erences Rick's lack of language skills, but it could also refer to the fact that, by blood quantum, he is "half" Navajo and "half" Pueblo. Because Rick's mother is Pueblo, in the Navajo way, clanwise this makes him more Pueblo than Navajo, as his first, maternal clan is Pueblo.[12] While he may enroll in the Nation based on his blood quantum, Rick is marginalized and without the sense of Navajo social citi-zenship he expresses a desire to feel. In an ironic twist, since his mother married out of her tribe, her children may or may not actually have Taos citizenship, even if they meet the minimum blood-quantum requirements for the tribe: one quarter Taos Pueblo blood.[13] Thus, because Taos Pueblo and Navajo Nation don't allow dual citizenship, Rick likely belongs politically to one tribe (Navajo Nation) and culturally and clanwise to another (Taos Pueblo). In both cases, however, Rick lacks an alignment of social and political belonging, and language plays a role in these assessments. As a result, he is a citizen of an Indigenous nation in which some fellow citizens label him as generic and where he feels he is without a voice.

But if Navajo language serves as an index of Navajoness, it is certainly not the only one. Early on in his study of Navajo poetry, for example, the linguistic anthropologist Anthony Webster confesses that he made a fundamental mistake in his early fieldwork, one he would later correct: "I had confused *being* Navajo," he states, "with *speaking* Navajo" (2009, 2; italics mine). He explains further:

"The use of Navajo can and does index Navajoness." However, "Navajoness can be indexed by traditional poetic devices that have been transferred to English. *Navajos can and do use English to index Navajoness*" (2009, 46; italics mine). As I show, this also holds true for Navajo performances of country-western songs sung in English and in humorous anecdotes.

For example, in a code-mixed joke that a friend from Crownpoint told me in August of 2011, we're told of a Navajo medicine man who is getting ready to conduct a ceremony in a *hooghan* somewhere in Eastern Agency. He is speaking to the younger people in attendance, and tells them, at length and in Navajo, that during the ceremony there will be no use of English because it can impact the efficacy of the ceremony. He continues in this vein, waxing eloquent about the beauty and centrality of the Navajo language in a Navajo ceremonial worldview, and then, at the end of the soliloquy, code-switches back into English. In a thick Navajo accent, he then says: "Bilagáana bizaad [the English language] éí [filler word], I DON'T LIKE IT!"

In this joke, we see through humor the "feelingful connection" for both languages, which can be played with to great effect (Webster 2009, 15). In the "I don't like it" joke, it is the code-mixing itself as it occurs within the single frame of the anecdote—perhaps an accurate commentary in its own right about the frequency of code-mixing, even in ceremonial contexts—that seems to make the joke funny and that made it resonate with my Navajo teacher, a speaker of an older, prestige variety of Navajo. Code-mixing is a frequent occurrence in Navajo, and English loan words are consistently peppered into Navajo language radio broadcasts with great humorous effect. We also hear this in traditional song forms such as skip dances, two-step songs, and round dance songs such as the well-loved "Cotton Candy/Lollipop" by the recording artist Jay Begaye.[14] By comparison, code-mixing and English loan-word incorporation in Hopi-language broadcasts like KUYI (88.1 FM) out of Hotevilla, Hopi Nation, occur much less frequently. The latter reflects a more conservative linguistic cosmology, where use of loan words of any origin other than Hopi can be perceived as a dilution of Hopi cultural expression (Hill 2002; Kroskrity 2004). For Diné speakers, however, English loan-word incorporation can express something quite different and often acts as an augmentative form of self-expression, giving a speaker a broader linguistic canvas from which to work. This playfulness focuses less on where the words are coming from or on the national boundaries they represent—the U.S. versus the Navajo Nation, for example—and focuses more on the pleasurable sound combinations that code-mixed phrases such as "wait/ałtsé" (wait/wait) and "tį'/let's go" (let's go/let's go) or "tį'/let's cruise" (let's go/let's cruise; also referred to as "TLC") have in dialogic settings.

Proper language use, however, also often secures public perceptions of belonging to a Nation where the "national" language is Navajo. The linguistic anthropologist Eleanor Nevins studied language revitalization in White Mountain Apache speech communities and observed that western Apache is articulated as the national language of the White Mountain Apache reservation, something reserved for White Mountain citizens alone (2004, 272). In contrast to a European nation, however, the Nation in this case specifically defines its citizenry based on a blood percentage, lineal descent traced back to a Bureau of Indian Affairs Census roll from 1940, and an a priori assumption that language is always already inside anyone who wishes to access it. Similarly, discourses around Navajo- and English-language use reveal a highly polarized linguistic field, where the tongue one speaks is tied to perceptions of racial identity, where "white people" speak English and "Navajos" speak Navajo. These ideologies of blood quantum, racial identity, and language partly explain how blood becomes so strongly tied to Navajo social authenticity.

In examining language as it relates to music genre, generational nostalgia and Indigenous authenticity, we see how the speaking voice, such as Vincent Craig's, can be used to secure one's place within the social field of Navajo relations. Conversely, voice (or perceived lack thereof) can be used, in the case of Rick Wilson, the Crownpoint chapter president, and the teenage cashier at the Mustang station, to exclude, silence, or marginalize. But to say that the only way to be Navajo is to speak one's heritage language would exclude the at least 26 percent of Navajos ages five through eighteen who do not speak Navajo. Many of these young people strongly identify as Navajo and continue to feel a strong affective tie to the language despite not speaking it (Parrish 2014; Thompson and Jacobsen forthcoming). These statistics are particularly powerful when we take into account that more than 50 percent of Navajo citizens are under the age of twenty-eight (Moroni Benally, personal correspondence, June 6 2014). This affective tie to the Navajo language for non-speakers was underscored for me by one Diné college student of mine in his mid-thirties who, although he didn't speak Navajo, considered Navajo "his" language and English someone else's.

Navajos today are trying to come to terms with what it means to be Navajo in a sociolinguistic field in which language shift has started to make English, in addition to Navajo, the national language of the polity known as the Navajo Nation. Thus, we see a shift where "marked forms of English," for example Navajo

English, can and do index a Native American identity (Peterson 2006, 87). Part of the anxiety, of course, stems from the very real need to make rights claims as a sovereign nation located within the larger settler colony of the United States, and the knowledge that having a national language distinct from English serves as an important tool—a sonic marker of social and cultural difference—in asserting Indigenous sovereignty for political, environmental, or cultural ends. When speaking to the Navajo Language Academy in Tsaile in July 2013, Rex Lee Jim, then vice president of Navajo Nation, voiced concern that "if we no longer use our language, just live in NHA [Navajo Housing Authority] housing communities and aren't really using the rangeland, who's to say the government won't come in and make this [the reservation] all public land?" (This is a fear, of course, born out on many parts of the Eastern Navajo Checkerboard.) For Jim, language and land use are outward manifestations of Navajo identity that legitimize continued claims to the use of tribal trust (and historically Indigenous) land in the eyes of the federal government. In reversing language shift and encouraging Navajos and non-Navajos to put in the time to learn *Diné bizaad*, Jim advocates dissolving the tidy isomorphism between Navajo citizens and Navajo speakers, instead making *Diné bizaad* an international language spoken by Navajos and non-Navajos. He also advocates for increased access and ease of use when it comes to heritage language. This can be accomplished in part by eliminating diacritics such as high tones, nasals, and glottal stops in Navajo writing so that, as he does, one can text message in Navajo using the English alphabet. Jim argues that because of their perceived difficulty, diacritics alienate Navajos and others from writing and learning the Navajo language. Tradition is once again resignified in varied forms of speaking, reading, and writing.

But what of our pageant, and what of genre, voice, and blood? By insisting that classical songs played on a Steinway in a concert hall are traditional, the reigning Miss Indian NAU refuses to be defined by the narrow confines of Indigenous musical tradition. Instead, she insists that because she—a traditionally oriented Diné speaker and Navajo woman—is playing these songs, they are not only Diné but also become traditional through the performative process. Undergirding such a performance, though, and also perhaps winning her the coveted title, was her ability to introduce herself comfortably in Navajo using the highly formulaic genre—the "Navajo language introduction"—in which the mother's clan, followed by the father's clan, the maternal grandfather's clan and then the paternal grandfather's clan, are presented along with place of origin and the speaker's identification as a Diné woman. The language introduction, therefore, gave her a broader musical maneuverability, buttresses claims to being heard in a public space and, by ascertaining her Diné heritage through her clans, lends credibility to her phenotype and Navajo blood.

Similar to Miss Indian NAU, other Navajo royalty are also trying to carve out alternative spaces that allow for more flexibility and mobility in how traditional and Diné identity are expressed and performed. For example, Former Miss Navajo Nation (2010–2011), Winnifred Bessie Jumbo of Two Grey Hills, New Mexico, a recent graduate of Brown University,[15] publicly acknowledges that she isn't fluent in Navajo. Despite this perceived shortcoming, and despite Navajo fluency being a criterion for being crowned Miss Navajo, in a feature article for the *Navajo Times* written shortly after her crowning, she stated, "I'm somewhat of a fluent speaker, but I'm always learning new terms as I go. I want to stress to people that it's OK to speak Navajo *even if you don't speak it fluently.* It's OK to learn Navajo even if it's just your [Navajo language] introduction or your clans" (Jumbo in Smith 2010, 1; italics mine). These comments show how the English-only policies of the past, and the place of Navajo language within a Navajo cosmology, live on in the heightened sensitivity and mindful attention to Diné language use and language performance. Inverting expectations that a full-blood from the reservation holding a position of visibility and authority must speak fluent *Diné bizaad*, Miss Navajo offers other models for prideful, effective, and proactive identification as a young Diné woman.

For Miss Jumbo, her utterance in *naabeehó bizaad* — imperfect, incomplete, and halting as it may be — and her insistence that it's still "her language" and not only that of an elder, a medicine man, or a speaker of a prestige variety of Navajo, speaks to a newer and more flexible structure of voicing that some younger Navajos are now adopting toward their heritage language. As such, in Miss Jumbo's process of "learning new terms as she goes," her own speech is dialogic: she is constantly learning new vocabulary from those who are better speakers than herself, but she's also offering up her own views on language use and language politics in return. Using her prestige as Miss Navajo and her cultural capital as a female culture bearer in Navajo society, Miss Jumbo calls attention to the issue of language stigmatization for second-language learners by insisting that speaking some Navajo is better than speaking none at all. As such, Miss Jumbo reverses the logic that only those who speak *Saadsání* "really" speak Navajo. In the process, she also challenges a linguistic politics of difference in which those who speak more or better Navajo are also understood to *be* more Navajo. By admitting her linguistic imperfections and yet insisting on making her own, imperfect voice heard *in Navajo*, she uses speech and song to transform the substance or stigma of learning Navajo—and the sociolinguistic disjunctures this creates for many speakers—into a symbol of power and grace in the face of historic challenges and devastating cultural loss.

Articulating her own stance toward a new Native-language pedagogy, Miss Navajo rearticulates social practice and a Navajo theory of voice and blood as being about maneuverability, doing one's best with what one has, and taking pride in the heritage language one is gifted with, regardless of one's level of fluency. Emphasizing the Navajo ethic of individual responsibility and the importance of following one's own path, Miss Jumbo follows another, equally forceful set of traditional teachings instead: "T'áá hó ájit'éego" ("If it is to be, then it's up to me").

CHAPTER THREE

Radmilla's Voice

Racializing Music Genre

Window Rock, Navajo Nation, Arizona, September 1997. A young woman butchers a sheep as the crowd at the Navajo Nation Fairgrounds watches. Her hair tied back in a *tsiiyééł*, a woman's hair bun, she wears a velvet top, a silver Concho belt, a long satin skirt, and leather moccasins — the markers of traditional Navajo femininity. As she expertly slits the sheep's throat to begin the arduous process of dissecting the animal, her skirt remains spotless: not a drop of blood touches it.

Sheep butchering, a traditional Navajo art of subsistence, makes up the first part of the Navajo Nation's annual Miss Navajo pageant. The second component is singing, and the same young woman — Radmilla Cody[1] — performs a traditional skipdance song in the Navajo language. But something makes her performance different. As Radmilla's voice carries across the fairground, she adds melismas, or vocal flourishes, note glides, and a bluesy inflection to the more nasal sound of traditional skip-dance songs, which are typically sung by men (McAllester 1954). Onlookers cock their heads to listen more closely, as they hear for the first time the singer who will become known as the "Navajo Whitney Houston."[2] The crowd responds ecstatically; Radmilla, a twenty-one-year-old from Grand Falls, Navajo Nation, is publicly crowned the forty-sixth Miss Navajo Nation, 1997–1998.[3]

When I introduced myself in Navajo to Radmilla in 2011 at a CD signing (for I had long been a fan of her music), she seemed amused to hear an Anglo, a *bilagáana*, speaking her language. She joked that we should try performing some skip-dance songs together in a perhaps improbable duo — a white woman and she, a half-black, half-Navajo one, performing old Navajo standards. As she autographed a glossy poster for my friend's nine-year-old niece, who is of Navajo,

ABOVE: Sheep butchering, Miss Navajo contestants, September 2012. Courtesy of the *Navajo Times*. Photograph by Sunnie Clahchischiligi.

RIGHT: Radmilla Cody, Miss Navajo Nation, 1997–1998. Courtesy of Radmilla Cody and Robert Doyle, photographer.

Korean, and French descent, she wrote in flowing cursive: "Beautiful you are! Many blessings to you. Always remember that, and walk in beauty."

Radmilla dramatically broke the mold in more ways than one. There was, most obviously, her distinctive, hybrid singing at the intersection of Navajo tradition and African American rhythm and blues—that style reflected Radmilla's own mixed heritage as the child of a Navajo (Tł'ááshchí'í clan) mother and a *Nahiłii*,[4] or African American, father. In the documentary *Hearing Radmilla* (2010), she recalled being singled out for her African American appearance as a child living on the Navajo reservation. There was also the later denouement to Radmilla's story, her arrest in 2003 for aiding an abusive, drug-selling boyfriend and her subsequent attempt to rehabilitate her public image as a citizen of the Navajo tribe. Fluent in Navajo and a citizen of the Navajo Nation, she embodies a story both unique and representative of contemporary Diné experience, where Radmilla's voice became a lightning rod for reflection and debate about the twenty-first-century politics of race,[5] blood, music genre, and belonging in Navajo country.

What, then, does Radmilla's story reveal about the relationship between sound, racial identity, and blood quantum on the Navajo Nation? And what, in particular, can be said about the role of the singing voice in the politics of Indigeneity? In this chapter, I use two case studies to show the tensions still surrounding black-Native parentage in Native American communities such as the Navajo and analyze reactions to Radmilla's voice as a partial reflection of larger racial stereotypes about blackness and criminality that permeate U.S. society. These ideas tie crucially into issues of tribal citizenship in Native North America in the era of casinos, where the affective and political stakes of belonging have been dramatically raised, and where citizenship and enrollment have come to signify more rigid demarcations between who belongs and who does not. Second, I demonstrate how sound itself becomes an ethnic trope—a symbol constructed as "allusions toward an ideal that has no living model" (Fast 2002, 23), where voice, musical genre, phenotype, and heritage language skills index a speaker as more or less "authentically" Diné. Here, I distinguish sound from music, defining sound as a broader framework encompassing both music and language, which allows me to discuss the singing and speaking voice within a single frame. In Radmilla's case, the supposedly black dimensions of both her phenotype and her traditional singing were used to single her out as less than fully Navajo. Since her crowning as Miss Navajo and, several years later, with her run-in with the law, itself the result of an abusive relationship,[6] Radmilla as a celebrity gained what

Daphne Patai (quoted in Starn 2011b, 123) has called "surplus visibility" about racial matters, "always put on the spot when controversy arises."

Using my own fieldwork singing and playing with Native Country as a counterpoint to Radmilla's experience, I examine how voices become marked by racial identities at the level of the collective group and of the individual. On the one hand, her voice, perceived racial identity, and idiosyncratic singing style designated Radmilla as a cultural outsider. At the same time, in other contexts and because of her ability to broker generational differences in her choice of recorded material and her fluency in the Navajo language, her voice was celebrated as being quintessentially Navajo, securing her insider status as a Diné citizen. Bringing sound into conversations about blood, belonging, and Indigeneity, I show how racial identities become marked, and I investigate the role played by voice in this marking. Music and language both reflect and reinforce ideas of inclusion, exclusion, and communal reckoning in contemporary Navajo communities and in U.S. society at large (Harkness 2010; Feld et al. 2004). My larger contention becomes, in the case of Radmilla, the Navajo Nation, and the U.S. nation, that aesthetics—and voice and sound in particular—matter in relation to politics, albeit often in divergent ways and on differing scales.

Radmilla's story epitomizes the internal heterogeneity of today's Navajo Nation, which is as internally diverse as the U.S. nation that surrounds it. Not all Diné people live on reservations, and approximately two-thirds of Navajo residents live on one of four Navajo reservations. The remaining one-third live in southwestern urban centers, elsewhere in the United States,[7] or abroad. Yet the politics of tribal belonging are far from simple. In fact, the legal criteria used for contemporary tribal membership conflict with other definitions Dine'é used and use to assay Navajo identity and social citizenship, and some scholars today (see Dennison 2012) see legal criteria such as blood quantum as a direct affront to tribal sovereignty and the future of Indigenous polities. Using a Certificate Degree of Indian Blood (CDIB or CIB) card as proof of one's legal recognition as an Indian is a fairly recent phenomenon in Navajo and Indian Country.[8] Significantly, this shift in the legal definition of Indian disregards historical and community-internal criteria—such as kinship (k'é), maternal clan, and number of years lived in a Navajo community—in determining Indigenous belonging and social authenticity. In many ways, Radmilla's story embodies these tensions, foregrounding the shifting sands of social citizenship in Indigenous communities.

Radmilla herself comes from Leupp Chapter, in the reservation's southwest corner on the Arizona side. After finishing her studies at Coconino High School in Flagstaff, an off-reservation border town, Radmilla moved to Phoenix, where she was encouraged to enter the Miss Navajo contest by her mother and maternal grandmother (Naylor 2006) and was befriended by the rising R & B/hip-hop star Adina Howard.

Since the 1950s and 1960s, the Navajo and other federally and state-recognized U.S. tribes have hosted similar hybrid beauty-culture pageants, open exclusively to their female citizens: the Seminole tribe of Florida, the Lumbee tribe of North Carolina, and the White Mountain Apache tribe of Arizona (Jenkins 2010; Schröder 2004).[9] Unique to these pageants is their dual emphasis on both contemporary and traditional skills (in the Navajo case including singing, food preparation, heritage language abilities, and sheep butchering). Thus successful contestants must demonstrate their knowledge of global culture and politics, but they must also be deeply grounded in their respective cultural traditions, however those might be defined by the pageant and the host tribe. Miss Navajo specifically "must exemplify the essence and characters of the Navajo deities First Woman, White Shell Woman and Changing Woman."[10] The winner of the Miss Navajo pageant then becomes the official ambassador to the tribe for one calendar year. Notably absent from these pageants is the archetypal category of traditional Western beauty competitions: the swimsuit contest.

But the Navajo pageant is by no means entirely different from its counterparts around the globe. Echoing the familiar gender politics of conventional contests, Miss Navajo contestants are expected to be single and "available." As one Diné critic has noted, "Although Miss Navajo Nation embodies Navajo cultural values associated with ideal womanhood, we must also acknowledge that beauty pageants are rooted in white middle-class values that present femininity as a marker of chastity, morality, and virtue" (Denetdale 2006, 20). We can observe these values at play in the Miss Navajo pageant itself, which awards its runners-up trophies for Miss Congeniality and Miss Photogenic (Bitsoi 2011).

Radmilla's mother, Margaret Cody, and her father, Troy Davis, had Radmilla when Margaret was eighteen (Cutwright 2011). Shortly after giving birth to Radmilla on the reservation in Tuba City, Margaret moved to Georgia, leaving Radmilla to be raised by her maternal grandmother, her *másání* Dorothy Cody, in Grand Falls. Troy was a driver for a Ford dealership in Flagstaff and had very little contact with his daughter as she grew up (Banks 2011). Radmilla attended Leupp Boarding School, a Bureau of Indian Affairs school on the reservation, and during her elementary school years lived without running water or electricity, two salient privations of rural reservation life. She was taught to herd sheep

Radmilla Cody and her *másání*, the late Dorothy Cody. Courtesy of Radmilla Cody and John Running, photographer.

and weave. At age seven, she also began attending a Pentecostal church, Church of the Nazarene,[11] with her grandmother, where she began singing in the choir. By junior high, Radmilla had decided she wanted to be a professional singer; she met her uncle, the noted traditional singer and composer Herman Cody, at a Miss Navajo engagement in 1997 or 1998, and they have been collaborating professionally since then.

Because she was raised in the Navajo way (*Dinék'éhjí*), it was not until high school that Radmilla became more conscious of her African American identity, learning about Malcolm X, Martin Luther King Jr., and gaining a black political consciousness that related to her own identity (Gordy 2011). As she frequently notes in interviews, she has since often been asked to choose between these two identities. These larger cultural expectations specifically came to the fore in mandates about what a Miss Navajo should look and sound like, as well as in op-ed pieces in the *Navajo Times*, and in press reviews of the pageant.[12] Radmilla has largely responded by refusing these mandates in both her music and her identity politics, insisting, like her late maternal grandmother, that *k'é*, or kinship, determines Navajo belonging and identity.

For Radmilla, she is Diné because she was raised on the Navajo reservation, has a maternal clan, and was socialized into the world as a Diné woman by the first teacher in her life, her másání, the late Dorothy Cody. Her grandmother, knowing that Radmilla would need to fight for her right to belong and be accepted as Diné, made the conscious decision to speak to her granddaughter exclusively in Navajo; she also showed Radmilla that *k'é*, or establishing relationality with others through systems of responsibility and obligation, is a muscle that needs to be actively practiced, and some exercise it more than others. *"K'é,"* as Radmilla noted in one conversation, "doesn't discriminate." Armed with the Navajo language as her shield, Radmilla then acquired a second shield, singing, with which to battle the politics of belonging as a *Nahiłii* Diné woman—a battle she continually fought not only on the reservation at Boarding School and in her home community, but also within her own family.

For example, building on her ability to successfully claim an audience and on the fundamentally Diné tenet on the power of language to bring things into being through repetition, Radmilla is now on a linguistic mission to eradicate usage of the term *zhinii*, a Navajo racial slur referring to African Americans and an elided version of the term *Naakaii Łizhinii* ("Black Mexicans") from everyday parlance.[13] As she explained in Navajo to the elderly women sitting in the audience after a screening of *Hearing Radmilla*, over the years *zhinii* (and *Naakaii Łizhinii*, as well) have been very hurtful, always singling her out and making her feel less Navajo and, ultimately, less human (in her own family, her uncle referred to her as "chocolate mama," an equally dehumanizing term). In the interest of supplanting a hurtful word with a more descriptive one, she is calling for the introduction of the term *Nahiłii*, to her ears, a respectful term denoting African American peoples; it translates to "the black ones that came across, persevered and have become one."[14] At the Chinle High School graduation on May 18, 2013, where she was a featured performer, Radmilla refused to self-identify in Navajo using the standard term Naakaii Łizhinii, introducing her four clans instead as "Tł'ááshchí'í nishłį [I am of the red ochre on cheek clan], Nahiłii báshíshchíín [I am born for the African American people], Naakaii Dine'é dashicheii [my maternal grandfather's clan is Mexican], dóó [and] Nahiłii dashináłí [my paternal grandfather's clan is African American]."

Throughout Native North America, Indian-white and Indian-black parentage has been understood in dissimilar and contradictory terms (Brooks 2002; Miles and Holland 2006). While Navajo–African American relations date back to the Spanish colonial period, they are today sometimes selectively depicted as a phenomenon of the past fifty years. As scholars of U.S. racial politics and the one-drop rule have shown (Sanjek and Gregory 1994; Starn 2011b), whiteness is often depicted as a tabula rasa or blank slate, while blackness becomes the stigmatized racial category (Gillborn 2010; McIntosh 1990; Omi and Winant 1994; Sullivan 2006, 22). In other words, whiteness in relation to blackness is understood as a mere "absence of pigmentation" (Roediger 2002, 326), whereas blackness—and black "blood" in particular—reads as that which overdetermines one's racial identity regardless of one's total racial background. Thus, within the logic of the one-drop rule, "it may take one drop of blood to make a black person, but it takes a lot of blood to make an Indian" (Arica Coleman in Schilling 2013, 1; see also Coleman 2013, 33).

While Navajo citizenship is determined by a minimum blood quantum of one-quarter Navajo blood and having at least one enrolled parent on the 1940 Bureau of Indian Affairs base roll (Spruhan 2008, 5, 11), sometimes Diné citizens with mixed Navajo-black ancestry are expected to prove their Native identity in ways that so-called full-bloods, and those of Indian-Anglo mixture, do not. Indeed, this held true for Radmilla, as the legitimacy of previous Miss Navajo winners with Indian-Anglo parentage was not questioned to nearly the same extent. Thus, while anthropologists understand race as a social construction and not a given, natural fact, perceptions of race and racial identities profoundly influence Navajo citizens' day-to-day lives and sense of belonging. As Thomas Biolsi (2004, 400) has noted, "race is a *concrete* abstraction, and to be black in the United States, for example, is to live on the receiving end of the fiction of 'race' in deeply brutalizing ways. And, as scholars have only recently come to recognize, to be white is to inherit racial privilege in profoundly material ways."

Blood quantum is also a social construction that is treated as real, often employing the language of biomedicine to substantiate its manifest realness: thus, blood is "tangible, traceable, curable, transfusible and transportable" (Bond, Brough, and Cox 2014). Similar to discussions of race, however, blood is also a concrete abstraction, where blood talk is locally salient, meaningful, and helps Diné citizens make sense of their own place in their respective Diné and non-Diné worlds. In its local usages in Diné social spaces, blood is a multipart index not only of belonging, authenticity, race, heritage language ability, connection to tradition, and cultural knowledge but also to temperament, body functions, physiology, and kinship (Bond, Brough, and Cox 2014, 2). Thus, while blood is socially constructed and not premised on biological accuracy, this fact doesn't take away from its import and social realness for those that employ this discourse and find it meaningful as a form of expressing identity.

Determining the blood percentage of a given individual, Native or not, is never straightforward. This is the case in part because blood quantum is measured based on ancestry rather than by a DNA test or actual percentages of Indian blood. Yet it is also because the administrative record was and is selective, strategic, and premised on the inaccurate notion that blood can, at base, measure "Indianness" and be used as a litmus test for looking Native in some prescriptive way. Moreover, depending on one's tribal enrollment, only the blood of the tribe in which the individual is enrolled shows on one's CIB, as dual enrollment in American Indian nations is not permitted by the Bureau of Indian Affairs (Fletcher 2011; Dennison 2012). For example, if an enrolled Navajo citizen's parentage is Southern Ute on her father's side and Diné on her mother's side, and each parent has a blood quantum of 100 percent, blood quantum on her CIB would show up as simply 50 percent, as the Ute "blood" will not be taken into account in this case. Assessing blood quantum presents an additional challenge because it is determined in part by who is present at a child's birth to sign the paperwork: a child's degree of Indian blood is calculated based on lineal descent but relies on the birth certificate as the starting point for calculating a child's blood quantum (Begay 2011, 21). This means that if a Navajo father is absent at the birth or chooses not to sign the birth certificate for any other reason, the child's blood quantum will be calculated using only the mother's Indian blood. Thus "the child may legitimately be a full-blooded Navajo, but due to the father being absent, the child is considered one-half or less depending on the mother's blood quantum" (Begay 2011, 22).

Additionally, Navajos have long intermarried with non-Navajos, and numerous Navajo clans[15]—a matrilineal kinship system used to determine systems of obligation and reciprocity—are so-called adopted clans. These adopted Navajo clans include the Mescalero Apache Clan (Naashgali Dine'é), the Chiricahua Apache Clan (Chíshí Dine'é), the Tewa Clan (Naashashí), that is, the Tewa-speaking peoples of New Mexico, and the Mexican People Clan (Naakaii Dine'é). Recall that this last clan is Radmilla's maternal grandfather's clan; it is also Tommy Bia's first maternal clan, which in the Navajo way makes Tommy and Radmilla cousins. The sixty or so Navajo clans influence everything from whom a person can marry, to whom one socializes with or calls a clan brother or sister, to the profession one chooses. Clans and the incorporation of non-Navajos into Navajo society also predate colonial forms of reckoning and belonging, which, importantly, based their criteria on *k'é* or kinship systems rather than blood quantum. Moreover, although many adopted clans were introduced into Navajo society as a result of war captives (mostly women and children) taken during retaliatory Navajo raids on Ute, Apache, Hopi, Spanish, and Mexican communities, once on Navajo land, these individuals were fully integrated into Diné society and were afforded the social and political rights of any other Diné individual.[16] Through affiliation, place of residence, and learned cultural practices, outsiders unproblematically became part of the Diné kinship system. Thus adopted clans are subsumed under the Navajo clan system, losing their separate status as an indicator of an ethnic or racial group. Further confounding these demarcations, the Bureau of Indian Affairs (BIA) and the Navajo Tribe count these adopted clans as Navajo when it comes to issuing CIB or tribal ID cards to Navajo citizens. For example, someone with three non-adopted Navajo clans and one adopted clan, such as Naakaii Dine'é, is considered a full-blooded or "4/4" Navajo according to his or her CIB.

The adaptability and mobility of Diné peoples has historically led scholars, including anthropologists, to question the authenticity of Navajos as Indigenous, especially when compared to their more sedentary, culturally conservative, and closest neighbors, the Hopi. Since Navajos are relatively recent arrivals to the Southwest and Hopi is the longest continually occupied Indigenous pueblo in the United States, anthropologists have portrayed Navajos as mere cultural borrowers, lacking a core Indigenous identity (Bsumek 2004). These differing perceptions of time depth, autochthony, and authenticity, have, in turn, laid the foundation for federal policy decisions that have negatively impacted Diné peoples' abilities to claim land, sacred sites, and their sovereignty in the twentieth and twenty-first centuries. More recently, Diné historians and archeologists (Denetdale 2006, 7; Thompson 2009) have responded to these critiques by acknowledging the flexibility of Navajo identities but refusing the deculturizing implications of the "cultural borrower" thesis, insisting instead that Navajos carried their Diné values with them wherever they traveled.

These earlier anthropological perceptions and federal Indian policy decisions, however, have also impacted present-day cultural politics and tribal policies. In particular, non-Native expectations of a prescriptive Indigenous authenticity have led to a retrenchment of Diné identities on the part of many Diné peoples, where the authenticity represented in many of the activities required of Miss Navajo contestants is strategically performed for community-external consumption. But this shift also affects how Navajos see and treat each other. Notably, this retrenchment of identity often excludes alternative sexual orientations and gender expressions, and is often a defensive stance pitting Navajos against non-Navajos. This prescriptive identity, or what I call a new Navajo nationalism, is often but not always grounded in blood politics and the language of biology, authenticity, and exclusion: language first created by federal bureaucrats and anthropologists but now used by Navajo people themselves. One way to understand responses to Radmilla's voice and appearance, therefore, is as one such retrenchment of Navajo nationalism, a reflection of a particular moment in the shifting landscape of Navajo cultural politics and history. And one way to understand Radmilla's voice and her own performance politics is as an explicit refusal of such nationalistic expression.

But debates about who belongs and who is authentically Navajo are not just limited to Diné individuals with a lower blood-quantum threshold. Indeed, assessing citizenship, belonging, and policing identity[17] are questions that citizens of many Indigenous nations within and beyond the United States grapple with today.[18] In the U.S. context, the stakes of Indigenous belonging have been raised particularly in the casino era (1979–present), where tribal citizenship can signal additional benefits such as per capita payments among casino-owning tribes, which has caused some tribes to further restrict their enrollment criteria (Debenport 2011; Painter-Thorne 2010).

In matrilineal Diné society, clans and land are traditionally passed down through one's first clan—the clan of one's mother. Using even the strictest criteria, a child whose first clan is Diné, as in Radmilla's case, is Navajo. As Theda Perdue and others have noted, matrilineal forms of determining belonging and Indigenous citizenship in the Cherokee and other matrilineal Native nations preceded the federal government's implementation of blood quantum (Kauanui 2008; Perdue 2003). In Cherokee and Navajo contexts, categories of citizenship and belonging were previously more inclusive and allowed for affiliation based on cultural identity, community connection, and in-depth knowledge of cultural practices. Although blood quantum is today used in a vaguely scientific, highly racialized way, its roots in English common law as a method for determining inheritance "long predates the question of mixed-race ancestry" (Spruhan 2006, 4). Its specific application in determining legal recognition for Indians and citizenship in tribal nations dates only to the early 1900s (Spruhan 2006, 4, 39).

In Radmilla's case, phenotype, blood quantum, kinship, and culture held a precarious balance, with some commentators, such as tribal citizen Orlando Tom (1997), arguing that phenotype was more important: "There is a duty and responsibility to procreate within our own kind, so we can perpetuate our existence in the years to come. If we fail in this endeavor, within 200 years from now, there will be no Indian people. . . . That is why inter-racial unions and the children it brings forth is nothing other than ethnic genocide. . . . Miss Cody's appearance and physical characteristics are clearly black, and thus representative of another race of people." Others, like Radmilla herself, argued that culture trumped phenotype, insisting that her ability to speak Navajo and butcher superseded her physical appearance (Gordy 2011). By claiming her identity as a Diné woman, singer, and a former Miss Navajo, Radmilla shows how voice is a uniquely malleable form of expressive culture. At the same time, voice can become fixed and rigid when categories of race, blood quantum, and expectations about musical genre are superimposed onto it. We see this in popular music, where singing voices are often raced and marketed as black or white depending on the music genre performed and the tone color of the singer's voice. Radmilla's singing foregrounds tensions about how voice—the way we hear it, interpellate it, categorize it, and project it—can stretch ideas of phenotype. Concurrently, her singing demonstrates how vocal tone color, diction, and register can mark and calcify expectations about phenotype.

While phenotype marks some Navajo individuals, sound can also mark Diné identities, especially when associated with music genre. Even within the narrow confines of country, the type (old or new) played by our band, Native Country, often determined our ability to get gigs on the reservation, and also influenced who would come and dance to our music. Traces of a rez band sound—such as a lack of twang, the use of Navajo English pronunciation and code-mixing, a focus on up-tempo songs, performing from a known repertoire of honky-tonk standards, male lead singers, and relatively self-contained performances with less swagger onstage than a standard country performance would warrant—became conscious decisions that we strategically embraced or rejected, depending on the gig. For example, during a Native Country band rehearsal in Many Farms, Tommy brought up the ever-present need to expand our repertoire to include more two-step songs, or up-tempo songs to which couples can dance in the style originating in Texas dance halls and honky-tonks. In an effort to bring in repertoire I already knew, I suggested Alison Krauss's version of the up-tempo bluegrass classic, "I'll Fly Away," a song commonly performed at country and bluegrass jam sessions I had attended in North Carolina. There was a momentary pause in the conversation, followed by chuckles from Tommy and Arlondo and a side-to-side headshake from LeAnder, our lead guitar player. Tommy then explained that this song, originally a religious song about death then popularized by the popular film and soundtrack, *O Brother, Where Art Thou?*, was the song played each Sunday morning after the obituaries are read on one local reservation radio station, KTNN AM 660. So, for him, this lively, up-tempo song is the quintessential dirge, and certainly not material a band would play in a bar or a chapter house on a Saturday night.[19]

In a conversation a few months later about expanding our repertoire to stand out a bit more as a band, I suggested Patsy Cline's classic shuffle song, "Walking after Midnight." This song the band gladly learned, but our first performance at an off-reservation Native biker bar in Page, Arizona, turned into a complete flop —no one danced—and we never performed it again. In fact, it was the only time in the history of performing with the band that we stopped partway through and ended the song with an apology to our fans. Discussing that experience with band members in subsequent years, I learned that my Patsy choice was really a problem with tempo. As a shuffle song, it was neither a ballad—a "cry in your beer" song—nor a two-step song, but something ambiguous and in between, a swung sound that, for Native Country's set list and many fans, was matter out of place. Not only had we chosen a song with the wrong tempo, we had also chosen a song that has little to no sonic precedence in the rez band canon. Songs I covered by Loretta Lynn and Kitty Wells, although also outside this canon, fit stylistically with their male counterparts covered by Tommy and Errison Littleben— songs by Waylon Jennings, Merle Haggard, Johnny Horton, and George Jones. Patsy's smooth croon, jazzy chords, lack of diphthongs, and Arlondo's inexperience playing a shuffle beat destined "Walking after Midnight" for failure in a rez band context and with a rez band audience, on reservation and off. Genres become localized and sedimented in ways that expand our understandings of place, language, tempo, and the social roles radio performs in rural communities.

In most cases, Native Country didn't twang, or diphthongize, their vowels. For example, in singing the George Strait hard-country ballad, "Amarillo by Morning," Tommy avoids diphthongizing words such as "mind" ["ma-eennd"] in the line, "Amarillo's on my mind," singing the more standard "mind" instead. Incorporating Navajo words into English-language cover songs is another common part of rez country performance, and something that Tommy also obliged when he was in the mood. Most commonly, in performing George Strait's "One Night at a Time," Tommy would commonly insert *shí* (my) into the line in the third verse, "Come on, baby, now what do you say?" singing "Come on, *shí*baby, now what do you say?" instead.

Most musicians in Navajo country-western bands are male,[20] as are many vocalists singing traditional Navajo skip-dance and round-dance songs, [21] so having me as a female vocalist was both a draw and a liability. Among on-reservation Diné forty and older, country music is often the genre of choice, so branching outside of it, singing in public, and even just the sight of a female performer can elicit surprised or shocked responses from these older listeners. Thus the choice of musical genre not only marks a musician's identity and class positioning but also determines a band's ability to succeed as a musical entity.

Music genre also dictates the types of physical spaces, radio stations, and built environments at which one performs—for example, on the reservation versus off it; chapter house, outdoor parade, or bar—and thus music genre itself is understood as the performance of a Navajo cultural identity. As I chronicle in chapter 4, when seeking airtime on a reservation radio station, one highly skilled Navajo blues band, Chucki Begay and the Mother Earth Blues Band,[22] was refused airplay by a radio announcer who told them that "they didn't sound Navajo enough."[23]

My main band, Native Country, was composed of four Diné men[24] born and raised on the Navajo reservation and myself; in our case, questions of Navajo identity and belonging frequently surfaced in casual conversation during band practice, particularly because of my own non-Native identity. Because the name *Native Country* implies Indigenous origins, early on in my fieldwork our band-leader Tommy suggested we tell audience members that I was a Lumbee Indian, as I had been living in North Carolina (where the Lumbee Tribe is located) and because, according to Tommy, some Lumbee Indians "look white like you." At the same time, the drummer for Native Country, Arlondo, was quick to note that he considered those with a lower blood quantum—he often referenced citizens of tribes "back east"—to be "less Indian," effectively putting an asymmetrical emphasis on blood over culture or other markers of identity.

Media descriptions of Radmilla Cody's voice mirror this polarization, couched as a distinction between a black blood essence ("soul") and a Navajo cultural essence ("spirituality"). Radmilla herself, employing language that reflects the earlier anthropological debate regarding nature versus culture (Ortner 1974), links vocal tone color (timbre) to racial ideologies about voice. Speaking about her own voice, she notes that "the soul comes from the black side" and that "the 'spiritual' side of songs springs from her Navajo side" (quoted in Contreras 2010, 1). This spirituality is also sometimes portrayed as something Diné women possess in greater abundance than men, exemplified by Navajo Nation presidential hopeful Carrie Lynn Martin's comment that "Navajo women are more spiritual."[25] Building on the idea of women as spiritual culture bearers and transmitters of linguistic knowledge, Radmilla cites her own ability to showcase the beauty and sound of the Navajo language, Diné bizaad. Her recording label, Canyon Records, in its most recent press release describes her voice as "soaring vocals that deliver both traditional and contemporary sounds with a hint of gospel and soul" (Rodgers 2011).

Such descriptions stem perhaps from Radmilla's technique of collapsing tone color, and from her singing style that indexes soul and rhythm and blues female vocalists—popular genres historically associated with African American singers —within a genre of male-dominated traditional Navajo songs. The term "rhythm and blues" (R & B) is attributed to the *Billboard* writer Jerry Wexler in 1947; by 1949, R & B replaced the *Billboard* chart category of "race" records, or music that was marketed to a primarily African American audience (Scaruffi 2003). In her performances of "Kéyah baa Hózhǫ́" ("My Country 'Tis of Thee"), "Chidí Nayiiłniih" ("Buy a Vehicle"), and the national anthem sung in Navajo, these differing styles buttress the expressivity and unique sound quality of Radmilla's voice. For example, in contrast to more typical performances of social dance songs, Radmilla employs a generous amount of wide vibrato (the signature sound of many opera singers and also used in slower soul, R & B, and pop ballads) and also glides between notes, as did her childhood musical idols Whitney Houston and Diana Ross. Further, many social dance songs are typically performed in a nasal, compressed "head" voice, described by some listeners as "a monotone, with almost no flourishes." Radmilla employs less nasality, and, as the cultural critic Felix Contreras notes, she "projects more and uses techniques like bending notes, common among blues, jazz and pop singers" (2010, 1). In Radmilla's own words, singing in a nasal style is simply "not an option; it's not how I hear those songs."[26] We can also hear the musical influence of her grandmother's church choir and traces of a classically trained singing voice in Radmilla's singing. In songs such as "Frybread Song" (*Precious Friends*, 2007), Radmilla liberally uses vibrato and attacks notes more directly, avoiding the vocal glides between notes she commonly utilizes when singing in other genres.

In contrast to other Navajo performers singing social dance songs in a traditional vein, Radmilla also sings with a breathier style, punctuating the beginnings and endings of phrases with anticipatory in-breaths and slower, more audible exhales and releases. By contrast, well-known performers of social dance songs such as the Tódí Néésh Zhéé Singers, the Navajo Nation Swingers, the Sweethearts of Navajoland, and the Chinle Valley Boys sing with a more focused, nasal sound, where connections between notes are generally deemphasized. Radmilla also consciously manipulates volume and a wide variety of vocal textures for expressive effect, contrasting rougher, more pharyngealized timbres with smoother, fully voiced sections of singing. These breathing and textural techniques have become part of the stylistic aesthetic of many R & B singers, and are part of what is sometimes called the "heterogeneous sound ideal" in African American vernacular vocal performance (Wilson 1999, 159–60).

At the same time, Radmilla's style also encompasses some of the most salient markers of the Navajo language, including her improvised introductions to some songs, delivered in an animated, reservation-inflected Navajo English for humorous and endearing effect. Navajo as a spoken language makes audible the manipulation of wind or air (Witherspoon 1977, 30–31) through the use of glottal stops (marked as l'l in written Navajo) or as "a speech sound articulated by a momentary, complete closing of the glottis in the back of the throat,"[27] as heard in the English expression "uh oh." In her expressive rendition of "Kéyah baa Hózhǫ́," we hear Radmilla's use of the glottal stop and the voiceless alveolar lateral fricative, more commonly referred to as the lateral or "slash l [ɬ]."[28]

A conscious attention to breath and air is also a prominent feature of artful country singing (Fox 2004a). We hear this most prominently in what Urban (1988, 389) calls "icons of crying," or the simulation of crying within the frame of a song or a lament, where a vocalist "breaks" between her head and chest voice. A stylized manipulation of air is also heard in what Aaron Fox terms the "ravaged voice," a pharyngealized singing style that the lead singer for our band, Tommy Bia, sometimes employed. This held especially true in songs that were affectively charged or, at the end of a long night, when his voice would start to give out from singing in a bar room clouded with cigarette smoke.

Despite the critiques she has received, many listeners identify Radmilla as a quintessentially Navajo singer precisely because of her singing style and how it reflects the complexity and multiple cultural influences indexing contemporary Navajo experience. But Radmilla's story is also representative of Diné experience in another more sobering sense: Native women are disproportionately affected by domestic violence (Deer 2008), often at the hand of non-Native men, as was the story in Radmilla's case. This is the backdrop against which many prison sentences are given for Indigenous women across Indian country—acts of self-defense, self-protection, and abrupt decisions made out of fear for one's life

(2008, 80–81).[29] Using that difficult experience and expressing it through her talent as a singer is exactly the lesson Radmilla's másání, Dorothy, taught her: that as a human being (bíla'ashdla'ii, or five-fingered person), you can be a broad vessel, maintain strength after experiencing setbacks, incorporate different cultural traditions, musical styles, and languages, and still, absolutely and unequivocally, "remain Diné through it all."[30] In her ability to reach multiple generations through a wide variety of musical genres and through her performances in English, Navadlish (Navajo, code-mixed with English), and Navajo, Radmilla's choice of songs — social dance songs, patriotic songs, rap, light classical, traditional songs composed by her uncle Herman, and, most recently, a fusion album with a fully electrified band — manifest the breadth of her Navajo and Native identity. Of course, Radmilla's own consistent identification first as a Diné woman holds even more weight.

Descriptions of Radmilla's voice by Canyon Records perpetuate the idea of Navajo cultural continuity while also marking and marketing her voice as different or exceptional. For example, even though her albums feature songs influenced by Western art music, gospel, country, hip hop, and rap, including the spoken-word performance of "Old School Sheepherder's Rap" (Precious Friends, 2007), Canyon Records describes the songs on her most recent album (Shí Kéyah or "My Land/Country," 2011) as "sung in the traditional style of the Diné." In her bio, the label also refers her as a "traditional Navajo recording artist."[31]

Radmilla also reminds us that the singing represented by her recordings is but one drop in her own larger musical and spiritual life and should also be heard in that context. "We are a nation of singers," reporter Marley Shebala reminds us about the Navajo Nation,[32] and traditional Navajo ceremonies are sung prayers. Patients are sung over for protection and for healing, and the song cannot be separated from the prayers themselves; they are one in the same. From this vantage point, songs — ceremonial or popular — are a form of protection infused into daily life, and it is only fitting that Radmilla has marshaled her own songs not only as armature but also as a means of connecting back to her beloved Diné Bikéyah.

Race and Musical Genre: The Whiteness of Country Music

While black musical styles are sometimes marked in and through Radmilla's voice, other musical genres remain initially unmarked when performed by Navajo musicians, only to become re-marked when they become identifiably Navajo again. Take country music, what are locally referred to as rez bands, and how whiteness and Navajo identity intertwine in complicated and unsettling ways. The following scene illustrates the impact of internalized racism and settler colonialism (Wolfe 2006; Rohrer 2016) on Navajo senses of self and musical ability: Francine, a driver for the dialysis clinic in Crownpoint, once mentioned to me in the clinic that she that had heard me singing with Native Country on the local radio station.[33] After announcing to the others in the waiting room how much she liked my singing of Kitty Wells's "It Wasn't God Who Made Honky Tonk Angels," she lowered her voice and said confidentially, "I could *tell* it wasn't a Navajo singing." When I asked her to explain, she said she just "knew" the vocalist had to be an Anglo because the voice sounded more professional and I did not sing with a rez or Navadlish accent.

What does Francine's blanket ascription mean, and what can we actually learn about racial identity through listening to voices on the radio? Francine was linking her perception of musical skill with sociophonetic ideologies of whiteness and upward mobility. Here, to tell someone they sound "white," is meant as a compliment. For Francine, who knew I was singing with a Navajo band and had been actively listening for us on the radio, my whiteness became correlated with a cultural capital, diction, and singing style that she associated with places beyond Crownpoint and the reservation.

As a female lap-steel player and vocalist, I auditioned for each of the bands I played with. Although the members of Native Country expressed some hesitation about the research portion of my band membership at the outset, my Anglo identity, my education level, and ability to play a lead instrument that few musicians on the reservation had ultimately led them to include me as a full band member. In a strange twist, my membership in the band also gave it the cultural capital needed to help us get off-reservation gigs. From a marketing perspective, the contrast between four Navajo men and one Anglo woman in the band, a rarity in Native bands, became an informal branding strategy that marked our band and made our gigs memorable for many fans, even if, as I chronicled in the introduction, it merely prompted them to suggest new band names. The same things that made me a potential asset also at times made me a liability, particularly in off-reservation musical spaces where fans, bar owners, or managers might have been expecting an all-Native or all-Anglo band and felt invested in policing boundaries in racially fraught border-town environments. The unexpected element of my membership in the band thus foregrounded not only others' expectations for our band but also various audience and music-management expectations in maintaining these boundaries.

But Francine's comment may also reflect a dominant cultural and musical narrative, something we "tell ourselves about ourselves" (Geertz 1973, 448), that correlates whiteness with country music and blackness with genres like jazz, blues, and gospel (Hughes 2015; Roy 2004; Pecknold 2007, 2013). This narrative may also include gendered identities and performance in reservation spaces, where lead singers are rarely women, thus further marking this recording as white or, at the very least, as non-Navajo for Francine's ears. These correlations, which date back to the division between so-called race records and hillbilly records in the early 1920s, continue to affect our perceptions of music, race, gender, and genre today (Pecknold and McCusker 2016). For example, Mann (2008) shows how country singing styles have historically indexed primarily white, working-class identities, many successful Native, African American, and Mexican American country singers notwithstanding.[34] Mann (2008, 75) attempts to denaturalize the supposed link between whiteness and country music, arguing that whiteness is not *reflected* in country music so much as it is consciously produced and reinstantiated by it through the entertainment industry and by early hillbilly records moguls targeting white audiences in particular (Jensen 1998; Pecknold 2007; Peterson 1997). This production of whiteness depended on thematic material, instrumentation, the consistent use of a southeastern U.S. dialect in singing, and the utilization of an instrumental and vocal twang (Fox 2004a; Feld et al. 2004). Defined as "gliding a single vowel sound to give it two audibly distinct segments," twang is so consistently used in country performance as to have become a "virtually substitutable marker of 'country' and 'racial' identification" (Mann 2008, 79).

In my own experience playing, teaching about, and singing country music in both Native and non-Native spaces, twang is also the element of country that elicits the strongest reaction from listeners, becoming an easy target for what people either love or hate about country music (Fox 2004b, 29–46; Feld et al. 2004, 339). As Mann notes, tongue-in-cheek, about the cultural politics of race and musical genre in the United States, "There is little in contemporary American popular culture more 'obvious' than the 'colour' of music. We simply 'cannot fail to recognize' . . . the blackness of hip-hop or soul, the whiteness of heavy metal or country" (Mann 2008, 77–78).[35] The point is thus to inquire into "the American-born social grounds of racially attributable stylistic procedures," since the "perception of musical difference [has] grown so thoroughly racialized that music [has come] to epitomize racial differences generally" (Radano 2003, 8, 9). The racialization of musical genres stands in for perceived racial difference, marking its performers in limiting and sometimes stigmatizing ways (Radano and Bohlman 2000, 8; Bigenho 2012, 21). Just as clean corollaries between social difference and identity need to be complicated and unpacked, so, too, do ideas of musical genre, race, and identity in locally made musical contexts.

Less evident in discussions of race and musical genre is the long and deep history of Dine'é performing country music in reservation spaces, as evidenced in Navajo given names like Garth Brooks Yazzie, George Strait Begay, Shelby Lynne Henry, and Shelby Lynne Arviso, all common Navajo surnames appended to the stage names of famous country vocalists. Because of country music's long history in Diné communities dating back to the 1930s, musicians and music fans on the Navajo Nation also frequently reference country music as a traditional genre of music (Jacobsen 2009). Country is a genre that resonates deeply with many rural Navajo ranchers, poetically and expressively narrating the loss, heartache, triumphs, and challenges of working-poor families across the United States. Nowhere is this truer than on the Navajo reservation, where 30 percent of residents still live without electricity, at least 10 percent "haul" their water because they don't have running water, and unemployment currently hovers around 50 percent (McCloskey 2007). Such appellations, of course, complicate our ideas of tradition and its link to time depth and supposed Native authenticity. At the same time, they also point to a pair of long-standing Navajo practices, ranching and rodeo competition (Downs 1972; Iverson 1994b), which are also often framed as traditional, or as "something Navajos have always done." In Navajo spaces, then, country singing signals not whiteness but a generation-specific, time-capsuled Navajo—and even Indian—identity.

In contrast to the sometimes-stigmatizing responses to Radmilla and Chucki Begay singing supposedly black styles of music, Navajos singing allegedly white musical genres such as country do not elicit similarly stigmatizing responses among the Diné citizenry. In fact, bands performing country music are considered quite unremarkable and commonplace: there are currently more than fifty country bands active on the Navajo Nation. Most Diné people I've met know someone—a friend, a family member, a coworker—who plays or has played in a rez band. As Diné country musician Frankie Marianito puts it, Navajo country bands today are "a dime a dozen" (in Ashley 1985).

Yet when country bands such as Native Country sing in thick rez accents, employ monotone, nasal singing styles, or use older public-address systems with low-fidelity speakers or no monitors, these bands re-mark their sound as explicitly Navajo. Samuels describes it as sounding "like a gym" (2004, 210–11), and the Diné comedian Vincent Craig refers to it as "Jung Jigga Jung" (discussed in chapter 4). Thus, country music is distinctively Navajo only when it is perceived as being historically, aesthetically, and linguistically placed within generation-specific Navajo social spaces. When choosing to perform in this older style, a sound that explicitly indexes the first Navajo country bands of the 1950s, fans often approvingly comment that it sounds "Navajo," "mono," or "rez" again. Straying from this sound, as the pop country or "countrypolitan" band Stillwater, from the New Mexico border town of Farmington, has sometimes done, risks being labeled as sounding "not rez" or "too white." As a result, Stillwater lacks the ability to capitalize on the nostalgic connection many older reservation fans hope for when they come out to dance to a live rez country band (Jacobsen 2009). But this sound also opens up other venues, such as playing at the all-white Elks Club in Farmington, or playing at the exclusive, Navajo-owned Fire Rock Casino in Gallup, which, until recently, refused to hire Navajo bands on the weekends until Stillwater came along.[36] Sounding Navajo and playing country correspond, but often only when country is played in a certain way and when a narrow canon of older country songs is performed. Country can be both white and Navajo, but "white country" is most often associated with the present, while "Navajo country" is associated with the past.

Just as white lineage is considered blood dilution and African American ancestry has been considered a one-drop pollutant, white musical styles such as country are more easily subsumed into Indianness than are black musical styles such as hip hop, soul, and the blues. Although Radmilla herself classifies her music as Native American, those who listen to her, market her, and describe her music for the press consistently mark it as black first and Native American second. For example, most commentators emphasize her singing style over the Navajo lyrics and her songs' referential content. Just as "sounding Navajo" can be overdetermined in and through the performance of older country music, blackness becomes equally essentialized through its assumed links to musical genres and singing styles historically associated with African American performers (Radano 2003, 8).

On returning to the reservation following her incarceration in 2004, Radmilla once again encountered some trepidation and anger from a small but vocal minority, much of it stemming from the sense that she had not lived up to the role-model responsibilities of a Miss Navajo and, by extension, of White Shell Woman, First Woman, and Changing Woman. However, for the vast majority of Diné people, k'é remained central through it all, and they have continued to support Radmilla. Since her return, she has reestablished herself within the

Navajo Nation: she was a recent Grammy nominee (the 2013 "Regional Roots" category), has an active recording career, and is pursuing a master's degree in sociology. Radmilla has also started a domestic violence nonprofit for teenagers — the "Strong Spirit: Life Is Beautiful, Not Abusive" campaign — and stars in the award-winning documentary, *Hearing Radmilla*. Like many other national U.S. celebrities and politicians from Bill Clinton to Tiger Woods (see Starn 2011b), Radmilla sought public forgiveness and, in her case, found redemption through her public activism, her artistic talent, and a successful recording career.

Native Country, on the other hand, continues to cultivate its highly localized rez-band sound, these days choosing to perform mainly on reservation for weddings, family celebrations, and work-related functions. In the end, we chose not to release the album we had been working on, and have instead focused on cultivating fans through live performance. In this way, the band continues to actively disavow a more modern country sound and an associated cosmopolitanism that would put us at odds with reservation-based fans.

How we hear the singing and speaking voice is informed by deeper cultural expectations and assumptions surrounding racial identity, gender, blood, and sound. When voices do not match our expectations or when identity and musical genre appear not to align, we are challenged to broaden our understandings of self in relation to society, and aesthetics in relation to politics. Radmilla's voice does this work because of the aesthetic and cultural mixture it represents, but also because it is simultaneously socially inscribed and yet inimitable, unique to one singer and to one body.

As auditory creatures socialized into sound, we are uniquely vulnerable to sound and voice: including voice as part of our ethnographic inventory is essential not only because of how deeply and unconsciously we internalize sound but also because voices represent the meeting point between the individual and the social. If words are the "sign" of the voice (Frith 1988, 121), then voice and vocality are "among the body's first mechanisms of difference" (Feld et al. 2004, 341). Sonic differences carry social differences because sound is value laden, socially embedded, and often inextricable from ideas of genre, nation, and identity.

Sound and voice matter to a politics of Indigeneity because voice indexes identity almost instantaneously; through this process, voices cement and challenge our expectations for how Native peoples sound and signify their own varied attachments to being Indigenous. Voices stretch and change our expectations of phenotype because, ultimately, we are more forgiving and open to experimentation in the world of aesthetics than we are in our cultural politics about race. Thus voices carry weight because recognition itself—at both the individual and tribal level—is often on the line. Aesthetics and politics matter because they mutually inform how we hear sound and how we assess belonging to a given social body.

Fusing musical elements from Navajo traditional culture, Christian hymnody, and popular genres of music preferred by a younger generation of Navajos, Radmilla's voice in many ways epitomizes and unifies contemporary Navajo experience, cultural influences, and listening practices. As Radmilla (quoted in Cordova 2012) recently noted: "People forget that there are more similarities than differences. . . . They get caught up in trying to dissect and break things apart when it comes to race and culture, and they wind up separating people rather than bringing them together." Building on this, she articulated a tenet of her own life philosophy to graduating seniors at the 2013 Chinle High School graduation ceremony: "When someone gets in your way or tries to put you down, bless them and move on."

"Welcome to Navajo Nation." Photo by the author.

The late Navajo Codetalker Andrew Bia, father to bandleader Tommy Bia and grandfather to Arlondo Bia. Anaheim, California, 1940s. Photographer unknown.

Candice Craig performing at
Eastern Agency Fair Parade.
Photo by the author.

Female *hooghan* and author's residence in Rough Rock, Navajo Nation,
Arizona. Photo by the author.

Letting out the goats in Rough Rock, Navajo Nation, Arizona.
Photo by the author.

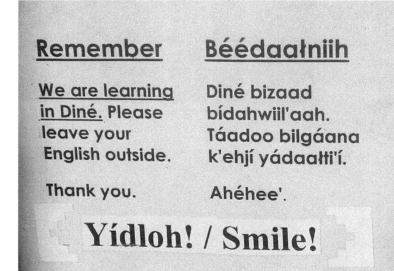

Sign posted on main door of Navajo Language Immersion School in Fort
Defiance, Navajo Nation, Arizona. Photo by the author.

Sovereign Interdependencies: Navajo Nation, Arizona, and U.S. flags, Canyon de Chelly National Monument, Chinle, Arizona. Photo by the author.

CHAPTER FOUR

Sounding Navajo

The Politics of Social Citizenship and Tradition

t's late afternoon at a bar in the Navajo reservation border town of Gallup, New Mexico, and rock music is blaring through the house speakers as waitresses gear up for the night shift. I am talking with the lead singer for a Navajo blues, rock, and soul band, Chucki Begay, as we drink coffee and eat chocolate cake. A fifty-two-year-old grandmother of four, Chucki is sleekly dressed in all black and looks at least ten years younger than her age. She recalls the first time she and lead guitar player Richard "Ritchi" Anderson Jr. took a CD of their music to the local country radio station, KTNN AM 660, in the tribal capital of Window Rock. They were hoping to get some coveted radio airplay. As mentioned in chapter 3, after listening to the CD, the Navajo deejay informed Ritchi that he would not be able to air his music, telling him "you guys don't sound Navajo enough." This comment really irked the band, as all its members are Navajo, and this station plays many local Diné bands, though more typically country and metal bands.

These questions about what "sounding Navajo" might mean were very much on Chucki's mind after her visit to KTNN. She continues: "What does that mean? KTNN plays a lot of Navajo country. . . . The chapter-house [country] bands are big on the reservation. They've got their own sound. A lot of times it's not a professional sound. That's what the [KTNN deejays] mean, I think. We sound too mainstream for them."[1] Thus, from Chucki's perspective, sounding Navajo for this deejay meant sounding like the chapter-house bands, or sounding less mainstream or professional. Those were the first Navajo groups, back in the 1960s and 1970s, to perform popular music, all male and playing mostly country (Jacobsen 2009).

How do sonic differences carry social differences, and what *does* it mean that, for some older Navajo listeners and fans, sounding Navajo becomes equated with sounding country, and that, among other things, this sound is often gendered as a Navajo man's voice? How does country music become a nationalist project specific to the Navajo Nation?[2] In this chapter, I compare two contrasting bands by focusing on their lead singers, Chucki Begay of Mother Earth Blues Band (MEBB) and Tommy Bia of Native Country,[3] examining how a Navajo politics of gender, social class, and tradition are heard through the singing voice.

As Jennifer Denetdale (Diné) has shown us, tradition is not without a political context, and often "becomes a tool that Navajo men and women use to legitimate claims about appropriate gender roles" (2006, 21, 17). A word used by many Diné in daily discourse, "tradition" is a fraught term that variously indexes proficiency in one's heritage language, ceremonial knowledge, and an aesthetic oriented more generally toward a historic Navajo past. Nationalism, in the way I use it here, refers to the political and cultural entity known as the Navajo Nation, and points to the status of Indigenous nations as "nations within nations," semisovereign entities nestled within the larger United States. Taking tribal sovereignty seriously in part means analyzing Indigenous nations and expressive cultures on their own terms, taking into account all the complications that such national boundary-making entails.

By contrast to "tradition" and "nationalism," "gender" is a term not often used in local contexts, and is usually only referenced in local discourse through adjectival forms such as "manly" or "girly." Here, I treat gender as an analytic category to be questioned, a "social category imposed on a sexed body," and thus not a stable and "natural" social identity (Scott 1999, 32). In fact, the Navajo language makes no distinction in the third-person singular between "he" and "she": linguistically, gender is defined by context and the subject of the sentence alone. Here, I focus on heteronormative distinctions between male and female that rest on a series of characteristics associated with each gender, such as speaking voice, singing voice, and associated gender roles in sociomusical contexts. In everyday discourse, these distinctions are typically foregrounded only when they are challenged or disregarded, marking the identity of the nonconforming individual, such as someone like Chucki.

In Diné creation scripture and journey narratives, we find four gendered identities: first gender (*asdzáá*—woman, or feminine female), second gender (*hastíí*—man, or masculine male), third gender (*nádleehí*—the one who changes, or feminine male), and fourth gender (*dilbaa'*—masculine female). Accordingly, two-spirit or third-gender intersex (TGI) individuals have a deep history in Navajo society, and each gender plays a central role in these origin stories, often referred to as *Diné Bahane'* (Zolbrod 1984; Thomas and Jacobs 1999; Jacobs, Thomas, and Lang 1997; Nez 2015). From these stories, we also have evidence that acceptance of the difference between biological sex and gender roles was historically commonplace among Dine'é. Navajos are also historically matrilineal and matrilocal,[4] where men live with their wives' families once married. Thus, traditionally Navajo women played important roles in family, community, and national decision making. However, influenced by the dramatic rise of charismatic Christianity and tent revivals on the reservation since the 1950s (Marshall 2011,70–89; 2016; see also Smith 2008) and echoing the gender norms of larger U.S. society (Denetdale 2006), since the 1930s matrilocality and the diversity of gender roles in Navajo country have shifted significantly. Today, hypermasculine and hyperfeminine depictions of men and women are often the norm in contemporary Indigenous contexts (Rifkin 2011; Smith 2003). This heterosexual gender performativity often becomes foregrounded in reservation rodeo events and in country music performance, where male performers in the latter often take leadership roles and female family members tend to play the essential but background roles of promoter, long-haul driver, ticket taker, and food vendor.

Chucki resists country music gender ideologies by refusing to perform and sing country music, although she is well versed in both the country rez band canon and in Christian liturgical music. She also resists these gender norms by unapologetically fronting and managing her own musical group, Mother Earth Blues Band, and by singing in a lower, alto range with a pharyngealized or rough blues voice, sometimes also described by listeners as sounding manly.

As Chatterjee (1989) and others have shown, nations are gendered using a variety of expressive resources, including music. Thus, vocal tone color, register, and timbre—and the ways a gendered voice, class, and production value conjoin—can affect the difference between a performer's sense of belonging and what Salamishah Tillet has called "civic estrangement" (2009, 125): "Legal citizenship that is complicatedly coupled with a persistent sense of . . . estrangement from the rights and privileges of the contemporary public sphere" (124). Arguably, one of the rights and privileges of a performing artist is to play and get gigs in one's community of origin, but aesthetics and taste often play a role in civic estrangement. For Navajo citizens, the question is often from *which* nation and *which* public sphere do they choose to estrange themselves? One way to understand this tension between belonging and estrangement in the cases of Chucki and Tommy is as a struggle between two sets of contrasting aesthetics— a local, inwardly directed aesthetic sometimes described as sounding *jaan,* and a cosmopolitan, more outwardly directed sensibility whose target audience lies beyond the Navajo Nation (Peterson 2006, 111).

Viewed from this perspective, we can see that when a band's recording sounds rez or *jaan*, this becomes a sound of inclusion on the reservation, but also a sound of exclusion beyond the confines of the Navajo Nation in the larger non-Navajo music scene, mainly because the *jaan* sound is a local, noncosmopolitan sound.

Conversely, *not* sounding *jaan*—sounding mainstream or professional, as Chucki earlier noted—excludes bands from a sense of belonging within reservation musical contexts, but it signals a larger acceptance and incorporation into non-Navajo musical circuits. This professional sound furthers a band's ability to get off-reservation gigs at venues such as bars, casinos, and music festivals. These two contrasting sounds, and the label of a band sounding *jaan*, have material consequences, most notably in determining where a band can and cannot play. Thus, sounding country, and sounding *jaan* in particular, produces and enables a particular kind of on-reservation sociality, where making do, and helping one another make do, becomes central to the musical aesthetics of rez country itself. Ultimately, this either-or model of labeling Navajo musical styles and identities proves equally constraining and essentializing for both kinds of bands, as it too neatly divides aesthetics and orientations that share significant crossover. Such categorizations limit possibilities of self-expression for these musicians as artists, Diné citizens, U.S. citizens, and contemporary Native peoples living civically engaged, successful artistic and professional lives.

I. The Sound of Exclusion: Gender, Cultural Roles, and Belonging

As a female musician, Chucki Begay often sees her authority as a bandleader and lead singer challenged by Navajo men. Her lead guitar player, Ritchi Anderson—who is also her husband—is the major exception to this rule. Male discomfort with her being a female musician is expressed most vocally, she tells me, in Navajo cultural spaces where the band sometimes tries to get gigs. In a story that weaves together social roles, gender expectations, and musical belonging, she recalls a comment posted on a website created for the promotion of Navajo bands called rezbandz.com. Shortly after Mother Earth Blues Band posted its contact information on the site, the male lead singer for a well-known Native band that plays primarily gospel and country posted the following comment for all to read: "Chucki Begay does not belong in music. Native women don't belong in music."

Chucki Begay. Courtesy of
Terry Jackson, photographer.

Unsurprisingly, this comment generated heated discussion and dissent, particularly from the offending musician's female promoter and from the site host of
rezbandz.com. While it didn't go uncontested, the comment reveals important
ways in which the Navajo popular music scene is experienced as a boys club,
a place where men belong and women often feel they do not. Much as Navajo
political office is often portrayed as an exclusively male space (Denetdale 2006;
Lee 2012) using the language of tradition to bolster this claim, music is often used
strategically to demarcate gender roles as well. Exclusion from the rights and
privileges of the public sphere holds particularly true for Navajo women trying
to perform genres other than country in public spaces on the Navajo reservation.
Indeed, Chucki's interpretation of the male musician's comment is even more
Navajo specific. What he's really trying to say, she explains, is that that *Navajo*
women don't belong in music.

Here, we see a double standard where Diné men prescribe the type of music and venues where Navajo women can perform. At the same time, these standards are much more flexible for non-Diné performers such as myself, and for female musicians performing off the reservation in general. At stake in this case was a sense of threat, with the fear being that MEBB would take away this male musician's on-reservation gigs. The band could play off-rez wherever they wanted, but posting their information on a website designed to promote live performance on the reservation was another matter entirely.

Other Diné female vocalists also experience forms of civic estrangement from the Navajo Nation based on their decisions to perform in public or certain set lists and musical repertoire. For example, the bandleader of Re-Coil, Stephen Etsitty, expressed frustration with on-reservation audiences in their refusal to welcome the band's female vocalist, Doreen Begay (who is married to Etsitty), stating "people on the reservation don't appreciate my wife's voice." He specifically cited the fact that fans weren't used to hearing female lead vocalists singing country and rock music. This exclusion is visible on social media, where Navajo fans are more critical of Doreen, a talented singer, than they are of the band's male vocalists. Obtaining on-reservation gigs has proven challenging for the band, and as a result, Re-Coil still plays primarily off-reservation gigs in Arizona, Colorado, and New Mexico. Thus, social citizenship (Marshall 1950, 10–14) is denied to certain female singing voices and the bands that back them. The numbers reflect this estrangement: in about sixty country bands throughout the reservation, only four female vocalists performed publicly during my fieldwork—and I, a non-Navajo, was one of them.

Chucki's take on why music has become an exclusively male domain is rooted in her own understandings of Navajo tradition and historical Diné gender roles, in which women possessed most of the material goods—*hooghans*, property, vehicles—but men had "side projects" outside of the home to assert their own individuality, such as taking care of livestock or, more recently, participating in politics, military service, or playing in a band (Lloyd Lee, personal correspondence., April 20 2015). Since historically women held more authority in issues relating to family decision making, the men wanted their bands to remain exclusively male, a patricentered space uniquely their own. In 2010, Chucki explained to me:

It's because of the music that it's a man's world. My uncle was in a band when he was young, before he went to Vietnam; back then there was no women [in bands]. It wasn't the woman's place I think. Traditionally and culturally, I think the woman had the home—that was her place. The men, they had the live-stock. And if they leave [their women], all they take is a saddle and the horse. The woman takes everything else, because that's her property. The mind-set is still there. The man has the band, that's his, the women don't belong in there. [Man says to woman:] "You take care of the home, that's your *hooghan* that I built for you, that's your sheep, but this is *my band, my guitar.*"

From Chucki's perspective, Navajo bands have become an almost sacred male do-main, a gender-segregated hallowed ground carved from the margins of a largely matrilineal and matrilocal society. In these musical spaces, women often tread lightly, if at all. Thus, going against this sonic grain—playing other genres besides country and singing "like a woman," in the vocal registers typical of women— has direct implications for geographic spaces of inclusion/exclusion and for where one can secure gigs and feel musically appreciated for one's talent.

Moreover, Diné ceremonial singing and healing ceremonies are traditionally led by men (Frisbie 1993, Mitchell and Frisbie 2001; Schwarz 2003; Lee 2013).[5] Women who are permitted to conduct ceremonies often identify as *dilbaa'*, or fourth gender, having the biological sex of a woman but playing the social role of a man. Crucially, the word for "singer/chanter" and "healer"—*hataałii*—in Diné bizaad is one and the same term, and many Diné hold strong associations between sound and healing—mental, physical, spiritual—and the ability to reg-ulate one's voice for such efficacies is of utmost importance. As the Diné reporter Marley Shebala noted in the film, *Hearing Radmilla*, Navajos are a nation of "singer-healers" (Webb 2010). Attesting to the sound-healing linkage, the Mother Earth Blues Band recently formed a non-profit called Music Is Medicine that focuses on teaching musical instruments to reservation youth. In fact, women healers are often distinguished and referred to using a broader term, *nahałaii*, or "practitioner,"[6] rather than the more male-exclusive *hataałii*, with the latter indicating "exceptional knowledge of ceremonial matters" (Schwarz 2003, 5). So, with the exception of *hataałii* who identify as *dilbaa'*, singing in public is more typically seen as a masculine behavior.

In response to the civic estrangement they experience as female vocalists, mu-sicians like Chucki actively step beyond the traditional reservation fan base, per-forming in off-reservation venues such as border-town bars (Gallup, Holbrook, and Farmington, for example), at open mics and Battles of the Bands (Farming-ton, Sky Ute Casino, Dancing Eagle Casino, and Albuquerque), and at music festivals and jam sessions (Chaco Rio, Albuquerque, Gallup). The Mother Earth Blues Band also performs at the most coveted and lucrative of off-reservation venues, gigs at places like Sky Ute (Southern Ute) and Dancing Eagle (Laguna Pueblo) casinos.

On the rare occasion when the Mother Earth Blues Band does play for primarily Native crowds, listeners often express surprise (and sometimes delight) in finding out that Chucki can sing. Chucki notes, "when people hear us, [they often say,] 'I never heard a Navajo band play blues before, especially a woman singing.' It's always that response: 'I never knew a Navajo woman could sing like that!'"

Strongly influenced by XIT, a Native rock band that sang politically charged songs influenced by the Red Power movement of the late 1960s and early 1970s, Chucki describes MEBB's sound as more "contemporary Native rock kind-of-blues." Like XIT, Chucki also tries to promote social justice with her music and to "spread a political message," for instance, by encouraging young Dine'é to play music and be in a band, but without the "sex, drugs, and rock and roll" lifestyle. Just as many Navajo country musicians and fans insist that country music is traditional Navajo music, Chucki sees the blues as an equally apt sonic marker of Navajo tradition and authenticity. For one, she notes the intertwined commercial origins of country and blues in the late 1920s, insisting that if country is traditional Navajo music in some sense, then so is the blues. Chucki also observes that both genres share the same soulfulness and pathos that she believes is so often a part of Navajo peoples' lives today, a testament to the settler-colonial legacy. She describes how she tries to put blues music "into a story," so that Navajo women in particular can relate to it and understand that the thematic content really concerns their *own* lives. For example, Chucki uses songs like Etta James's "I'd Rather Go Blind" as a metaphor for Navajo women's collective experiences of love, loss, and heartbreak. Similar to the early jazz singer Billie Holiday, Chucki uses her own life experiences — and the sense of double marginalization experienced as both a woman and a person of color — to buttress the believability of the music she sings. As the cultural studies scholar David Brackett notes about Holiday, Chucki incorporates a "sense of struggle as part of her self-created image" (1988 [2000], 54) to connect with a larger audience. Chucki notes:

> Country came from blues . . . came from people's soul, heart, singing about their experiences, mostly sad. We Indians do have a sad history, tragic — why not sing about it? Why not sing about a broken heart, your baby left you, it's us, it's who we are, a lot of women can relate to those songs I sing. Like the Etta James song, "I'd Rather Go Blind." I'll put that into a story for them. I dedicate it to all the women, [I'll say] "this is for you. You're giving your heart to one man,

Chucki Begay and Ritchi Anderson perform "The Thrill Is Gone" at Evangelino's in Santa Fe, New Mexico. Courtesy of Nancy Smith and Lightninghorse Photography.

but he's over there with someone else . . . he's over there texting and emailing somebody else you know." It's heart-and-soul kinda music. That's really who we are.

When listening to Chucki sing, it's clear that she has strong affective ties to Etta James's songs and voice.[7] We hear this in the beautiful, highly pharyngealized and tortured vocal style—another example of what Aaron Fox calls the "ravaged voice" (2004a, 328)—that Chucki employs while performing James's songs, and also during her performance of the band's original song "Geronimo." James's voice has also influenced Chucki's singing range, which is considerably lower than that of many female singing voices, approaching a man's vocal range.

The ravaged voice, employed as a performative device to convey crying in the frame of a song (Feld, Fox, Porcello, and Samuels 2004, 328), is part of what gives Chucki her masculinist aesthetic as a performer. In contrast, traditional Navajo songs such as social dance songs, when performed by women, are sung in a higher vocal register, employing a highly nasalized "head" voice, while male singing and speaking voices are associated with "chest" voices and pharyngealization. Chucki's ravaged singing style, her non-nasal sound, and the use of her chest voice flaunt these conventions. Thus, her voice is associated with a more avant-garde, masculine sound in reservation spaces. This impression is augmented by her style of dress, combining a gender-neutral "blues hat" (seen in the picture) with attractive, low-cut shirts that many Navajo women her age wouldn't feel comfortable wearing in public settings. Chucki's choice of clothing, her singing style, and her body language on stage solidify the aesthetic orientation of the band as one targeting audiences beyond the Navajo Nation. Other Navajo bands use the reverse tactic and direct their artistic energy almost exclusively toward other Diné citizens living on the reservation. Sounding like a rez or *jaan* band is one way to secure an on-reservation fan base and, along with that, a sense of Diné social citizenship.

II. The Sound of Inclusion: Performing the *Jaan* Band

The sound of the *jaan* band exemplifies the multifaceted and contradictory ways that Navajo identity is expressed through music. In chapter 1, I discussed the ways in which the term *jaan* acts as both a laudatory and derogatory designation of contemporary Navajo identity. The same holds true for Navajo musical styles labeled as *jaan*. Thus, analyzing how *jaan* is used in everyday musical and linguistic contexts gives us deeper insight into ambivalent responses to settler colonialism and Indigenous modernity more broadly.

But how exactly *does* a band sound *jaan*, and how does this ambivalence translate into the Native band sound? As a term referencing one fraught ideology of rural, Indigenous authenticity, *jaan* essentializes and leaves nothing untouched. Yet in lighter-hearted contexts, *jaan* is also used teasingly about oneself. Here, the meaning can shift: it's still a disparaging term but invites others—most often other Navajos—to see the humor in a given situation and to join in on the joke.

It's a Saturday morning. I am with the Bia family at a softball field called Gorilla Mountain, a butte with a profile resembling a gorilla located between Bídahochii (Indian Wells) and Holbrook, Arizona. We're facing the field, watching players warm up, and waiting for the day-long tournament to begin. We'll be competing as a team called District 10,[8] and Tommy Bia, our team captain, excuses himself to get ready for the day ahead. To energize the group, I pull out my purple iPod and small speaker set and place them on the tailgate of my pickup behind us. I decide to play the songs from Native Country, in particular some older songs featuring Tommy's voice that the group had recorded before I joined. To my ear, the songs sound good: they're not quite properly mixed—the lead

We go up   to the ro - oo - om   at the top   of the stairs

Transcription 1, "Jung Jigga Jung."

Tommy Bia with bass guitar, Windy Mesa Bar, Page, Arizona, July 2009. Courtesy of Doug Reilly, photographer.

singer's voice is muffled and the lead guitar tracks are a bit too loud — but there's still a lot of affect and energy audible in each track. At the start of the second song, "Room at the Top of the Stairs,"[9] Tommy returns to the group. After the first line of the chorus, where the exposed lead voice swoops down from an A to a low C on the word "room" ("we go up to the *ro-o-oom* at the top of the stairs"), cracking slightly, Tommy stops, cocks his head to indicate he's listening closely, and then, in an expressive, animated voice, exclaims: "I just said to myself, now *that* sounds like a *rez* band — and I was right!!"

How did Tommy know, and what signaled this association for him? What was rez or *jaan* (as other musicians might describe a similar sound) about this recorded song, and what caused Tommy to label his own band as such, from the distance of the softball field? The term is self-referential in a prideful way but also serves as a delimiter, a sound that locally emplaces a band as provisional and precludes the possibility of making it big, whatever that might look like.

Tommy's quip references a host of signifiers. Native Country is a dance band that plays only up-tempo songs. They recorded "Room at the Top of the Stairs" before I joined the band in an improvised home studio with less-than-ideal equipment, at a time when vocal nodes were starting to change Tommy's singing voice. This commentary thus reveals Tommy's ambivalence about hearing his own recorded voice in a racially mixed public space, and reflects his own mixed emotions about how his band actually sounds from a distance.

Tommy's comment also recalls the ambivalence and performative aesthetics expressed by the first Navajo country bands about their own performances. Performing during a time when many Navajo cowboys were still excluded from participation in the national rodeo circuit, the chapter-house bands began to perform in all-Indian spaces, in part simply to show people that "Indians can play too" (Emmett "Toto" Bia Jr. 2002).[10] Bands in the 1960s like the Wingate Valley Boys, the Fenders and, a decade later, the Navajo Sundowners, gained huge fan bases and could attract up to five hundred people at a single dance. Spurred by cheap gas prices, the beginning of the American Indian Movement in 1959, and a relatively prosperous economy, the 1960s marked the heyday of chapter-house bands; today the sixties are often referenced as an economic and artistic golden age both for Navajo bands and for the Navajo Nation at large (Iverson 2002; Jacobsen 2009).

Like Native Country, the chapter-house bands and their protégés were—and still are—live dance bands. This is one way in which Native Country fits the rez-band image, and Mother Earth Blues Band, a group that doesn't play two-step songs, defies it. The chapter-house bands played up-tempo country songs so that fans could dance the two-step to their music. By contrast, playing waltzes, ballads, or slow songs that are in three-quarter or nine-eighths time (triple meter),[11] something common if a band were performing the music of Patsy Cline, for example, is generally not encouraged by fans and listeners. The two-step is a "progressive" dance step where couples move counterclockwise around the dance floor in waltz-like fashion. This dance is accompanied by songs in duple meter,[12] between 130 and 200 beats per minute (Casey 2010). It features four steps: "quick-quick, slow-slow," or "step-together, walk, walk." Playing two-step songs for reservation bands and fans has become part of musical tradition and country performance practice on the reservation. Thus, being a dance band and playing

The Wingate Valley Boys, 1967. Courtesy of Bruce Hamilton,
Hamerhouse Productions.

The Fenders, *Once More Around*, 1969. Courtesy of Bruce Hamilton,
Hamerhouse Productions.

songs that dancers know, as Native Country does, is given a high premium in
reservation spaces. For example, one creative take on the two-step mandate is
a remake of the reggae-inspired song "Beautiful Girls" by the Stateline Band,[13]
rendering the tune into an up-tempo two-step song that became popular during
my fieldwork.

In the beginning, the chapter-house bands often used substandard PA systems,
amplifiers, and microphones — whatever they could get their hands on — and as

a result, their listeners often described their sound as "tinny" and "monotone," or "mono." So, although these groups were talented, their own equipment often undermined their efforts. But distinctions existed within the category: Rival bands like the Valley Boys and the Fenders became especially recognized for the voices of their male lead singers and their contrasting personae. Fenders lead singer Johnny Emerson sang in a thick Navajo accent and employed a rougher, more nasalized tone when singing. In contrast, Valley Boys lead singer Ernest Murphy had a much more polished, cosmopolitan singing voice, sang with a more open-throated sound, and pronounced lyrics with a more standardized, American-broadcast variety of English. While Emerson had an edgier, hard-country vocal tone color and a style akin to country singer Ernest Tubb, Ernest Murphy's style resembled that of the early crooners such as Bing Crosby, Faron Young, and Webb Pierce: he sang closer to the mic, had a more fluid vocal range, and employed vibrato and a smoother, bel canto singing style. These two voices created the templates for two different vocal aesthetics, influencing the sounds and technologies that contemporary Native bands, including Native Country, use today to guide their own musical endeavors.

Two sonic shorthands also buttress the Native band sound. When the late Navajo comedian and musician Vincent Craig started recording in the 1980s, he codified the chapter-house band sound—perhaps using a phrase that was already in circulation at the time—with the onomatopoeic descriptor *jung jigga jung.* Jung jigga jung, also called the "chapter-house beat," became a sonic shorthand for the chapter-house bands and their unique, unpolished sound. "Jung jigga jung" can be spoken—typically in a low, monotone voice in the way Vincent Craig did it—or played, as my bandmates sometimes did for humorous effect during rehearsals, on an electric guitar, strings muted, with a pick repeatedly striking the same note, emulating the chunky, dry guitar sound associated with the chapter-house beat (see figure 10).

Jung jigga jung also signals the actual beat—the rhythm and tempo—of most chapter-house band songs—usually a quarter note equaling about 130 beats per minute, so that songs remain danceable.

A second sonic shorthand for the chapter-house sound involves a highly stylized, humorous form of mic checking. This was recently performed on a live broadcast of the Navajo presidential debate. Before the debate began, the veteran KTNN deejay Ray Tsosie halfheartedly checked the microphone on air and, in doing so, built on the trope of the chapter-house bands first learning to use their own microphones and public-address systems. Blowing into the mic with

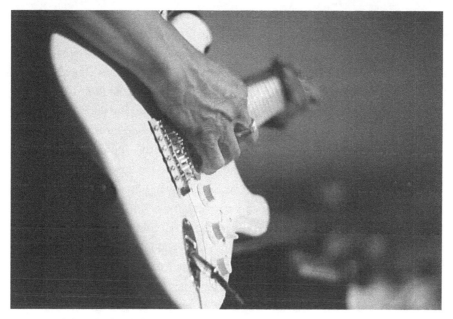

Errison Littleben, lead and rhythm guitar player, Native Country Band, emulating the chapterhouse beat. Courtesy of Doug Reilly, photographer.

Transcription 2, "Jung Jigga Jung."

his mouth rounded in an "O" shape, Tsosie made an owl-like whooshing sound, "whoo whoo," followed by "Dinits'ash?" (Can you hear me?). The loud whoosh causes microphone static and feedback from the PA on air, and the question produced giggles from older audience members and candidates sitting nearby (Ray Tsosie, Navajo Presidential Debate Live Broadcast, Shiprock, New Mexico, June 5, 2014). Emulating the way in which Emerson allegedly used to check his microphone, Tsosie draws on those early memories to execute his joke. In doing so, he both pays homage to Emerson while also emphasizing how out-moded and comical his version of a mic check now seems. Versions of the Johnny Emerson mic check were also frequently performed by Native Country band members, always resulting in chuckles from other band and audience members.

Imitating—and sometimes making fun of—Emerson in particular, Craig created a series of musical skits based on the chapter-house dance experience: people "rubbing belt buckles" (partner dancing), sporting western "banana peel" boots with the seams split down the side so the tops flopped over, and wearing "ten gallon" cowboy hats ("An O' Fender Song," *Cowboys 'n Stuff*, vol. 4). These skits are slices in time for many Navajo baby boomers, taking them back to their adolescence and giving them a space-time to feel nostalgic for it.

Native Country's use of the chapter-house beat, the Johnny Emerson mic check, low-fidelity listening through tinny playback speakers to make the band sound mono, and Tommy's voice—expressive, scratchy, and slightly hoarse—all mimicked the *jaan* band sound in this moment at the Gorilla Mountain softball field. Like country music and the image of the rural hillbilly in American public culture, the sound of the *jaan* band is both abject and celebrated, something on which Craig capitalized in his comedic routines. In Navajo country music, this hillbilly or *jaan* sound almost always features the male singing voice.

As a result, the sound of the *jaan* band is generation-specific and resonates most deeply with Navajos in their forties and older. This divide parallels generational differences in heritage-language speaking abilities discussed in chapter 2, where adults approximately fifty and older are most often fluent speakers, those ranging from their thirties to late forties are often semispeakers and passive users, and citizens aged thirty and below sometimes understand Navajo but often don't speak it. Thus, speaking Navajo and enjoying Navajo country music are closely linked, and are activities enjoyed particularly by Navajos of a certain age.

In contrast, many Navajo youth today refer to these bands and the chapter-house spaces in which they performed as "rez" or "rezzed out." They associate them with an older, retro generation from which they often actively distance themselves by seeking out heavy metal, hip hop, and punk music instead (Cyganik, forthcoming; Dehyle 1998). Chapter houses and chapter-house bands therefore become "a marked space for some Navajos, indexing the traditional or the local" (Peterson 2006, 97) and represent a distinctly anticosmopolitan aesthetic and worldview for younger Diné'é. At the same time, ties with family are strong—as I experienced in my own allegiances when choosing between bands with which to perform—and younger musicians and fans who *do* listen to and like rez country often do so because of connections to older family members: younger generations are introduced to this music through playing it with older family members. This was very much the case with Tommy and Arlondo: playing shows together, traveling together, rehearsing, and planning an album together gave father and son—

two men who grew up in very different worlds, with different educational levels and career trajectories—a way to connect, share a common purpose, and spend quality time with one another. And although Arlondo held less affection for rez-band tunes than his father did, he was willing to play these tunes with him as a way to honor his father's own life experience and aesthetic. In this way, the intergenerational affect for rez country is tied to family—both immediate and through kinship—and place as a means of connection through musical expression. Try as they might, there is also the sense that younger folks can never completely escape the "total sonic fact" that is the rez band sound, legacy, and pervasive performative aesthetic.

But we should also situate Tommy's comment about Native Country being a rez or *jaan* band vis-à-vis his own vocal attachments and in the context of the physical diminishment of his voice. Since being diagnosed with vocal nodes in the late 1980s, Tommy has continued to sing and front his own bands. During gigs, however, he has had to cut back on the number of songs he sings as his voice now tires more quickly. In addition, while he could perform up to two hundred songs from memory in his younger days, he has come to rely on what he calls "cheat sheets" or lead sheets in middle age—a common practice for many vocalists regardless of age. But using lead sheets for Tommy signals that he is getting older and beginning to lose the acuity of his memory. Thus, while his voice still remains his son Arlondo's all-time favorite country singing voice—described to me by Arlondo as a deep, rich, and strong voice—Tommy's himself believes his voice is beginning to show signs of "wear," having become "dull" and "hoarse," without the crispness that he associates with his bandmate Errison's singing voice.[14] Tommy now hears his own voice as *jaan* in a way he didn't before, and this is amplified when listening to recordings of his own voice made at home and played through computer speakers.

In fact, Tommy's struggle to sing a full, fifty-minute set on his own was the main factor driving him to add other vocalists to Native Country. By sharing the singing three ways with Errison and myself, Tommy could rest his voice between songs during the course of the standard, four-hour-long gig. In the song "You're Gonna Miss Me," Tommy would often begin the song and then sometimes have me sing the highest notes for him in the short bridge section, explaining that he could no longer hit those notes comfortably. Thus, his own ailing voice directly provoked his decision to open band membership to an Anglo female vocalist.

In referring to his own band and his more recent singing voice as rez, Tommy indicates that he recalls and nostalgically remembers what his voice used to

sound like. In comparing his own band's sound against the slicker, professionally recorded sound of his musical idol, Waylon Jennings, he concedes that the
recording production, the tinny playback speakers, and the lead vocalist make
Native Country sound like a *jaan* band.

Jaan as an ascribed status indicates the uneasiness with which older Navajos
view Anglo influences on a traditional Navajo worldview. As such, the figure
of the *jaan*—and the frequency with which it currently surfaces in Navajo linguistic discourse—marks an implicit critique of Indigenous modernity and the
particular forms it takes on the reservation. It includes the Anglicization and
bureaucratizing of Navajo worlds, exemplified by the presence of the Bureau of
Indian Affairs and Indian Health Service clinics and hospitals on the reservation.

In rez country music, the figure of the *jaan* is specifically embodied and performed as the abject male. As Ching (2003) has elsewhere elaborated, many male
country singers perform the role of "abject burlesque" on stage, but in Navajo
contexts this abjection is more culturally specific and takes on a prescribed stage
patter, vocal timbre, and body language. Although women are also described as
jaan, in the musical context it is mostly men who are thus denoted. Thus, Tommy
can say that a Native Country recording sounded *jaan* because "Room at the Top
of the Stairs" sonically marked many of the characteristics associated with the
so-called *jaan* band described above. The track featuring a slightly nasal, male
singing voice was recorded in a home studio, and as Tommy puts it, "isn't properly mixed."[15] This particular country song is one covered by many older Native
bands and forms part of the Native band canon.

In October 2009, a live, on-air interview and performance of Native Country
on the Gallup NPR affiliate station KGLP (91.7 FM) shone a light on the precarious relationship between sound, social belonging, and what it means to sound
"manly." The show, called *Kindbeat*, featured worldbeat music and was hosted
by Lester Kind, an Eastern Agency relocatee who grew up in California and
returned to Navajo country as an adult. This was the only time the band ever performed acoustically, either in public or during rehearsal, and it was therefore the
first time I had heard my bandmates playing without the mediation of a PA system. Their responses to playing back the interview were instructive not only for
what an ideal rez band should sound like but also for what it means to sound one's
masculinity when playing rez country music. I read my bandmates' responses as
a retrenchment back into the rez band sound after a temporary excursion away
from it. They seemed to be in active pursuit of the social citizenship associated
with the rez band sound.

From my perspective, this acoustic set was the best the band had ever sounded in my two and a half years playing with them. The performance was intimate: we listened more deeply and with great attention to each other's instrumental solos, and were able to make lots of eye contact because we were sitting in a circle, facing each other, rather than all facing out to perform in front of an audience. Because we were playing acoustically, the sound was much more raw, reflecting more accurately what we each actually sounded like. To my ear, we sound less like a *jaan* band in this recording and more like the acoustic country or folk bands one might hear on alternative country stations or on worldbeat shows such as Lester's throughout the United States.

Playing acoustically also brought about changes in the instrumentation itself. For this interview, LeAnder played acoustic guitar rather than his electric Fender Telecaster, and Arlondo played brushes on a snare drum rather than using sticks and a full drum kit. Tommy played electric bass, but with the volume turned down to a level matching the other acoustic instruments, and I played lap steel through a tube amplifier, also with the volume turned down. Since playing louder was one of the ways band members typically expressed emotional affect, performing in the KGLP studio forced us to express heightened emotion through other means. However, while the music sounded good, the live radio-interview format was new for all of us, and Tommy was uncomfortable promoting or even talking about the band on air. A number of dead-air moments resulted during the interview, making the deejay have to cajole Tommy into speaking at all, much to band members' later amusement and chagrin. At one point, the deejay mentioned he would like to have us back on air during the next NPR pledge drive, an invitation to which none of us responded, causing the deejay to say with a bit of exasperation: "Anyone? Could someone please respond to my question?"

Two weeks later, the band discussed their responses after playing back the interview at the family sheep camp in Many Farms. While I wanted to put the recording on the band's MySpace page as promotional material, my bandmates were less enthusiastic and found the recording both disorienting and disconcerting. Tommy noted that his voice sounded "too raw" and "too rough," commenting that there was no reverb on his vocals, a sound he'd become accustomed to hearing when singing through the PA. He also felt that the effects of the vocal nodes on his voice were much more obvious in this recording than in others he'd made. LeAnder noted that the acoustic guitar, too, sounded "plain," that without volume and special-effects pedals, the guitar didn't sound expressive or even like a country guitar. Arlondo's reaction to the recording was perhaps the strongest:

playing with just the snare and using brushes not only sounded "wimpy" to him but also watered down the band's sound in general and made us sound like "some other band." When he heard that I thought the drums sounded really good—the playing was much subtler with the brushes than with the sticks—he interpreted this as a commentary on his ability to play well with a full drum kit, including the large, boomy Ludwig bass drum he had owned since high school. As a result, he announced that he would no longer agree to play brushes on a snare drum and that, when he played drums, he would be playing with a full drum kit or not at all.

This conversation was instructive in rez band aesthetics, but it also reflected my own middle-class taste grounded in playing folk and acoustic music. Where our acoustic sound to me signaled intimacy and effective performance strategy differentiating us from other rez bands using too many special effects, for Tommy it was as if the band had been stripped of its core sound, vulnerable and naked. The mask of the rez band—the reverb from the PA, the bass drum, and the guitar player's special-effects pedals—had been removed, and he didn't like what he heard in the spaces in between. While I suggested that we begin practicing acoustically to really hear one another and correct our mistakes—we always practiced through a full PA—what happened instead was just the opposite.

Prior to the KGLP interview, LeAnder had begun using my acoustic guitar when he was playing "rhythm" guitar during performances:[16] after this discussion he returned to playing electric guitar at all times. Tommy's reverb at gigs was intensified, mics and guitars were turned up, and bass drums were more closely miked. The acoustic sound we produced that day became a foil that Native Country sought to actively work against and disavow; the KGLP experience was "heard" as emasculating and acted as a catalyst for the retrenchment of a rez band sound. Ultimately, Native Country didn't accept the invitation to return to KGLP, and that was the last radio interview we have given since.

Both the KGLP interview and Tommy's reference to Native Country as a *jaan* band reflect Tommy's ambivalence to the sound of his own band. On the one hand, his use of the term *jaan* is a commentary on less-than-successful mediations, which to him sound fragile and provisional—not as he might ideally have them sound—and which bring attention to "bad sound quality" as an expressive resource in its own right (Meintjes 2010, 1). On the other hand, when given the opportunity to stray from this sound and branch beyond the rez band aesthetic, Tommy opted to continue targeting older Navajo country fans and creating sociality primarily for listeners living on the reservation.

Significantly, it's not that Tommy doesn't hear the cracks: he does, but he is also constrained by what David Samuels has termed the "political economy of musical sound" (2004, 203)—the very real financial and time limitations in his own life as a full-time rancher, family man, and Indian Health Services supervisor. As Samuels notes regarding the political economy of musical sound in his work with the San Carlos Apache band the Pacers, "it's a question of what you do if you can afford only rice when what you'd like to eat is caviar" (2004, 205). Tommy's commentary ultimately reflects an outsider's perspective on how "they" might hear the band and this song, pointing to the complex mediations and perceived valuations of Anglo and non-Navajo cultural influences on Navajo land and musical sounds.

The figure of the *jaan* offers us important insights into the multifaceted, criss-crossing, and often contradictory ways that Navajo identities are constructed and articulated in musical performance. It's a term that Tommy uses to describe his affection for and attachment to his band's sound while acknowledging that it doesn't necessarily sound like the professional country bands he hears on Top 40 country radio—though it *does* sound like what he hears on local AM radio. Significantly, it's also a term he very rarely uses around non-Navajos, because he knows it could be misconstrued to buttress misguided stereotypes. *Jaan* is a term that reflects a space he and fellow musicians have carved out, controlled by neither the gatekeepers of tradition nor by aspirations of off-reservation capital and consumption.

Jaan is also a gendered term of inclusion indexing a highly localized, male civic belonging—over and beyond one's legal citizenship as a Navajo—to the Navajo Nation. By contrast, social citizenship is denied to Navajo citizens, like Chucki, who sound too cosmopolitan, urban, professional, or mainstream. *Jaan* and *rez* are terms that include some and exclude others—they work as "rites of incorporation" into a gendered, generationally divided Navajo Nation (Van Gennep 1909 [1960], 11).

Examining the relationship between aesthetics, gendered identities, and musical tradition, we see how Chucki, by playing musical genres deemed less Navajo and by foregrounding a more professional sound, directs her attention toward a primarily non-Navajo, off-reservation audience. Thus, Tommy and Chucki position themselves differently in relation to a working-class, rez-based identity: while Tommy embraces this identity and makes it more regionally, technologically, and affectively specific through the incorporation of the Johnny Emerson mic check, Chucki aspires to a more middle-class and, in her words, less "rez-zie" sound and persona. As a female performer, however, she also struggles for a fuller sense of inclusion and belonging within her respective Navajo musical milieu. And, much as she would love to have a larger on-reservation fan base and actively cultivates the one she does have, Chucki isn't willing to compromise what she hears as her core sound to access this base.

At its most essentializing, sounding Navajo and playing country music are heard as a set of primordial essences pointing to Navajo social authenticity, a nationalist project that leaves little room for musical experimentation or variation in social roles and singing styles. Sonic differences carry social differences because sound is value laden, socially embedded, and often inextricable from social class, gender, generation, and nation. These sonic differences in turn are rendered socially intelligible through vocal grain, vocal register, linguistic labeling, timbre, and forms of gender-exclusive sociality. For Navajo country bands such as Native Country, sounding rez becomes a local way to belong, participate, and relate through music; it is an aesthetic choice that eschews upward mobility for its own sake and instead focuses on the affect this music generates for those that relish it, both past and present. Refusing to sound Navajo, as the KTNN deejay put it, makes bands vulnerable to broader critiques about place-based, gendered, and Indigenous identity; it's a sound representing musicians' refusal to rely on the cultural capital of nostalgia, place of origin, and the chapter-house beat, forcing them to invent new ways to connect with their Navajo listeners in the future.

CHAPTER FIVE

Many Voices, One Nation

t's early morning, and I am sitting in the first-grade classroom at Diné
Bi'Olta,' a Navajo-language immersion school in Fort Defiance, Arizona.
Eighteen energetic girls and boys swirl around me, asking for assistance with
their drawings, tying their shoes, and refastening their hair buns (*tsiiyéél*). The
classroom is phenotypically a microcosm of different cultural groups living in the
Southwest: some students look Navajo, others Anglo, others African American,
and still others Hispanic. But all are Navajo citizens. All of a sudden, at the direction of their teacher, they snap to attention. "Go ahead and introduce your clans
to our guest," she says to them in Navajo. Going around the room, each student
recites his or her introductions from memory, clearly and confidently, ad-libbing
in some cases after the formal introductions are over. One little girl then raises
her hand: "Há'áát'íí adóoné'é nílį?" [What are your clans?], she asks me. As I
did so many times throughout my time in Navajo country, I introduce myself,
substituting my European ethnicities for Navajo clans. "Swedish nishłį́, Danish
báshíshchíín, English dashicheii dóó Danish dashinálí. Kót'éego asdzání nishłį́."[1]
An hour later, we end the morning session by singing "Mary Had a Little Lamb"
("Mary Bidibé Hóló") in Navajo. As I leave the classroom with their teacher for
morning recess, she reflects on how, for her, music is a resource for both language
learning and for cultural expression as Navajos, cementing new vocabulary in
students' minds without them even having to think about it and allowing them to
connect emotionally and viscerally to a Navajo identity through singing. Music is
that good, she says, at cementing new words. The Navajo vocabulary and melody
from "Mary Bidibé Hóló," she chuckles, will probably stay with her students long
into their adult lives, whether they like it or not.

As I hope to have shown, Navajo identities form not only around one's language, place of origin, or last name. They are also indexed by the speaking and
singing voice, through phenotype, claims to firstness, degree of Navajo blood,

and gendered personae. Voice, expressive culture, and the arts often act as litmus tests for the tribal, state, and federal politics of deciding who counts as Indigenous, while values continue to shift with time. Through a methodological focus on cultural intimacy and generational expressions of Navajo sociality, this study sheds light on how exclusion and marginalization form the flip side of the coin of Navajo cultural authenticity, belonging, and social citizenship. Thus, terms of linguistic approval traced throughout this book—"traditional," "deep rez," "rez," "mono," and "old Navajo"—are matched in frequency and intensity by terms of linguistic disapproval. Words like *jaan*, "apple," "generic," "urban," and even "New Mexico Navajo" speak to the privileged currency of cultural distinction that permeates so many layers of Navajo discourse, private and public. Terms of approval and disapproval also demonstrate beyond a doubt how varying identities become attached to different Navajo speaker types in often essentializing ways.

An implication of this study, therefore, has been to show how changing, evolving facets of culture come to be seen and heard as fixed and internalized essences. Expressive cultural forms—humor, music, oratory, dance, language play, code-switching—are particularly apt at revealing the cracks in these essentialisms, often cementing and refracting them at the same time. As we have seen, Vincent Craig's comedic routines attempt to poke fun at and expose the fallacy of a single Navajo essence through his impersonations of overdetermined cultural types. Essentializing expressive culture, in turn, not only restricts the range of movement and senses of possibility for those denoted as traditional; such strictures also limit our own ability as students of human culture to understand *all* social worlds as fundamentally experimental, creative, and based on movement, fluctuation, and change. Thus, while evolution and diachronic change within language structures are often a given from an anthropological perspective, the anthropological desire to document supposedly traditional expressive forms in Indigenous communities in particular has sometimes blinded us to seeing change and hybridity as cultural norms rather than anomalies.

If instead we understand voice as the instrument through which a politics of sameness and difference is expressed, we can then hear voice as the sign or signature of a particular identity. Affective attachments to voices—certainly those of Vincent Craig, Johnny Emerson, Waylon Jennings, Etta James, and Whitney Houston, but also those of fathers and uncles, mothers, teachers, and aunties—shape not only our politics and senses of self but also our own feelingful experiences of citizenship and belonging. Whose voices do we long to listen to, who do we emulate, and why? What kind of cultural work is performed by hearing a particular voice at a particular moment, in private or in public? How might knowing a voice or getting a joke about another person's voice (recall Arlondo's comment about the Navajo lead singer who sang with a Gary Stuart vibrato) shape us as fully fledged members of a social group or citizens of a nation? How do music and language craft specific senses of self that differ from one nation or community to another?

Senses of belonging and knowing one's place are also often highly gendered. As stories about Chucki, Candice, Doreen, and Radmilla demonstrate, women are often portrayed as the bearers and transmitters of that which lies within the nation. This includes depictions of women as the ones transmitting traditional culture and as prestige-group speakers of an Indigenous heritage language. From this perspective, Navajo identity is something that comes both from within the physical body and from within the symbolic nation, a private (and often idealized and imagined) center or cultural core. Men, in contrast, often represent that which aesthetically lies beyond the nation and thus emblemize its more public face: popular music, popular culture, recording technologies, and Western-style realpolitik realized at the level of Navajo tribal politics (most Tribal Council positions are held by men). These tensions between male and female voices also speak to larger slippages I track throughout the book between what is public and what is intimate, seen and unseen, heard and not heard, and the perceived right to belong based on one's success navigating these disjunctures.

The aim of this study has not only been to show how the grain of the voice constitutes the physical and symbolic locus of Navajo identity politics but also to demonstrate how recording technology itself informs how we hear and assign value to vocal and instrumental timbres. Grain marks the friction between language and a voice, but it's also the friction between a voice and a microphone, such as when musicians do the Johnny Emerson mic check. Thus grain is produced through the mono sound of early chapter-house bands, through low-fidelity recordings and temporary playback devices, and, by extension, through a high-fidelity male sociality privileging relatedness and reciprocity through family and kinship ties. Grain articulates with social structure because sound is not only value laden and socially enmeshed; grain carries the residual weight of nostalgia, the former affect and future hope of sounds and voices to come.

In a final return to the concepts of tradition, cosmopolitanism, and being Diné, Benjamin Barney, the director of the Navajo Teacher Education Program at Diné College, Tsaile, offers some thoughts for a future road map that is both courageous and, for some, unexpected:

I think a good map is the original Navajo map because the . . . map entails having to do with Utes, having to deal with Hopis, Tewas, and all these Pueblos and all these people in the tribe that are different customs, cultures, and ways and lifestyle. That original map was a good map. And that's much more necessary now. The older [generation], my great-grandparents' age, I think, were much better at dealing with cross-cultural, cross-language, cross-religion. And they had an ease, a flowing back and forth. That particular map, I think, is much more necessary for these younger Navajos than ever before, because they will end up in Germany, they will end up in France, they will end up in Korea. They will end up in New York City, Albuquerque, Phoenix, Denver. Some of them have gone mid-west; some of them have gone east. (Barney in House 2002, iv)

For Barney, making this observation in 1994, a return to Navajo tradition may actually mean opening up definitions of Navajo identity rather than sealing them off from outside influence. This return to the "original Navajo map" might include expanding these categories not only within and among Navajos living on the reservation but also broadening and deepening a set of intra-Navajo diplomatic relations, for example between Navajos living on the Big Rez and those residing on satellite reservations, in U.S. cities and stationed abroad in the U.S. military. Such an approach might also include a more serious look at international relations between the Navajo Nation and other tribal nations, state governments, and the federal administration, including an examination of how national imaginaries of both the Navajo Nation and the U.S. nation are co-created in this process.

In linking Navajo cosmopolitanism to traditional Navajo concepts of self before removal (known as the Long Walk), Barney also pushes us to reconsider the role of Navajos in larger U.S. society, in the U.S. international community, and vis-à-vis other U.S. tribes (Lee 2006). In the process, he prompts us to re-conceptualize how we think about home and abroad, about "us" versus "them." Showcasing this cosmopolitanism and "flowing back and forth" so typical of Navajo experience, it isn't uncommon to hear a Navajo park ranger living in the heart of the reservation make a casual reference to the time he spent in Belarus with his dance troupe, or a Navajo ceremonial practitioner declare his affinity for *Käsebrot*, a taste he acquired when he was stationed at a military base in southern Germany. A Native American Church (NAC) member may recount how Navajo grandmas look just like the older Athabaskan women in western Canada and the Canadian Shield he saw when he apprenticed to an NAC roadman, or he might remember the cherished visits to sons, nieces, cousins, and uncles who are stationed in North Carolina at Fort Bragg and Camp Lejeune. Since Navajos are nationally known as the tribe of the legendary Code Talkers,[2] how might a self-governing entity like the Navajo Nation argue for its right to belong—its social citizenship—to the U.S. nation based on its extraordinary legacy of military service? Ultimately, the stakes for gendered inclusion on the Navajo Nation are similar to the stakes for Indigenous belonging in broader U.S. contexts. Both are narrowly defined and currently reflect larger, settler-colonial definitions fused with the powerful, local language of tradition, authenticity, and what it means to be Diné. Determining who sounds Navajo follows similar criteria to those used to assess who is and isn't "Navajo enough." Sound and authenticity are linked much as gender and authenticity are.

More recently, the specter of Indigenous belonging and authenticity has force-fully reared its head under the guise of language politics at the executive level. In the fall of 2014, two candidates were vying for the Navajo Nation presidency, Dr. Joe Shirley Jr. and Christopher Clark Deschene. Shirley, age sixty-six, is a former two-term Navajo president fluent in *saadsání* (old Navajo), has a spiritually tradi-tional orientation, and hails from the heart of Diné Bikéyah, Chinle, Arizona. He also explicitly incorporates performances of traditional songs on the campaign trail. Deschene, forty-three, is a former Marine Corps officer, an engineer, a law-yer, and served one term in the Arizona House of Representatives. A child of the relocation era, Deschene was born in southern California and returned to the reservation and to Lechee Chapter, Navajo Nation, as an adult. Most important, as an urban Navajo, Deschene does not speak Navajo, a requirement written in the Navajo Tribal Code for those running for president, vice president, or the Tribal Council. Thus, although he "doesn't need a translator" (Morales, radio transcript, September 22, 2014), he isn't necessarily comfortable reproducing Navajo sounds himself. Coming in second in the Navajo Nation primary election, Deschene in-corporated his struggles with Navajo into his campaign-trail rhetoric, adding more Navajo words into his introduction during the last six months and promising the Navajo people that, by the end of his first term, he would be fully fluent (however that might be defined). In contrast to Shirley, Deschene didn't use traditional songs or prayers in his campaign and relied, instead, on his legacy of military service and academic credentials to bolster his credibility with Diné voters.

The Deschene-Shirley divide beautifully encapsulates many of the genera-tional, aesthetic, and place-based differences traced throughout this book, but it also ups the stakes because, in the end, Deschene was removed from the ballot as presidential candidate due to his lack of fluency (another candidate, Russell Begaye, also fluent in Navajo, was sworn in on May 12, 2015).[3]

On July 21, 2015, the Navajo Nation voted in a nation-wide referendum to remove the language-fluency requirement for the offices of president and vice president, thus allowing voters to decide at the time they vote whether or not the ability to read and understand English and Navajo is an essential qualification (Thompson and Jacobsen, forthcoming). Driving into Chinle that morning and listening to KTNN, it was clear that this marked a historic decision that didn't come lightly for Navajo citizens. Instead of following the regular country music format, morning airtime was dedicated to public service announcements (PSAs) for and against the language amendment. Significantly, most messages against the amendment were aired in Navajo and strongly linked Diné identity to language, language loss in the boarding-school context, and the need to continue Diné language and tradition to continue as a Diné people. The PSAs for the amendment — most but not all in English — targeted mainly older voters and explained that voting for the referendum didn't mean voting *against* the Navajo language, per se, but, rather meant giving voters the opportunity to decide how essential language fluency was to a candidate's ability to lead. Targeting the fear that voting *for* the referendum meant voting *against* one's heritage language, the pro-amendment PSAs hit close to the grain, nuancing what is often a polarized cultural and linguistic field where older Navajo speakers as a voting block hold significant sway. And then, ending the PSA segment, veteran deejay Ray Tsosie segued back to the musical format at hand, announcing in Navajo the artist and song name of honky-tonk artist Gary Stewart ("If Drinking Don't Kill Me, Her Memory Will"), followed by the rez band favorite played by so many bands during my fieldwork, "Indian Cowboy," performed by the White Mountain Apache band, Apache Spirit.

Although the referendum didn't retroactively change anything for Deschene, the debate over the fluency requirement has opened up a much larger and long-term public forum for a conversation about Navajo language speakers, fluency, cultural intimacy, and generational divides. As the Diné journalist Jaynie Parrish noted about the debate in the *Guardian*: "Our private narratives have been brought into the public realm" (October 13. 2014). In newspaper articles and on Facebook pages, Twitter feeds and newscasts, Diné citizens are now debating how important heritage language fluency is, how fluency is defined (for example, does understanding a language count as fluency, as Deschene claims?), and whether this requirement needs to be changed, given that 50 percent of the people

Deschene meant to lead aren't fluent in their heritage language either (Thompson in Morales, radio transcript, September, 22, 2014). Voters are asking: *Is* Navajo still the national language of the Navajo Nation, and, if it is and given the dwindling number of speakers, is Diné identity in a broader sense in peril? And if not, what makes it cohere? Is fluency the most important criteria for a Navajo leader, or is it the skill sets he or she brings to the job, regardless of mother tongue? As in the case of Radmilla Cody and Rick Wilson, language again has come into the limelight, this time taking away Deschene's right to run for president.

By extension, we might also ask: is there one national music genre that represents the Navajo Nation? No, but for one or two social generations — "people within a delineated population who experience the same series of events within a given period in time" (Pilcher 1994, 481–95) — there may indeed be one genre that expertly encapsulates Navajo expressive identity from their years coming of age and living on the reservation. And this music is often country. These answers again reveal the tremendous internal diversity of the Navajo Nation as both a political and a cultural entity, where Diné citizens have always privileged and created space for heterogeneity — in origin stories, gender roles, ceremonial practices, dialectal variation, weaving styles, silversmithing, and music. In examining the historical and archeological record, we see that there has always been room for multiple aesthetic fields within a Diné cosmology; the narrowing of these fields constitutes a relatively recent phenomenon (Thompson 2009, 2011). At this level, for Diné citizens the teachings of the maternal clan to which one belongs still typically hold sway over governmental, educational, or political narratives about what it means to be Diné. Indeed, this is the diverse canvas on which, in 1923, the first Navajo Nation Council was formed for the sake of signing oil and gas leases with outside entities. One might argue that, from 1923 until the present, much of Navajo cultural politics, including the material presented in this book, has resulted from the misalignments between the Navajo Nation as a political entity — a modern, semisovereign nation-state — and Diné Bikéyah as a kinship-based cultural entity, the latter imbued with preconstitutional or inherent sovereignty from at least the 1400s to the present. Political nationhood is new, but a sovereign peoplehood, and notions of inclusion and diversity of opinion on what is called Diné Bikéyah (the people's land) are not: these indices of cultural identity can be traced as far back as the historical record of Diné peoples can take us.[4] Music and language foreground the friction between these two competing structures in unique and powerful ways.

In a final return to how music genre reflects the internal diversity of the Navajo

Nation as a cultural field, I'll end with a recent interview given by Radmilla Cody. Known for her performances of traditional Diné songs sung in Navajo, Cody was asked to list her greatest musical influences. Predictably listing Whitney Houston, her uncle Herman Cody, other Navajo traditional singers and R & B singer Adina Howard, she went on to say that her real idol was the late hard country recording star and songwriter Merle Haggard. Her dream, she said, would have been to open for *him* in concert someday.

T'áá ákódí. The end.

"The Lights of Albuquerque"[1]

Fall 2015. The main events chronicled in this book took place between 2008 and 2011, roughly four years ago. Since that time, I returned to North Carolina to finish my degree, then came back to the Southwest to teach at Northern Arizona University in Flagstaff, and now I teach at the University of New Mexico (UNM) in Albuquerque. Because I now work close to the place where my research took place, I have had the great privilege to stay connected with the Navajo Nation, the various bands I played with, and community members with whom I became close during my fieldwork. Native Country, for example, continues to play occasional gigs, including the upcoming Chapterhouse Dance we're playing in Sawmill, Navajo Nation, for a friend's wedding.

Chucki Begay and Mother Earth Blues (now Chucki Begay and Family Band) no longer actively perform, but Chucki continues to perform as a solo act, and *Music Is Medicine* is going strong. Members of Candice's band, The Wranglers, still perform, although Carson has recently suffered health issues and is less active musically than he would like to be. Candice continues to sing, and she graduated with her bachelor's degree in science and technology at Navajo Technical University in the spring of 2015. She is looking for a country band with which to start singing either on the rez or in Albuquerque, soon. Last spring, she traveled to Albuquerque to perform for members of my country music class, where she sang "Redneck Woman" and "Okie from Muskogee," Candice style, a truly memorable and moving experience for all involved. I was also able to invite an old friend and former student from my line dancing class days in Crownpoint into that same class to teach students some line dances and the two-step. Re-Coil continues to be active, primarily off the reservation, and performed last fall for my class on Diné art and politics. The band has a new bassist, and they are writing and recording more original material now. They are still eager for the book to come out and have encouraged me to keep on playing, writing, to not spend too much time "thinking about stuff," and to publish the book. Amen.

LeAnder Bia of Native Country still sits in with various bands, and his lead-guitar skills are coveted among local bands in the communities of Chinle, Many Farms, Piñon, and beyond. He also wants to form his own blues and rockabilly band some day. Errison Littleben, too, continues to play, sitting in on rhythm guitar and lending his expressive voice and his performances of the song now iconic to his repertoire, "Mississippi," to various bands playing in Kayenta, Chinle, and beyond. He recently performed again at Apache House of Liquors (Jicarilla Apache Nation), one of Native Country's regular stomping grounds: the tribe has redone the bar, and he says the band should start playing over there again. Tommy continues to struggle with his vocal nodes; when he's not overly busy growing alfalfa, feeding, watering, branding, and rounding up cattle, and otherwise being a family man, we get to jam out and play old Anita Carter/Waylon Jennings and Gram Parsons/Emmylou Harris tunes on our box guitars, most recently working up a harmony for "If I Could Only Win Your Love." Tommy also recently sat in at the weekly open mic I hosted in Chinle in the *hooghan* behind Our Lady of Fatima Catholic Church last summer (2014). He sang a moving acoustic rendition of XIT's "Baa shił Hózhǫ́" (I Am Happy about It).

I now live in Albuquerque and make frequent trips to the Navajo Nation, and I eagerly look forward to the Bia family cattle branding and roundup on Carson Mesa every summer (I still can't rope to save myself). At UNM, I teach classes in anthropology, ethnomusicology, Native American studies, and songwriting, and I cofacilitate the UNM honky-tonk ensemble—classes that together form the intellectual and sonic impulses undergirding this book. Last Thursday, in my "Navajo Expressive Culture" class, I brought in my guitar and sang some of Native Country's classic songs—Loretta Lynn, Kitty Wells, and Merle Haggard classics—tunes frequently requested at our gigs. Singing the chorus from Charley Pride's hard country classic "Is Anybody Going to San Antone or Phoenix, Arizona?," I switched the lyric, as Tommy requested I do the first time we performed it at Hopi Nation's Kootka Hall seven years ago: "Is anybody going to San Antone/or Many Farms, Arizona?" Happily for me, many of my students now are from the Nation or its border towns and are fans of the very same bands I write about. They laugh when I tell them about the "rowdy" bars I've performed in, and they occasionally come to dances and observe me and the band for the ethnographic writing exercises I've assigned them in my classes. My students tune in to KTNN and listen to rez bands, they tell me, when they feel homesick for Diné Bikéyah, far away from home under the glowing lights of Albuquerque.

Notes

....

Introduction

1. *Ak'ah Kǫ' Bitoo'* (meaning "fat, fire, its juice"). To access songs and videos discussed throughout the book, please visit the author's website: www.kristina-jacobsen.com.

2. Diné (pl. Dine'é) is the preferred ethnonym for Navajo people, meaning "the people." When used in Navajo, this term can also simply mean "human being" or "person."

3. The tribal roll to which one needs to trace descent is the 1940 so-called base roll. Rolls were taken by the Bureau of Indian Affairs as a way to determine the total number of citizens in a given tribe eligible for federal services. By definition, these rolls are always partial and somewhat arbitrary in terms of who was included and who was left off.

4. Fieldwork was permitted through a Class C Ethnographic Permit issued by the Navajo Nation Historic Preservation Department under the guidance of Ron Maldonado and Ora Marek-Martinez.

5. Although the genre performed includes both country and western music and musicians identify as residents of the western or southwestern United States, most musicians refer to it simply as "country."

6. The recent police shooting of Loreal Tsingine in Holbrook, Arizona (Quintero 2016), and the brutal killing of two Navajo homeless men, Allison Gorman and Kee Thompson, at the hands of Hispanic teenagers in Albuquerque in July 2014 are some of the most recent and chilling examples (Landry 2016).

7. See http://www.nnhrc.navajo-nsn.gov/.

8. Pronounced "Bai-uh."

9. Chapter houses are town-hall-style municipal buildings on Navajo land where political and social events take place.

10. While the majority of musicians and Navajo speakers with whom I spent my time were at least ten years my senior, the major exception was younger family members of Native band musicians, many of whom also play in these family bands, though with more ironic distance toward the genre than their parents.

11. Groups included The Outlaws from Crownpoint; Dennis Yazzie and the Night Breeze Band from Thoreau, New Mexico; and Chucki Begay and the Mother Earth Blues Band, now Chucki Begay and Family Band (from Gray Mountain and Borrego Pass, New Mexico).

12. Female *hooghans* are round, have a varying number of sides with an east-facing door, and are built to represent the female womb. Male *hooghans*, also called "forked-stick" *hooghans*, are conical in shape. Most residential *hooghans* on the reservation today are female *hooghans*.

13. Following local usage, I refer to paternal aunts as "aunties."

14. Following the clan-system model, I was encouraged to substitute my predominant European ethnicity from each grandparent as follows: "Danish nishłį, Swedish báshíshchíín, English dashicheii dóó Danish dashinálí. Kót'éego asdzání nishłį" [I am born to the Danish people, born for the Swedish people, my maternal grandfather belongs to the English people and my paternal grandfather belongs to the Danish people. In this way I am a woman/human being].

15. Jacobsen 2009.

16. See, for example, Marcus and Fisher 1986 [1999], and Marcus 1998.

17. Person of "white" or Anglo descent.

18. These numbers are currently debated: some tribal citizens state there are more than seventy clans, while others insist there are significantly fewer (Lloyd Lee, personal correspondence, July 25, 2014,).

19. Many clans are affiliated with certain occupations, and some are considered higher status than others (Shirley Bowman, personal communication, October 15, 2009).

20. Adopted clans were often created when descendants of Ute, Apache, Pueblo, Spanish, and Mexican war captives were incorporated into Diné society (Thompson 2009, 134). This includes present-day clans such as the Mexican People Clan (Naakaii Dine'é; actually a reference to slaves taken of Iberian descent), the Ute clan (Nóóda'í Dine'é), and Apache clans such as the White Mountain Apache clan (Dziłghą'í Dine'é), the Mescalero Apache clan (Naashgalí Dine'é), and the Chiricahua Apache (Chishí Dine'é) clan. Adopted Pueblo clans include the Hopi clan (Kiis'áanii), the Tewa Clan (Naashashí), that is, the Tewa-speaking peoples of New Mexico, the Zuni clan (Naasht'ézhí) and the Zia [Weaver] clan (Tł'ógí).

21. For example, most members of Re-Coil belong to the Salt Clan (Ashįįhí).

22. Referred to by most Diné citizens as a "CIB."

23. See Ching and Creed 1997; Fox 2004a; Tichi 1994; R. Peterson 1997; Williams 1973 [1985].

24. Smith 1994; Gibson and Davidson 2004; Fox 2004a; Dent 2009.

25. Linguists refer to vocal "twang" as a type of diphthongization, where the "insertion of a tensing of the vowel is followed by an offglide to the lax form" (Feld, Fox, Porcello, and Samuels in Duranti 2004, 337). However, instruments can also twang (Mann 2008), as heard, for example, when a skilled guitar player plays the iconic twanging lead instrument, the Fender Telecaster.

26. As Samuels points out, country performance practice is also considered more authentic if one actually *speaks* the regional dialect one uses in performance. In country performance, this is often a variant of Appalachian American English. While country artists can and do perform in dialects different from that of their place of origin—indeed, the use of the southeastern U.S. twang is part of country music performance practice even for Australian country artists—the alignment of place and dialect buttresses one's credentials in country music, as is the case with the Oklahoma artist, Reba McEntire (Feld, Fox, Porcello, and Samuels in Duranti 2004, 337).

27. Reservations refer to Indigenous homelands in the United States, and reserves refer to Indigenous homelands in Canada.

28. Fox and Yano forthcoming; Dent 2009; Fast 2002; Pecknold 2013.

29. Fox 2005; Aaron Fox, keynote speaker, University of Chicago *EthNoise* conference, October 2005.

30. Often referred to as "cry breaks," country's crying sound is described by Fox as a sharp deformation of the air stream, akin to a fast yodel, and typically sung on a semi-vocalic segment (Fox 2004a, 280–81). Cry breaks are usually performed on nouns and verbs thematically related to sorrow.

31. Although not the focus of my ethnographic research, there are three smaller satellite reservations that also form part of the Navajo Nation and are all in New Mexico: Tóhajilee', Alamo, and Ramah.

32. Cindy Yurth in *Navajo Times*, January 26, 2012. The number of off-reservation Navajos is disputed; Diné scholar Lloyd Lee suggests the number is much higher, closer to 45 percent of the total population (personal communication, July 25, 2014).

33. San Ramon Pueblo is a pseudonym.

34. See http://navajorenaissance.org/index.html.

35. These ideas about language literacy, its relative freedom of circulation and, as a result, the permission granted (in some cases) for non-Navajos to learn Diné Bizaad also had important implications for my own ability as a non-Navajo to learn Navajo and receive tutelage and mentoring by veteran language teachers such as Shirley Bowman.

36. Fernandez et al. 1974; Gilroy 1995; Feintuch 2003; Cook 2010; Brulotte 2012.

37. Notable exceptions include Barker 2011; Sturm 2011; Dennison 2012; and Simpson 2014.

38. Songs associated with the public portion of the Navajo Enemyway (*Ndáá'*) ceremony.

39. Songs associated with the Native American Church.

40. A local designation for code-mixed Navajo and English. Examples include *solice* for "police" (Navajo *siláo* combined with English "police") and *móógashii* for "cow" (Navajo *béégashii* combined with the English sound "moo").

41. KTNN AM 660, Window Rock, Navajo Nation, Arizona.

42. "Pickin' White Gold," Waylon Jennings, 1970.

43. "Sundowners" is local slang for "sheepherder."

44. I was recently reminded of this when a Navajo Technical University welding instructor casually shared with me that, for him, Waylon Jennings "is Jesus." Each time a Waylon Jennings' song comes on the radio, he crosses himself, and he explained with pride and amusement that he has taught his four kids to do the same.

45. This is often referred to in some country circles as "countrypolitan."

46. Pedersen and Elkins 2005; Wolfe 2006; Smith 2010; Veracini 2010.

47. Hemispheric Institute of Performance and Politics, http://hemisphericinstitute.org/hemi/en/about-this-website.

48. For a discussion of the intertwining of the legal and social politics of difference, see Barker's discussion of what she terms "consequential differences" of Native identity and community making, which she describes as being "in contradiction, in disagreement, and in complexity" about what "unique cultures and traditions are and how those cultures and

traditions matter . . . in the governance, territorial integrity, and cultural autonomy that they seek" (2011, 13).

49. The so-called checkerboard comprises the eastern portion of the Navajo reservation, known as Eastern Agency. It is made up of various landowners in addition to the tribe, so that on a map it resembles a literal checkerboard.

50. Barker 2011; Biolsi 2004; Denetdale 2006; Dennison 2012; Perdue 2003; Sturm 2002.

51. Brooks 2002; Omi and Winant 1994; Roediger 2002.

52. Feld 1982, 1984a, 1990; Meintjes 2003; Brenneis and Feld 2004; Fox 2004a; Samuels 2004a.

53. Jakobson 1960; Bakhtin 1981; Feld et al. 2004; Weidman 2006; Gray 2007; Ninoshvili 2010, 2011.

54. Hymes 1964; Tedlock 1983; Bauman 1977 [1984]; Urban 1988; Bauman and Briggs 1990; Feld and Fox 1994; Feld et al. 2004.

55. Cowlishaw 1987; Strong and Van Winkle 1996; L. T. Smith 1999; Povinelli 2002; Sturm 2002; Brown 2003; Niezen 2003; de la Cadena and Starn 2007; Kauanui 2008; Barker 2011; Dennison 2012; Coleman 2013.

56. Fox 2004a; Samuels 2004; Weidman 2006.

57. Begaye is from Shiprock Chapter and Shelly is from Thorough Chapter, both in New Mexico.

Chapter One

1. Now Navajo Technical University.

2. Many rural areas on the Navajo reservation (approximately 30 percent of families) don't have running water for drinking, washing, or ranching. Families often carry large water tanks (typically 55-, 250-, and 500-gallon drums) in their pickup trucks to haul water from the nearest community pump.

3. In contrast to an income-based definition of wealth, traditionally oriented Diné also covet owning livestock and land as a form of wealth.

4. Yazzie and Begay are two of the most common Navajo surnames. Yazzie is an Anglo transliteration of the Navajo word *yázhí* (small, little), and Begay is an Anglo transliteration of *biye'* (kinship term from a man to his son, meaning "his son").

5. See, for example Dyk 1938 [1996]; Haile 1926; Hill 1943; Frisbie 1967 [1993]; Kluckhohn and Leighton 1962; Kluckhohn and Wyman 1940; Matthews 1897; McAllester 1954; Mitchell 1978; Peterson 2006; Reichard 1928; Sapir 1936; Witherspoon 1977.

6. The original boundaries were Bear Springs as the eastern boundary, Fort Defiance as the southern boundary, Canyon De Chelly as the western boundary, and the thirty-seventh degree latitude north as the northernmost boundary (http://dine.sanjuan.k12.ut.us/heritage/people/dine/organization/government/treaty.htm/).

7. There are 110 chapters on the Navajo reservation, and each chapter has its own chapter house; Eastern Navajo Agency is one portion of the reservation that lies within northwestern New Mexico.

8. The town of Crownpoint, New Mexico, is located within Crownpoint Chapter, Eastern Agency, Navajo Nation.

9. Archeological evidence shows us that Diné peoples gradually made a shift from hunter-gatherer subsistence to increased pastoralism around 1700 (Thompson 2009, 50), but continued to combine hunting-gathering, horticulturalism, and pastoralism as forms of subsistence (Thompson 2009, 151). However, semimobility likely also predated the introduction of sheep and horses (Thompson 2009, 241, 250).

10. Dziłná'oodiłii (Turning Mountain Mesa).

11. The Place Where the Water Flows In.

12. There are also some Navajo stories and vocabulary that support a migration over the Bering Land Bridge, or at least an origin from as far north as Alaska. For example, one Navajo term for the Native peoples of Alaska is "Diné Náhódló̜" which, according to the bandleader Tommy Bia and his wife, Helen Bia, is a term that probably refers to "the people that stayed behind" (Tommy and Helen Bia, September 2010, personal communication).

13. Some of the strongest evidence for the so-called Bering Strait theory is the shared vocabulary of Athabaskan speakers from Alaska, down the western coast of Canada, into the Pacific Northwest, Northern California, and then the American Southwest and northern Mexico (Sapir 1936; Young and Morgan 1987).

14. Begay and Roberts 1996; Kelley and Francis 2003; Warburton and Begay 2005; Denetdale 2007; Thompson 2009.

15. Reasons for its adoption include that it was learnable, clear, and linguistically inclusive; there is evidence that this southern Athabaskan language may have even been used as a trade language on the Hopi reservation and along the Camino Reál going to Mexico City (Kerry Thompson, personal correspondence, September 2015).

16. On most maps of the reservation, the Navajo checkerboard does not appear as Navajo reservation land.

17. The 2010 Census listed 2,729 residents living in Crownpoint (https://docs.google .com/file/d/0B9Ys0__F67YfQoIwRHJ3aHRLUDQ/edit).

18. Vincent Craig is the paternal uncle of the country artist Candice Craig, who also hails from Crownpoint.

19. Rugs today are rarely used as actual floor coverings. Rather, they are coveted collectors' items typically hung and framed, or they are made into women's traditional dresses and reserved for other special occasions.

20. For an overview of Navajo governmentality, see Wilkins 1999 and Austin 2009.

21. According to a Robert Wood Johnson Foundation report, Gallup became a civic enabler for Native-specific alcohol abuse in a number of ways, including sixty-one liquor establishments for a city of less than 21,000 residents and a number of "quick-cash" establishments, including twenty-one pawnshops, a blood plasma donation center, numerous payday loan establishments, and two bottle-recycling centers (Brodeur in Isaac and Knickman, 2003, 3).

22. The frozen bodies of Native men and women who have died of exposure while intoxicated and have been found on the streets of Gallup are so common that police officers and ambulance drivers sometimes glibly refer to them as "popsicles" (Brodeur 2006, 3).

23. Nálii is an Anglicization of *nálí hastíí* (paternal grandfather).

24. Garden Deluxe has been replaced by other popular fortified beverages such as Thunderbird wine and High Gravity malt liquor.

25. As described by Barbara Ching (2001), "hard country" is a subgenre of country defined more by its oppositional stance than by a sound per se. It is exemplified by members of the Country Outlaw movement, a group of musicians reacting to the slicker "Nashville sound" of the late 1950s and including musicians such as Waylon Jennings, Kris Kristofferson, David Allan Coe, Merle Haggard, Willie Nelson, and Jessi Colter.

26. Such studies typically focus on differential rates of alcohol metabolism among Native and non-Native populations. Contrary to popular belief, studies by the Wisconsin Department of Health and Human Services and at the University of Colorado's Alcohol Research Center (1999) have shown that Native Americans metabolize alcohol at the same rate as non-Natives (May 1995; Brodeur 2006, 5–6).

27. "Tanya Tucker" is replaced in subsequent choruses with "Charlie Daniels" and "Old Bocephus."

28. This was done for marketing purposes, with "hillbilly" music targeted toward rural, white southerners and "race" music marketed to African American listeners.

Chapter Two

1. Pieces by the Diné classical composer and pianist Connor Chee, inspired by melodies from the Enemyway ceremony but learned off an early recording, *Navajo Songs*, by the ethnomusicologist Laura Boulton.

2. Billy Luther's film, *Miss Navajo* (2007), documents some of these struggles in the life of the 2005–6 Miss Navajo contestant Crystal Frazier.

3. Webster uses the term "Navlish" to describe the same phenomenon. In the speech communities where I worked, "Navadlish" was the more common term used to describe this form of code-mixing.

4. American Indian suffrage was granted in 1924. However, according to Diné citizens and veterans to whom I've spoken, in the Southwest, most Native citizens were not actually allowed to vote at polling stations until 1948.

5. The Mormon Placement Program is usually referred to on the reservation simply as "Placement."

6. While depicted in a relatively positive light by many of my interlocutors, the legacy of Indian Boarding Schools and the Placement program also includes documentation of physical and sexual abuse along with forced sterilization (Pegoraro 2015). Although they lie beyond the scope of this study, such accounts have been powerfully told by Archuleta, Child, and Lomawaima (2000), Reyhner and Eder (1924), Gilbert (2010), Rehyner and Eder 2006 [2015], and Child (1998), among others.

7. An example of a compound noun is the Navajo word for pickup truck, *chidí bikée'jį' adeez'áhí* ("car," "behind it extending," "the one that juts out"), also glossed as a "car with an extension to the back of the vehicle."

8. The Navajo Nation Election Code for each elected office states that candidates for

president and vice president must "speak and understand Navajo and read and write English" (11 N.N.C. Sec. 8[A][4]). Similarly, candidates for council delegates "must be able to speak and understand Navajo and/or English" (11 N.N.C. Sec. 8[B][8]).

9. The non-code-mixed version in Navajo would be *Há'át'íísh baa naniná?*

10. See http://www.navajobusiness.com/fastFacts/demographics.htm (accessed July 29, 2014).

11. A sheep camp is local terminology for a family ranch where livestock is kept, usually with an adjacent *hooghan* or house. A sheep camp might have full-time residents, or it might have a designated person who does daily feedings, the house itself serving as a meeting place for family reunions, butchering, and branding, and as a gathering place for family members on weekends and holidays.

12. Clans are typically given in the following order: mother's first clan, father's first clan, maternal grandfather's clan, paternal grandfather's clan.

13. I thank Taos Pueblo Tribal Enrollment Office specialist, Micheleigh Lujan, for her clarification of enrollment requirements for Taos Pueblo (personal correspondence, April 4, 11).

14. "Cotton Candy/Lollipop," from *The Colorful World* (2010). A mixture of vocables — formulaic, non-referential syllables — and English-language lyrics, the refrain is playfully sung by Begaye in a falsetto voice: "Who's gonna buy you candy, [if] I won't be there?/ If you be nice I will buy you lollipop/Maybe cotton candy/weyo weyo we."

15. Jumbo majored in anthropology at Brown with an emphasis in linguistic anthropology and Indigenous language revitalization.

Chapter Three

1. Thank you to Radmilla Cody for reading multiple drafts of this chapter and for generously offering her insights and feedback. Ahéhee'!

2. Chip Thomas, "On the Road with Miss Navajo Nation," *Ruminations*, last modified May 27, 1998 (http://www.chipthomasphotography.com/ruminations/miss_navajo_97.htm).

3. Radmilla also won in the following categories: most photogenic, most applause, and the frybread-making Contest.

4. The more standard terminology for this clan is *Naakai Łizhinii* [Mexican People Clan]. This is a term Radmilla avoids for its racialized overtones.

5. The American Anthropological Association's Project Race states: "Physical variations in the human species have no meaning except the social ones that humans put on them" (Smedley 1998). While I acknowledge that race is indeed a social construct, for the purposes of this chapter, here I foreground what Biolsi has termed the "social fact" of race, or the way that race is assigned social meaning in its lived, everyday contexts (Biolsi 2004, 400; Smaje 2014).

6. Statistically, indigenous women are disproportionately affected by domestic violence, and domestic violence is often linked to the reasons for their incarceration (Deer 2015; https://www.futureswithoutviolence.org/userfiles/file/Violence%20Against%20AI%20AN%20Women%20Fact%20Sheet.pdf). Native women experience violence and sexual assault at

2.5 times the national average. This was also true in Radmilla's case, where she was sentenced for lying to a Grand Jury in order to protect herself from an abusive and vindictive partner.

7. For example, the 2000 census reported Navajos living in every state of the union with the exception of Vermont, Rhode Island, and Delaware (Y. Begay 2011, 29).

8. Officially called Certificate Degree of Indian Blood cards, in Navajo reservation discourse these cards are typically referred to simply as "CIBs."

9. Miss Navajo, 1952; Miss Florida Seminole, 1957; Miss Lumbee, 1968; Miss White Mountain Apache, 1954.

10. In Navajo, these deities are *Ałtsé Asdzą́ą́, Yoołgaii Asdzą́ą́*, and *Asdzą́ą́ Nádleehí*, respectively. The biographical information is taken from Garth Cartwright's website, http://www.garthcartwright.com/radmilla-cody (accessed February 17, 2014).

11. Church of the Nazarene is a Protestant church in the Wesleyan-Holiness tradition (www.nazarene.org).

12. See these letters to the editor in the *Navajo Times*: "Interracial Marriages Have Deep Ties" and "Sense of Identity," December 30, 1997; "What's Your Beef?!" January 22, 1998; "Superior Disgust," April 2, 1998; "Mothers Love Their Children, Who They Are," April 16, 1998.

13. For an analysis outlining the pros and cons of banning racial epithets, see Kennedy 2002.

14. In an e-mail from Radmilla (March 1, 2011), she writes that "the new term that I now use for African Americans is Nahiłii, or "those who have come across, are dark and calm, have persevered, and are one," which is broken down in the following way: Na (across), hip (dark, calmness, have overcome and persevered), ii (oneness)." See another translation at http://radmillacody.net/biography.html.

15. Clans are also in place to reinforce kinship, to prevent incest, and to allow Diné people to connect to and recognize one another as Diné.

16. In fact, there is evidence that, once freed, many war captives would "often immediately return to the Navajo families of which they had become members" (Thompson 2009, 134; Price 1884; Walker 1872).

17. For some of the more acrimonious debates regarding the policing of Native identity, consult Byrd 2007; Churchill 2001; Harjo 2007; and Red Shirt 2002.

18. Allen 2002; Beckett 1982 [1988]; Bond 2007; Bond, Brough, and Cox 2014; Dennison 2012; Perdue 2003; Povinelli 2002; Smith 1999; Sturm 2002, 2011.

19. Diné taboos about death and the deceased made this song even more inappropriate for me to have suggested.

20. For example, out of about sixty country bands on the Navajo reservation in 2011, I knew of five female musicians: three lead singers, one drummer, and one bass player.

21. These are songs comprising the public portion of Navajo ceremonies or "sings." As a whole, they are often referred to by McAllester (1954) and others as "social dance songs" in English and in Navajo as *Ndáá biyiin*.

22. Charlene "Chucki" Begay, interview with the author, March 1, 2010, Gallup, New Mexico.

23. Ibid.

24. Each band member referred to blood quantum when referencing their own Diné identity in conversation with me, and each referred to themselves as "full blooded."

25. Live Presidential Forum, June 23, 2014, Grey Hills Academy, Tuba City, Navajo Nation.

26. Phone conversation with author, July 6, 2016.

27. Http://www-01.sil.org/linguistics/GlossaryOflinguisticTerms/WhatIsAGlottalStop .htm.

28. The IPA symbol is [ɫ].

29. As *Navajo Times* reporter Marley Shebala (Diné) observed about this element of partner violence in the documentary *Hearing Radmilla*, "Radmilla was going through something that a lot of our Navajo women experience."

30. Phone conversation with author, July 6, 2016.

31. See the Canyon Records website, http://store.canyonrecords.com (accessed June 13, 2013).

32. Quoted in *Hearing Radmilla*, 2010.

33. KTNN AM 660, Window Rock, Arizona.

34. Examples include the performers Stoney Edwards (Cherokee Nation), Charley Pride, and Baldemar Huerta (aka Freddy Fender).

35. The internal quote ("cannot fail to recognize") is to Althusser 1971 [1989], 172.

36. I learned this when I tried to book Native Country at Fire Rock in 2011 and was told by the manager that Fire Rock "didn't hire rez bands." They have since changed their policy.

Chapter Four

1. Chucki Begay, interview by the author, March 25, 2010, digital recording, Coal Street Pub, Gallup, New Mexico.

2. See Chatterjee 1989.

3. I had different relationships with Native Country and Mother Earth Blues Band. I played with Native Country for two and a half years while in the field and continue to intermittently play with this group at the time of this writing. I only sat in with Mother Earth Blues Band, and my primary role was that of a listener, fan, and supporter of their non-profit, Music Is Medicine.

4. Because Navajos have two maternal clans and two paternal clans, some scholars describe Navajos as being matricentered and bilateral rather than matrilineal (Lloyd Lee, email correspondence, June 1, 2015).

5. I thank my colleague Lloyd Lee for reminding me of this crucial connection.

6. This term is applied to singers, curers, prayer-makers, diagnosticians ("hand tremblers"), and "anyone who attempts to influence the course of events by ceremonial means" (Schwarz 2003, 5; Kluckhohn and Wyman 1940, 15).

7. To hear performances of some of MEBB's songs, visit http://www.myspace.com /chuckibegay (accessed April 17, 2016).

8. This is the name of the Bia family's livestock grazing district.

9. Original version recorded by Eddie Rabbitt, *Eddie Rabbitt*, 1975.

10. Emmett "Toto" Bia Jr., interview by author, July 24, 2002, Many Farms, Arizona, digital recording, author's personal archive.

11. The time signature would be written as 9/8 or 3/4.

12. This means the song has a time signature of either 2/2 or 4/4.

13. "Beautiful Girls," original recording by Sean Kingston, 2007.

14. Tommy Bia, interview by author, May 14, 2009, Carson Mesa, Arizona, digital recording, author's personal archive.

15. To hear Tommy sing other songs in a similar style, listen to "Cindy" and "Thanks a Lot" on our Myspace page, http://www.myspacemusic.com/nativecountryband (accessed April 17, 2016). Please also visit the author's website: www.kristina-jacobsen.com.

16. This refers to the style of playing a rhythmic background texture, as opposed to playing "lead" guitar. In country music, it often consists of playing alternating bass strings and strumming between the alternations.

Chapter Five

1. "I am born to the Danish people, born for the Swedish people, my maternal grandfather belongs to the English people, and my paternal grandfather belongs to the Danish people. In this way I am a woman/human being."

2. Other tribal nations also participated as Code Talkers, including Hopi and Choctaw nations.

3. For an annotated timeline of the election events, see Paul Spruhan's "The Complete Timeline of the Navajo Nation Presidential Dispute," April 21, 2015, http://papers.ssrn.com /sol3/papers.cfm?abstract_id=2598541 (accessed July 9, 2016).

4. Scholars generally agree that Diné peoples arrived in the Southwest by around 1400. According to Diné peoples, however, Navajos migrated from elsewhere and existed as a people long before this date.

Epilogue

1. James William "Jim" Glaser, "The Lights of Albuquerque," 1986. Locally recorded and covered by rez country band Stillwater (Farmington, New Mexico).

Works Cited

Abasta, R. 1997. "Disturbed by Racial Attack." *Navajo Times*, December 30.

Aberle, D. 1966. *The Peyote Religion among the Navaho.* Chicago: Aldine.

Archuleta, M. L., Brenda J. Child, and K. Tsianina Lomawaima, eds. 2000. *Away from Home: American Indian Boarding School Experiences, 1879–2000*. Phoenix, Ariz.: Heard Museum.

Ahlers, J. 2006. "Framing Discourse: Creating Community through Native Language Use." *Journal of Linguistic Anthropology* 16 (1): 58–75.

Alexie, S. 2003. "What You Pawn I Will Redeem." *New Yorker Magazine*, 168–77.

Allen, C. 2002. *Blood Narrative: Indigenous Identity in American Indian and Maori Literary and Activist Texts*. Durham, N.C.: Duke University Press.

Althusser, L. 1971 [1989]. *Lenin and Philosophy*. Trans. Ben Brewster. New York: Monthly Review Press.

Altinay, A. G. 2004. *The Myth of the Military-Nation: Militarism, Gender, and Education in Turkey*. New York: Palgrave Macmillan.

Anderson, B. 1983. *Imagined Communities: Reflections on the Origin and Spread of Nationalism*. London: Verso.

Archuleta, M., B. J. Child, and K. T. Lomawaima. 2000. *Away from Home: American Indian Boarding School Experiences, 1879–2000*. Heard Museum, Santa Fe: Museum of New Mexico Press.

Ashley, R. 1985. "The Wingate Valley Boys." *Maazo Magazine* (Spring): 34–37.

Associated Press. 2010. "In-Situ Leach Mining." September 17.

Austin, R. D. 2009. *Navajo Courts and Navajo Common Law: A Tradition of Tribal Self-Governance*. Minneapolis: University of Minnesota Press.

Baker, L. D. 2010. *Anthropology and the Racial Politics of Culture*. Durham, N.C.: Duke University Press.

Baker, M. A. 1990. *Being on the Moon*. Winlaw, British Columbia: Raincoast Books.

Bakhtin, M. 1981. *The Dialogic Imagination: Four Essays by M. M. Bakhtin*. Edited by M. Holquist. Translated by C. Emerson and M. Holquist. Austin: University of Texas Press.

Balibar, E. 1988. "Propositions on Citizenship." *Ethics* 98 (4): 723–30.

Banks, L. W. 2011. "An Unusual Miss Navajo." *High Country News*, March 7, http://www.hcn.org/issues/43.4/an-unusual-miss-navajo.

Barker, J. 2011. *Native Acts: Law, Recognition, and Cultural Authenticity*. Durham, N.C.: Duke University Press.

Barrett, J. E., and D. Roediger. 2002. "How White People Became White." In *White*

Privilege: Essential Readings on the Other Side of Racism, edited by Paula S. Rothenburg. New York: Worth Publishers.

Barthes, R. 1968 [1977]. *Elements of Semiology*. Translated by Annette Lavers and Colin Smith. 1st American edition. New York: Hill and Wang.

Basso, K. H., S. Feld, and School of American Research. 1996. *Senses of Place*. Santa Fe: School of American Research Press.

Battistella, E. L. 2012. "Bad Language: Bad Citizens." In *Making Sense of Language: Readings in Culture and Communication*, by Susan D. Blum, New York: Oxford University Press.

Battles, R. 1998. "Superior Disgust." *Navajo Times*, April 2.

Bauman, R. 1977 [1984]. *Verbal Art as Performance*. Prospect Heights, Ill.: Waveland Press.

Bauman, R., and C. L. Briggs. 1990. "Poetics and Performance as Critical Perspectives on Language and Social Life." *Annual Review of Anthropology* 19: 59–88.

———. 2003. *Voices of Modernity: Language Ideologies and the Politics of Inequality*. Cambridge: Cambridge University Press.

Beauvais, F. 1998. "American Indians and Alcohol." *Alcohol Research and Health* 22 (4): 253–59.

Becker, B., and P. Spruhan. 2010. "Navajo Tribal Sovereignty." Presentation given to Diné College class, Chinle, Arizona, June 29.

Beckett, J. R. 1982. "The Torres Strait Islanders and the Pearling Industry: A Case of Internal Colonialism." In *Aboriginal Power in Australian Society*, edited by M. C. Howard. Honolulu: University of Hawaii Press.

———. 1982 [1988]. *Past and Present: The Construction of Aboriginality*. Canberra, Australia: Aboriginal Studies Press.

Begay, L. 1998. "Response to Orlando Tom." *Navajo Times*, March 26, A4.

Begay, R. 2004. *Great Gambler*. http://www.kued.org/productions/thelongwalk/links/index.php. Accessed December 12, 2011.

Begay, R. M., and Alexandra Roberts. 1996. "The Early Navajo Occupation of the Grand Canyon Region." In *The Archaeology of Navajo Origins*, edited by Ronald H. Towner, 197–210. Salt Lake City: University of Utah Press.

Begay, Y. 2011. "Historic and Demographic Changes That Impact the Future of the Diné and Developing Community-Based Policy." B.A. thesis, University of New Mexico, Albuquerque.

Bigenho, M. 2012. *Intimate Distance: Andean Music in Japan*. Durham, N.C.: Duke University Press.

Biolsi, T. 2004. "Race Technologies." In *A Companion to the Anthropology of Politics*, edited by David Nugent and Joan Vincent. Malden, Mass.: Blackwell.

———. 2001 [2007]. *Deadliest Enemies: Law and Race Relations on and off Rosebud Reservation*. Minneapolis: University of Minnesota Press.

Bitsoi, A. L. 2011. "The New Miss." *Navajo Times*, September 15.

Blu, K. 1980. *The Lumbee Problem: The Making of an American Indian People*. Cambridge: Cambridge University Press.

Boas, F. 1927. *Primitive Art*. Cambridge, Mass.: Harvard University Press.

Boas, F., and G. Hunt. 1897. *The Social Organization and the Secret Societies of the Kwakiutl Indians*. Washington, D.C.: U.S. Government Printing Office.

Bohlman, P. V., and R. Radano. 2000. *Music and the Racial Imagination*. Chicago: University of Chicago Press.

Bond, C. 2007. "'When You're Black, They Look at You Harder': Narrating Aboriginality within Public Health." Ph.D. diss., University of Queensland.

Bond, C., M. Brough, and L. Cox. 2014. "Blood in Our Hearts or Blood on Our Hands? The Viscosity, Vitality, and Validity of Aboriginal 'Blood Talk.'" *International Journal of Critical Indigenous Studies* 7 (2): 2–14.

Borstadt, L. F., R. S. Lee, and S. O. Feather. 1997. "Educating Native Americans about Free Enterprise." *Journal of Entrepreneurship Education* 1 (1): 33.

Bourdieu, P. 1984. *Distinction: A Social Critique of the Judgement of Taste*. Translated by R. Nice. Cambridge, Mass.: Harvard University Press.

Brackett, D. 1988 [2000]. *Interpreting Popular Music*. Berkeley: University of California Press.

Briggs, C. L., and R. Bauman. 1992. "Genre, Intertextuality, and Social Power." *Journal of Linguistic Anthropology* 2 (2): 131–72.

Brodeur, P. 2006. "Combating Alcohol Abuse in Northwestern New Mexico: Gallup's Fighting Back and Healthy Nations Programs." In *To Improve Health and Health Care*. Vol. 10 of *Robert Wood Johnson Anthology*, edited by S. L. Isaacs and J. R. Knickman. Published by Jossey-Bass.

Brooks, J. 2002. *Confounding the Color Line: The Indian-Black Experience in North America*. Lincoln: University of Nebraska Press.

Brown, J. N. 2005. *Dropping Anchor, Setting Sail: Geographies of Race in Black Liverpool*. Princeton: Princeton University Press.

Brown, M. F. 2003. *Who Owns Native Culture?* Cambridge, Mass.: Harvard University Press.

Browner, T. 2002. *Heartbeat of the People: Music and Dance of the Northern Pow-Wow*. Urbana: University of Illinois Press.

Brugge, D., T. Benally, and E. Yazzie-Lewis. 2007. *The Navajo People and Uranium Mining*. Albuquerque: University of New Mexico Press.

Brugge, D., and M. Missaghian. 2006. "Protecting the Navajo People through Tribal Regulation of Research." *Science and Engineering Ethics* 12 (3): 491–507.

Brugge, D. M., and R. Wilson. 1976. *Administrative History, Canyon de Chelly National Monument, Arizona*. U.S. Dept. of the Interior, National Park Service.

Brulotte, R. L. 2012. *Between Art and Artifact: Archaeological Replicas and Cultural Production in Oaxaca, Mexico*. Austin: University of Texas Press.

Bsumek, E. 2004. "The Navajos as Borrowers: Stewart Culin and the Genesis of an Ethnographic Theory." *New Mexico Historical Review* 79 (3): 319–51.

Bufwack, M. A., and R. K. Oerman. 1993 [2003]. *Finding Her Voice: Women in Country Music, 1800–2000*. Nashville: Vanderbilt University Press and Country Music Foundation Press.

Burnham, P. 2000. *Indian Country, God's Country: Native Americans and the National Parks*. Washington, D.C.: Island Press.

Byrd, J. 2007. "'Living My Native Life Deadly': Red Lake, Ward Churchill, and the Discourses of Competing Genocides." *American Indian Quarterly* 31 (2): 310–32.

de la Cadena, M. 1997. "Women Are More Indian: Gender and Ethnicity in Cuzco." In *Ethnicity, Markets, and Migration in the Andes: At the Crossroads of History and Anthropology*, edited by B. Larson, O. Harris, and E. Tandeter, 319–28. Durham, N.C.: Duke University Press.

de la Cadena, M., O. Starn, and Wenner-Gren Foundation for Anthropological Research. 2007. *Indigenous Experience Today*. Oxford, UK: Berg.

Cantwell, R., 2003. *Bluegrass Breakdown: The Making of the Old Southern Sound*. Urbana: University of Illinois Press.

Cantwell, R. 1996. *When We Were Good: The Folk Revival*. Cambridge, Mass.: Harvard University Press.

Casey, B. 2010. *Dance across Texas*. Austin: University of Texas Press.

Cattelino, J. R. 2008. *High Stakes: Florida Seminole Gaming and Sovereignty*. Durham, N.C.: Duke University Press.

———. 2010. "The Double Bind of American Indian Need-Based Sovereignty." *Cultural Anthropology* 25 (2): 235–62.

Chatterjee, P. 1989. "Colonialism, Nationalism, and Colonialized Women: The Contest in India." *American Ethnologist* 16 (4): 622–33.

Cheever, F. 2006. "Confronting Our Shared Legacy of Incongruous Land Ownership: Notes for a Research Agenda." *Denver University Law Review* 83: 1039–56.

Ching, B. 2001. *Wrong's What I Do Best: Hard Country Music and Contemporary Culture*. New York: Oxford University Press.

Ching, B., and G. W. Creed, eds. 1997. *Knowing Your Place: Rural Identity and Cultural Hierarchy*. New York: Routledge.

Churchill, W. 2001. "'Some People Push Back': On the Justice of Roosting Chickens." *Dark Night Field Notes, Pockets of Resistance* (11) 12: 1–19.

Clevenger, S. 2010. *America's First Warriors: Native Americans and Iraq*. Santa Fe: Museum of New Mexico Press.

Clifford, J. 1988. "Identity in Mashpee" In *The Predicament of Culture: Twentieth-Century Ethnography, Literature, and Art*, edited by James Clifford. Cambridge, Mass.: Harvard University Press.

———. 2007. "Varieties of Indigenous Experience: Diasporas, Homelands, Sovereignties." In *Indigenous Experience Today*, edited by M. de la Cadena and O. Starn. Oxford, UK: Berg Press.

Cocheo, S. 1994. "Can Banks Lend in Indian Country?" All Business, www.allbusiness.com. Accessed December 11, 2011.

Cohen, M. 2009.*The Networked Wilderness: Communicating in Early New England*. Minneapolis: University Of Minnesota Press.

Coleman, A. L. 2013. *That the Blood Stay Pure: African Americans, Native Americans, and the Predicament of Race and Identity in Virginia.* Bloomington: Indiana University Press.

Contreras, F. 2010. "Two Cultures, One Voice." Transcript of interview for National Public Radio. May 10.

Cook, G. W. 2010. *Renewing the Maya World: Expressive Culture in a Highland Town.* Austin: University of Texas Press.

Coolen, M. T. 1984. "Senegambian Archetypes for the American Folk Banjo." *Western Folklore* 43 (2): 117–32.

Cordova, R. 2012. "A Musician's Life Is a Rich Tapestry." *Arizona Republic*, February 8.

Cornsilk et al., dir. 2006. "Spiral of Fire" and "A Seat at the Drum." In *Indian Country Diaries.* Lincoln: Native American Public Telecommunications and Adanvdo Vision.

Cowlishaw, G. 1987. "Colour, Culture, and the Aboriginalists." *Man* 2 (22): 221–37.

Cutwright, G. 2011. "Radmilla Cody." Blog. http://www.garthcartwright.com/radmilla -cody. Accessed May 2, 2016.

Cyganik, J. Forthcoming. "Navajo Metal Music." Ph.D. diss., University of New Mexico.

Darling, E. J. 2009. "O Sister! Sarah Palin and the Parlous Politics of Poor White Trash." *Dialectical Anthropology* 33 (1): 15–27.

Davis, J. L. 2015. "Language Affiliation and Ethnolinguistic Identity in Chickasaw Language Revitalization." *Language and Communication* 47: 100–111.

Debenport, E. 2011. "As the Rez Turns: Anomalies within and beyond the Boundaries of a Pueblo Community." *American Indian Culture and Research Journal* 35 (2): 87–109.

Deere, T., dir. 2008. *Club Native: How Thick Is Your Blood?* Lincoln: Native American Public Telecommunications. Documentary film.

Deloria, P. J. 1998. *Playing Indian.* New Haven, Conn.: Yale University Press.

———. 2004. *Indians in Unexpected Places.* Kansas City: University Press of Kansas.

Deloria, V. 1969. *Custer Died for Your Sins: An Indian Manifesto.* New York: Macmillan.

Deloria, V., and C. M. Lytle. 1985 [1998]. *The Nations Within: The Past and Future of American Indian Sovereignty.* Austin: University of Texas Press.

Denetdale, J. 2006. "Chairmen, Presidents, and Princesses: The Navajo Nation, Gender, and the Politics of Tradition." *Wicazo Sa Review* 21 (1): 9–28.

Dennison, D., dir. 2010. *Indian Rodeo on the Navajo Nation.* Available for live streaming at http://vimeo.com/10780353. Accessed December 11, 2011.

Dennison, J. 2012. *Colonial Entanglement: Constituting a Twenty-First-Century Osage Nation.* Chapel Hill: University of North Carolina Press.

Densmore, F. 1913. *Chippewa Music.* Washington, D.C.: Government Printing Office.

Dent, A. 2009. *River of Tears: Country Music, Memory, and Modernity in Brazil.* Durham, N.C.: Duke University Press.

Deyhle, D. 1998. "From Break Dancing to Heavy Metal Navajo Youth, Resistance, and Identity." *Youth & Society* 30 (1): 3–31.

Diamond, B. 2002. "Native American Contemporary Music: The Women." *World of Music* 44 (1): 11–39.

Di Giovanni, L. 2002. "Diné in Shock over Cody's Crimes." *Gallup Independent*, December 11.

Dinwoodie, D. W. 1998. "Authorizing Voices: Going Public in an Indigenous Language." *Cultural Anthropology* 13 (2): 193–223.

Douglas, M. 1966 [1991]. *Purity and Danger; An Analysis of Concepts of Pollution and Taboo*. London and New York: Routledge.

Downs, J. 1972. "The Cowboy and the Lady: Models as a Determinant of the Rate of Acculturation among the Piñon Navajo." In *Native Americans Today*, edited by H. M. Bahr, B. Chadwick, and R. Day. New York: Harper and Row.

Duncan, C. 2014. "An Australian in Nashville: Style Shifting and Authentic Performance of Country Music." Presentation, New York University, September 18.

Duranti, A., ed. 2004. *A Companion to Linguistic Anthropology*. Oxford, UK: Wiley-Blackwell.

Dyen, I., and D. F. Aberle. 1974 [2010]. *Lexical Reconstruction: The Case of the Proto-Athapaskan Kinship System*. Cambridge: Cambridge University Press.

Dyk, W. 1938 [1996]. *Left Handed, Son of Old Man Hat: A Navajo Autobiography*. Lincoln: University of Nebraska Press.

Eckert, P. 2003. *Language and Gender*. New York: Cambridge University Press.

Edwards, D. 2014. "Michael Savage Stereotypes 'Drunk' Native Americans with Debunked Genetic Myth." *Raw Story*, June 23, http://www.rawstory.com/2014/06/michael-savage-stereotypes-drunk-native-americans-with-debunked-genetic-myth.

Elkins, C., and S. Pedersen. 2005. "Settler Colonialism in the Twentieth Century: Projects, Practices." *Legacies*, 1–15.

Epstein, D. J. 1975. "The Folk Banjo: A Documentary History." *Ethnomusicology* 19 (3): 347–71.

Essed, P., and D. T. Goldberg. 2002. *Race Critical Theories: Text and Context*. Malden, Mass.: Blackwell.

Fast, P. A. 2002. *Northern Athabascan Survival: Women, Community, and the Future*. Lincoln: University of Nebraska Press.

Fathers, F. 1910. *An Ethnographic Dictionary of the Navajo Language*. Saint Michaels, Ariz.: St. Michaels Mission.

Feintuch, B., ed. 2003. *Eight Words for the Study of Expressive Culture*. Urbana: University of Illinois Press.

Feld, S. 1982 [1990]. *Sound and Sentiment: Birds, Weeping, Poetics, and Song in Kaluli Expression*. Philadelphia: University of Pennsylvania Press.

———. 1984. "Communication, Music, and Speech about Music." *Yearbook for Traditional Music* 16: 1–18.

Feld, S., and D. Brenneis. 2004. "Doing Anthropology in Sound." *American Ethnologist* 31 (4): 461–74.

Feld, S., and A. A. Fox. 1994. "Music and Language." *Annual Review of Anthropology* 23: 25–53.

Feld, S., et al. 2004. "Vocal Anthropology: From the Music of Language to the Language of Song." *A Companion to Linguistic Anthropology*. Edited by A. S. Duranti. Malden, Mass.: Blackwell: 321–45.

Fernandez, J., et al. 1974. "The Mission of Metaphor in Expressive Culture [and Comments and Reply]." *Current Anthropology* 15 (2): 119–45.

Field, L. W. 2008. *Abalone Tales: Collaborative Explorations of Sovereignty and Identity in Native California*. Durham, N.C.: Duke University Press.

Finn, C. 1997. "'Leaving More Than Footprints': Modern Votive Offerings at Chaco Canyon Prehistoric Site." *Antiquity* 71 (271): 169–78.

Fletcher, M. L. 2011. "American Indian Tribal Law." Michigan State University Legal Studies Research Paper No. 09–05, Aspen Elective Series, Aspen Publishers.

Fletcher, A. C., and F. LaFlesche. 1893 [1994]. *A Study of Omaha Indian Music*. Lincoln: University of Nebraska Press.

Foucault, M. 1965 [1989]. *Madness and Civilization: A History of Insanity in the Age of Reason*. Translated by Richard Howard. New York: Random House.

Fox, A. 2004a. *Real Country: Language and Music in Working-Class Culture*. Durham, N.C.: Duke University Press.

———. 2004b. "White Trash Alchemies of the Abject Sublime: Country as 'Bad' Music." In *Bad Music: The Music We Love to Hate*, edited by Christopher Washburne and Maiken Derno. New Brunswick, N.J.: Rutgers University Press.

———. 2005. "Alternative to What? O Brother, September 11, and the Politics of Country Music." In C. K. Wolfe, and J. E. Akenson. *Country Music Goes to War*. Lexington: University Press of Kentucky.

Fox, A., and C. Yano. Forthcoming. *Songs out of Place: Global Country*. Durham, N.C.: Duke University Press.

Fox, P. 2009. *Natural Acts: Gender, Race, and Rusticity in Country Music*. Ann Arbor: University of Michigan Press.

Francis, K. 2010. "Presidential Candidates: Time for Change." *Gallup Independent*, June 28.

Frisbie, C. J. 1967 [1993]. *Kinaaldá: A Study of the Navaho Girl's Puberty Ceremony*. Middletown, Conn.: Wesleyan University Press.

Frisbie, C. J. 1980. "Vocables in Navajo Ceremonial Music." *Ethnomusicology* 24 (3): 347–92.

———. 1992. "Temporal Change in Navajo Religion: 1868–1990." *Journal of the Southwest* 34 (4): 457–514.

Frith, S. 1988. *Music for Pleasure: Essays in the Sociology of Pop*. New York: Routledge.

Gabriel, D. 2007. *Layers of Blackness: Colourism in the African Diaspora*. London: Imani Media.

Garrett, M. R. 2010. "Mormons, Indians, and Lamanites: The Indian Student Placement Program, 1947–2000." Ph.D. diss., Arizona State University.

Geertz, C. 1973. *The Interpretation of Cultures: Selected Essays*. New York: Basic Books.

Gibson, C., and D. Davidson. 2004. "Tamworth, Australia's 'Country Music Capital':

Place Marketing, Rurality, and Resident Reactions." *Journal of Rural Studies* 20 (4): 387–404.

Gilbert, M. S. 2010. *Education beyond the Mesas: Hopi Students at Sherman Institute, 1902–1929.* Norman: University of Nebraska Press.

Gillborn, D., and G. Ladson-Billings. 2010. "Critical Race Theory." *International Encyclopedia of Education* 6: 341–47.

Gilroy, P. 1996. "'. . . to Be Real': The Dissident Forms of Black Expressive Culture." In *Let's Get It On: The Politics of Black Performance*, edited by Catherine Ugwu. London: Institute of Contemporary Arts. Seattle: Bay Press.

Gordy, C. 2011. "Black, Red, and Proud." *Root*, February 22, http://www.theroot.com /views/black-native-american.

Gray, L. E. 2007. "Memories of Empire, Mythologies of the Soul: Fado Performance and the Shaping of Saudade." *Ethnomusicology* 51 (1): 106–30.

Green, R., 1988. "The Tribe Called Wannabee: Playing Indian in America and Europe." *Folklore* 99 (1): 30–55.

Grosz, E. A. 1994. *Volatile Bodies: Toward a Corporeal Feminism.* Bloomington: Indiana University Press.

Gupta, A., and J. Ferguson. 1997. *Anthropological Locations: Boundaries and Grounds of a Field Science.* Berkeley: University of California Press.

Harris, M. 1964. *The Nature of Cultural Things.* New York: Random House.

Haile, B., and L. C. Wyman. 1957. *Beautyway: A Navaho Ceremonial.* New York: Pantheon Books.

Haile, Fr. B. 1926. *A Vocabulary of the Navajo Language.* St. Michaels, Ariz.: St. Michaels Mission.

Hale, C. R. 1996. *Resistance and Contradiction: Miskitu Indians and the Nicaraguan State, 1894–1987.* Stanford, Calif.: Stanford University Press.

Hamill, C., 2012. *Songs of Power and Prayer in the Columbia Plateau: The Jesuit, the Medicine Man, and the Indian Hymn Singer.* Corvallis: Oregon State University Press.

Harjo, S. S. 2007. "Ward Churchill, the White Man's Burden." *Indian Country Today,* August 3.

Harkness, N. 2010. "The Voices of Seoul: Sound, Body, and Christianity in South Korea." Ph.D. diss., University of Chicago.

———. 2013. *Songs of Seoul: An Ethnography of Voice and Voicing in Christian South Korea.* Berkeley: University of California Press.

Harvey, D. 1996. *Justice, Nature, and the Geography of Difference.* Cambridge, Mass.: Blackwell.

Henson, E. C. 2008. *The State of Native Nations: Conditions under U.S. Policies of Self-Determination.* The Harvard Project on American Indian Economic Development. New York: Oxford University Press.

Herzfeld, M. 1997. Cultural Intimacy: Cultural Poetics in the Nation-State. New York: Routledge.

Hill, J. 2002. "'Expert Rhetorics' in Advocacy for Endangered Languages: Who Is

Listening and What Do They Hear?" *Journal of Linguistic Anthropology* 12 (2): 119–33.

Hill, W. W. 1943. "Navajo Humor." Menasha, Wisc.: George Banta.

Hinton, L. 1994. *Flutes of Fire: Essays on California Indian Languages.* Berkeley, Calif.: Heyday.

Hitt, J. 2005. "The Newest Indians." *New York Times Magazine,* August 21.

Hood, M. 1960. "The Challenge of 'Bi-musicality.'" *Ethnomusicology* 4 (2): 55–59.

House, D. 2002. *Language Shift among the Navajos: Identity Politics and Cultural Continuity.* Tucson: University of Arizona Press.

Hubbs, N. 2014. *Rednecks, Queers, and Country Music.* Berkeley: University of California Press.

Hughes, C. 2015. *Country Soul: Making Music and Making Race in the American South.* Chapel Hill: University of North Carolina Press.

Hymes, D. 1964. "Introduction: Toward Ethnographies of Communication." *American Anthropologist* 66 (6): 1–34.

Irvine, J. T., and S. Gal. 2000. "Language Ideology and Linguistic Differentiation." In *Linguistic Anthropology: A Reader.* Boston: Wiley-Blackwell.

Iverson, P. 1994a. "Speaking Their Language: Robert W. Young and the Navajos." In *Between Indian and White Worlds: The Cultural Broker,* edited by Margaret Szasz. Norman: University of Oklahoma Press.

———. 1994b. *When Indians Became Cowboys.* Albuquerque: University of New Mexico Press.

Iverson, P., and M. Roessel. 2002. *Diné: A History of the Navajos.* Albuquerque: University of New Mexico Press.

Jacobs, S.–E., W. Thomas, and S. Lang. 1997. *Two-Spirit People: Native American Gender Identity, Sexuality, and Spirituality.* Urbana: University of Illinois Press.

Jacobsen, K. 2003. "Native Bands of Diné Bikéyah: Country Music and Contexts." Master's thesis, Arizona State University.

———. 2009. "Rita(hhh): Placemaking and Country Music on the Navajo Nation." *Ethnomusicology* 53 (3): 449–77.

Jacobsen-Bia, K. 2014. "Radmilla's Voice: Music Genre, Blood Quantum, and Belonging on the Navajo Nation." *Cultural Anthropology* 29 (2): 385–410.

Jakobson, R. 1960. "Linguistics and Poetics." In *Roman Jakobson: Selected Writings III,* edited by S. Rudy. The Hague: Mouton Publishers.

Jenkins, C. C. 2010. "Miss, Jr. Miss Florida Seminole Crowned in 53rd Edition of Pageant." *Seminole Tribune.* August 27.

Jenks, C. 2014. *Social Interaction in Second Language Chat Rooms.* Edinburgh: Edinburgh University Press.

Jensen, J. 1998. *The Nashville Sound: Authenticity, Commercialization, and Country Music.* Nashville, Tenn.: Vanderbilt University Press.

Kauanui, J. K. 2008. *Hawaiian Blood: Colonialism and the Politics of Sovereignty and Indigeneity.* Durham, N.C.: Duke University Press.

Keil, C. 1985. "People's Music Comparatively: Style and Stereotype, Class and Hegemony." *Dialectical Anthropology* 10: 119–30.

Keller, R. H., and M. F. Turek. 1998. *American Indians and National Parks*. Tucson:
University of Arizona Press.

Kelley, K. B., and H. Francis. 2003. "Abalone Shell Buffalo People: Navajo Narrated
Routes and Pre-Columbian Archaeological Sites." *New Mexico Historical Review* 78
(1): 29–58.

Kennedy, R. 2002. *Nigger: The Strange Career of a Troublesome Word*. New York:
Pantheon Books.

Kluckhohn, C., and C. Leighton. 1962. *The Navajo*. Garden City, N.J.: Doubleday.

Kluckhohn, C., and L. C. Wyman. 1938. *Navaho Classification of Their Song Ceremonials*. Menasha, Wisc.: American Anthropological Association.

———. 1940. *An Introduction to Navaho Chant Practice*. Menasha, Wisc.: American
Anthropological Association.

Knickman, J. R., and S. L. Isaacs, eds. 2006. *To Improve Health and Health Care*.
Vol. 10 of *The Robert Wood Johnson Anthology*. San Francisco: Jossey-Bass.

Kroskrity, P. V., ed., 2000. *Regimes of Language: Ideologies, Politics, and Identities*.
Santa Fe, N.Mex.: School of American Research Press.

———. 2004. "Language Ideologies." In *A Companion to Linguistic Anthropology*,
edited by A. Duranti. Malden, Mass.: Blackwell.

Kroskrity, P., and M. Field, eds. 2009. *Native American Language Ideologies: Beliefs,
Practices, and Struggles in Indian Country*. Tucson: University of Arizona Press.

La Chapelle, P. 2007. *Proud to Be an Okie: Cultural Politics, Country Music, and
Migration to Southern California*. Berkeley: University of California Press.

Landry, A. 2016. "Police Kill Navajo Woman Allegedly Armed with Scissors." *Indian
Country Today*. March 29. https://indiancountrytodaymedianetwork.com/2016/03/29
/police-kill-navajo-woman-allegedly-armed-scissors-163955. Accessed July 22, 2016.

Lambert, V. 2007. *Choctaw Nation: A Story of American Indian Resurgence*. Lincoln:
University of Nebraska Press.

LaRoque, K. A. 2004. "The 1934 Indian Reorganization Act and Indigenous Governance: A Comparison of Governance of Santa Clara Pueblo and the Turtle Mountain
Band of Chippewa Nations: 1991–2000." Master's thesis, Virginia Polytechnic Institute
and State University.

Lassiter, L. E. 1998. *The Power of Kiowa Song: A Collaborative Ethnography*. Tucson:
University of Arizona Press.

Lee, L. L. 2006. "Navajo Cultural Identity: What Can the Navajo Nation Bring to the
American Indian Identity Discussion Table?" *Wicazo Sa Review* 21 (2): 79–103.

———. 2012. "Gender, Navajo Leadership and 'Retrospective Falsification.'" *AlterNative: An International Journal of Indigenous Peoples* 8 (3): 277–89.

———. 2013. *Diné Masculinities: Conceptualizations and Reflections*. CreateSpace
Independent Publishing Platform. Self-published.

———, ed. 2014. *Diné Perspectives: Revitalizing and Reclaiming Navajo Thought*.
Tucson: University of Arizona Press.

Lee, T. S. 2009. "Language, Identity, and Power: Navajo and Pueblo Young Adults' Perspectives and Experiences with Competing Language Ideologies." *Journal of Language, Identity, and Education* 8 (5): 307–20.

Lefebvre, H. 1991. *The Production of Space*. Trans. D. Nicholson-Smith. Cambridge, Mass.: Blackwell.

Lerma, M. 2010. Review of "Navajo Courts and Navajo Common Law: A Tradition of Tribal Self Governance," by R. D. Austin. *Indigenous Policy Review* 20 (8): 310–14.

Lévi-Strauss, C. 1964 [1994]. *The Raw and the Cooked: Introduction to a Science of Mythology*. Trans. J. and D. Weightman. New York: Harper and Row.

Lewis, G. H. 1997. "Lap Dancer or Hillbilly Deluxe? The Cultural Constructions of Modern Country Music." *Journal of Popular Culture* 31 (3): 163–73.

Lomawaima, K. T. 1995. *They Called It Prairie Light: The Story of Chilocco Indian School*. Lincoln: University of Nebraska Press.

Lotman, Y. 1990. *Universe of the Mind: A Semiotic Theory of Culture*. Bloomington: Indiana University Press.

Lott, E. 1995. *Love and Theft: Blackface Minstrelsy and the American Working Class*. New York: Oxford University Press.

Lowery, M. M. 2010. *Lumbee Indians in the Jim Crow South: Race, Identity, and the Making of a Nation*. Chapel Hill: University of North Carolina Press.

Luther, B., dir. 2007. *Miss Navajo*. Documentary film, www.miss-navajomovie.com. Accessed December 11, 2011.

Lynch, D. 1998. "What's Your Beef?!" *Navajo Times*, January 15.

Malkki, L. H. 1996. "Speechless Emissaries: Refugees, Humanitarianism, and Dehistoricization." *Cultural Anthropology* 11 (3): 377–404.

Malone, B. C. 1985. *Country Music, USA*. Rev. ed. Austin: University of Texas Press.

———. 2006. *Don't Get above Your Raisin': Country Music and the Southern Working Class*. Urbana: University of Illinois Press.

Mann, G. 2008. "Why Does Country Music Sound White? Race and the Voice of Nostalgia." *Ethnic and Racial Studies* 31 (1): 73–100.

Mannheim, K. 1923 [1952]. "The Problem of Generations." In *Essays on the Sociology of Knowledge: Collected Works*, vol. 5, edited P. Kecskemeti. New York: Routledge.

Marcus, G. E. 1998. *Ethnography through Thick and Thin*. Princeton, N.J.: Princeton University Press.

Marcus, G. E., and M. M. J. Fischer. 1986 [1999]. *Anthropology as Cultural Critique: An Experimental Moment in the Human Sciences*. Chicago: University of Chicago Press.

Marshall, K. J. 2011. "Performing Conversion among the Diné Oodlání (Navajo Believers)." Ph.D. diss., University of Indiana Bloomington.

———. 2016. *Upward, Not Sunwise: Resonant Rupture in Navajo Neo-Pentecostalism*. Lincoln: University of Nebraska Press.

Marshall, T. H. 1950. *Citizenship and Social Class*. Cambridge: Cambridge University Press.

Matthews, W. 1894. "Songs of Sequence of the Navajos." *Journal of American Folklore* 7 (26): 185–94.

———. 1897. *Navaho Legends*. New York: Houghton, Mifflin.

Mauss, M. 1966. *The Gift*. Translated by W. D. Halls. London: Routledge and Kegan Paul.

Maynor, M., dir. 1996. *Real Indian*. Women Make Movies. DVD.

McAllester, D. P. 1954. *Enemy Way Music: A Study of Social and Esthetic Values as Seen in Navaho Music*. Cambridge, Mass: Peabody Museum of American Archaeology and Ethnology, Harvard University.

———. 1979. "The Astonished Ethno-Muse." *Ethnomusicology* 23 (2): 179–89.

McCloskey, J. 2007. *Living through the Generations: Continuity and Change in Navajo Women's Lives*. Albuquerque: University of New Mexico Press.

McCusker, K. M., and D. Pecknold, eds. 2004. *A Boy Named Sue: Gender and Country Music*. Jackson: University Press of Mississippi.

M'Closkey, K. 2008. *Swept under the Rug: A Hidden History of Navajo Weaving*. Albuquerque: University of New Mexico Press.

McIntosh, P. 1990. "White Privilege: Unpacking the Invisible Knapsack." *Independent School* 49 (2): 31–35.

McLeod, C. et al., dirs. 2010. *In the Light of Reverence*. Bullfrog Films.

McNeley, J. K. 1981. *Holy Wind in Navajo Philosophy*. Tucson: University of Arizona Press.

Meek, B. A. 2010. *We Are Our Language: An Ethnography of Language Revitalization in a Northern Athabascan Community*. Tucson: University of Arizona Press.

Meintjes, L. 2003. *Sound of Africa! Making Music Zulu in a South African Studio*. Durham, N.C.: Duke University Press.

———. "Shoot the Sergeant, Shatter the Mountain: The Production of Masculinity in Zulu Ngoma Song and Dance." *Ethnomusicology Forum* 13 (2): 177–201.

———. 2010. "Luck with Bones: Post Apartheid Cultural Brokerage on the World Music Circuit." Paper presented at the annual American Anthropological Association Meeting, November 17.

———. Forthcoming [2017]. *Dust of the Zulu: Ngoma Aesthetics after Apartheid*. Durham, N.C.: Duke University Press.

Mercier, M. 2011. *Sur la route des Frères Patison* [On the Road with the Patison Siblings]. Éditions Atria.

Merriam, L. 1928. "The Problem of Indian Administration: Report of a Survey Made at the Request of the Honorable Hubert Work." Secretary of the Interior. *Baltimore: The Lord Baltimore Press*.

Miles, T., and S. P. Holland, eds. 2006. *Crossing Waters, Crossing Worlds: The African Diaspora in Indian Country*. Durham, N.C.: Duke University Press.

Mitchell, F. 1978. *Navajo Blessingway Singer*. Edited by C. J. Frisbie and D. P. McAllester. Tucson: University of Arizona Press.

Mitchell, R., and C. J. Frisbie. 2001. *Tall Woman: The Life Story of Rose Mitchell, a Navajo Woman, c. 1874–1977*. Albuquerque: University of New Mexico Press.

Montaya, R. 2010. "Glad, Concerned about Eastern Agency." *Navajo Times*, October 14.

Moore, D. S., J. Kosek, and A. Pandian. 2003. *Race, Nature, and the Politics of Difference*. Durham, N.C.: Duke University Press.

Moore, R. E. 1988. "Lexicalization versus Lexical Loss in Wasco-Wishram Language Obsolescence." *International Journal of American Linguistics* 54 (4): 453–68.

Morales, L. 2014. "Language Becomes Key Issue in Navajo Presidential Race." Radio Transcript, *Morning Edition*. September 22.

Morris, I. 1997 [2000]. *From the Glittering World: A Navajo Story*. Tulsa: University of Oklahoma Press.

Muehlmann, S. 2012. "Von Humboldt's Parrot and the Countdown of Last Speakers in the Colorado Delta." *Language and Communication* 32 (2): 160–68.

Murray, S. O. 1989. "A 1934 Interview with Marcel Mauss." *American Ethnologist* 16 (1): 163–68.

Nagel, J. 1998. "Masculinity and Nationalism: Gender and Sexuality in the Making of Nations." *Ethnic and Racial Studies* 21 (2): 242–69.

Naylor, C. 2006. "'Playing Indian'? The Selection of Radmilla Cody as Miss Navajo Nation, 1997–1998." In *Crossing Waters, Crossing Worlds: The African Diaspora in Indian Country*, edited by T. Miles and S. P. Holland. Durham, N.C.: Duke University Press.

Nevins, M. E. 2004. "Learning to Listen: Confronting Two Meanings of Language Loss in the Contemporary White Mountain Apache Speech Community." *Journal of Linguistic Anthropology* 14 (2): 269–88.

———. 2008. "'They Live in Lonesome Dove': Media and Contemporary Western Apache Place-Naming Practices." *Language in Society* 37 (2): 191–215.

Nez, A. 2015. "Third Gender Intersex (TGI) Identities on Navajo Nation." Paper presented at the Annual Navajo Studies Association Conference, Flagstaff, Arizona, May 30.

Nez, A., and M. Nez. 2011. "Changes Needed in Miss Navajo Contest." *Navajo Times*, September 22.

Niezen, R. 2003. *The Origins of Indigenism: Human Rights and the Politics of Identity*. Berkeley: University of California Press.

Novak, D. 2013. *Japanoise: Music at the Edge of Circulation*. Durham, N.C.: Duke University Press.

Nowlin, B. J. 2005/6. "Conflicts in Sovereignty: The Narragansett Tribe in Rhode Island." *American Indian Law Review* 30 (1): 151–64.

O'Brien, J. 2010. *Firsting and Lasting: Writing Indians Out of Existence in New England*. Minneapolis: University of Minnesota Press.

Omi, M., and H. Winant. 1994. *Racial Formation in the United States: From the 1960s to the 1990s*. New York: Routledge.

Ortiz, S. J. 1994. *After and before the Lightning*. Tucson: University of Arizona Press.

Ortner, S. 1974. "Is Male to Female as Nature Is to Culture?" In *Women, Culture, and Society*, edited by Michelle Rosaldo, Louise Lamphere, and Joan Bamberger. Stanford, Calif.: Stanford University Press.

Ottosson, Å. 2015. *Making Aboriginal Men and Music in Central Australia*. London: Bloomsbury Publishing.

Ottosson, Å. 2006. "Making Aboriginal Men and Music in Central Australia." Ph.D. diss., Australian National University, School of Archaeology and Anthropology.

Painter-Thorne, S. 2010. "If You Build It, They Will Come: Preserving Tribal Sovereignty in the Face of Indian Casinos and the New Premium on Tribal Membership." *Lewis and Clark Law Review* 14: 311–53.

Parrish, J. 2014. "The Future of Navajo Nation Depends on the Election Issue Everyone Should be Talking About." *Guardian*, October 13.

Patterson, J.-M. 2009. "Native Starts Provide Variety of Entertainment at Central Navajo Fair." *Navajo Times*, August 27.

Pecknold, D. 2007. *The Selling Sound: The Rise of the Country Music Industry*. Durham, N.C.: Duke University Press.

———. 2013. *Hidden in the Mix: The African American Presence in Country Music*. Durham, N.C.: Duke University Press.

Pecknold, D., and McCusker, K. M., eds. 2016. *Country Boys and Redneck Women: New Essays in Gender and Country Music*. Jackson: University Press of Mississippi.

Pegoraro, L., 2015. "Second-Rate Victims: The Forced Sterilization of Indigenous Peoples in the USA and Canada." *Settler Colonial Studies* 5 (2): 161–73.

Peile, A., and P. Bindon. 1997. *Body and Soul: An Aboriginal View*. Victoria Park, Australia: Hesperian Press.

Perdue, T. 2003. *Mixed-Blood Indians: Racial Construction in the Early South*. Athens: University of Georgia Press.

Perea, J. B. 2012. "Pamyua's Akutaq: Traditions of Modern Inuit Modalities in Alaska." *MUSICultures* 39 (1): 7–31.

———. 2013. "A Tribalography of Alaska Native Presence in Academia." *American Indian Culture and Research Journal* 37 (3): 3–28.

———. Forthcoming. *Sound Relations: A History of Music, Media, and Indigenous Self-Determination in Alaska*.

Perea, J. C. 2013. *Intertribal Native American Music in the United States: Experiencing Music, Expressing Culture*. New York: Oxford University Press.

———. 2006. "Technology, Ideology, and Emergent Communicative Practices among the Navajo." Ph.D. diss., University of Texas at Austin.

Peterson, R. 1997. *Creating Country Music: Fabricating Authenticity*. Chicago: University of Chicago Press.

Pilcher, J. 1994. "Mannheim's Sociology of Generations: An Undervalued Legacy." *British Journal of Sociology* 45 (3): 481–95.

Povinelli, E. A. 2002. *The Cunning of Recognition: Indigenous Alterities and the Making of Australian Multiculturalism*. Durham, N.C.: Duke University Press.

Powell, D. E. 2010. "Landscapes of Power: An Ethnography of Energy Development on the Navajo Nation." Ph.D. diss., University of North Carolina, Chapel Hill.

———. Forthcoming. *Landscapes of Power: Politics of Energy in the Navajo Nation*. Durham, N.C.: Duke University Press.

Perdue, T. 2003. *Mixed-Blood Indians: Racial Construction in the Early South*. Athens: University of Georgia Press.

Price, Hiram (Commissioner). 1884. "Report of the Commissioner of Indian Affairs for the Year 1884." Washington, D.C.: Government Printing Office.

Quintero, Donavan. 2016. "Maricopa County to Review Tsingine Report." *Navajo Times*, July 16. http://navajotimes.com/reznews/maricopa-county-review-tsingine-report/. Accessed July 21, 2016.

Rabinow, P. 1977 [2007]. *Reflections on Fieldwork in Morocco*. Berkeley: University of California Press.

Radano, R. 2003. *Lying Up a Nation: Race and Black Music*. Chicago: University of Chicago Press.

Radano, R., and P. Bohlman, eds. 2000. *Music and the Racial Imagination*. Chicago: University of Chicago Press.

Ramirez, T. 1998. "Mothers Love Their Children, Who They Are." *Navajo Times*, April 16.

Rave, J. 2005. "Feeling Isolated in Indian Country." *Bismarck Tribune*, December 3.

Red Shirt, D. 2002. "These Are Not Indians." *American Indian Quarterly* 26 (4): 643–44.

Reed, S. A. 1998. "The Politics and Poetics of Dance." *Annual Review of Anthropology* 27: 503–32.

Reed, P. F., T. G. Baugh, and L. S. Reed. 2000. "Melding Archaeology and Ethnohistory into a Contemporary View of the Early Navajo." In *The Entangled Past: Integrating History and Archaeology: Proceedings of the Thirtieth Annual Chacmool Archaeological Conference*, edited by M. Boyd, J. C. Erwin, and M. Hendrickson. Calgary, Alberta: Archaeological Association of the University of Calgary.

Reichard, G. 1928. *Social Life of the Navajo Indians, with Some Attention to Minor Ceremonies*. New York: Columbia University Press.

———. 1944. *Prayer: The Compulsive Word*. Seattle: University of Washington Press.

———. 1948. "Significance of Aspiration in Navaho." *International Journal of American Linguistics* 14 (1): 15–19.

Reichard, G. A. 1950. *Navaho Religion: A Study of Symbolism*. 2 vols. New York: Pantheon Books.

Reyhner, J., and J. Eder. 2015. *American Indian Education: A History*. Norman: University of Oklahoma Press.

Reyhner, J. 1993. "American Indian Language Policy and School Success." *Journal of Educational Issues of Language Minority Students* 12 (3): 35–59.

Reyhner, J., and J. Eder. 1992. "A History of Indian Education." In *Teaching American Indian Students*, edited by Jon Reyhner, 33–58. Norman: University of Oklahoma Press.

Rifkin, M. 2015. "The Duration of the Land: The Queerness of Spacetime in Sundown." *Studies in American Indian Literatures* 27 (1): 33–69.

———. 2011. *When Did Indians Become Straight? Kinship, the History of Sexuality, and Native Sovereignty*. New York: Oxford University Press.

Rink, H., and F. Boas. 1889. "Eskimo Tales and Songs." *Journal of American Folklore* 2 (5): 123–31.

Robins, R. H., and E. M. Uhlenbeck. 1991. *Endangered Languages*. Oxford, UK: Berg.

Rodgers, L. 2011. "Canyon Records Marks Sixty Years of Preserving, Promoting Native Heritage." *Arizona Republic*, November 6.

Roediger, D. 2002. "Whiteness and Ethnicity in the History of 'White Ethnics' in the United States." In *Race Critical Theories: Text and Context*, edited by Philomena Essed and David Theo Goldberg. Malden, Mass.: Blackwell.

Rohrer, J., 2016. *Staking Claim: Settler Colonialism and Racialization in Hawai'i*. Tucson: University of Arizona Press.

Rosaldo, R. 1994. "Cultural Citizenship and Educational Democracy." *Cultural Anthropology* 9 (3): 402–11.

Rosenberg, N. V., ed. 1993. *Transforming Tradition: Folk Music Revivals Examined*. Urbana: University of Illinois Press.

Roy, W. G. 2004. "'Race Records' and 'Hillbilly Music': Institutional Origins of Racial Categories in the American Commercial Recording Industry." *Poetics* 32 (3): 265–79.

Samuels, D. W. 1999. "The Whole and the Sum of the Parts; or, How Cookie and the Cupcakes Told the Story of Apache History in San Carlos." *Journal of American Folklore* 112 (445): 464–74.

———. 2004. *Putting a Song on Top of It: Expression and Identity on the San Carlos Apache Reservation*. Tucson: University of Arizona Press.

Samuels, D. W., et al. 2010. "Soundscapes: Toward a Sounded Anthropology." *Annual Review of Anthropology* 39: 329–45.

San Juan School District. 2012. "How the Diné Clans Are Related," http://dine.sanjuan .k12.ut.us/heritage/people/dine/organization/clans/clans.htm. Accessed November 4, 2016.

Sanjek, R., and S. Gregory, eds. 1994. *Race*. New Brunswick, N.J.: Rutgers University Press.

Sapir, E. 1936. "Internal Linguistic Evidence Suggestive of the Northern Origin of the Navaho." *American Anthropologist* 38 (2): 224–35.

Sax, J. L. 1986. "Symposium on Law and Community: The Trampas File." *Michigan Law Review* 84 (7): 1389–1414.

Scales, C. A. 2012. *Recording Culture: Powwow Music and the Aboriginal Recording Industry on the Northern Plains*. Durham, N.C.: Duke University Press.

Scaruffi, P. 2003. *A History of Rock Music: 1951–2000*. Lincoln, Neb.: iUniverse.

Schilling, V. 2013. "Exploring the Political Exploitation of Blood Quantum in the U.S." *Indian Country Today*, May 7.

Schröder, I. W. 2004. "Parades and Beauty Pageants: Encountering Authentic White Mountain Apache Culture in Unexpected Places." *Etnofoor* 17 (1/2): 116–32.

Schwarz, M. T. 2003. *Blood and Voice: Navajo Women Ceremonial Practitioners*. Tucson: University of Arizona Press.

Scott, J. W. 1999. *Gender and the Politics of History*. New York: Columbia University Press.

Sedgwick, E. K. 2002. "The Beast in the Closet: James and the Writing of Homosexual

Panic." In *The Masculinity Studies Reader*, edited by R. Adams and D. Savran. Malden, Mass.: Blackwell.

Seizer, S. 2005. *Stigmas of the Tamil Stage: An Ethnography of Special Drama Artists in South India*. Durham, N.C.: Duke University Press.

Shepelwich, S., and R. Zalneraitis. 2000. "McKinley Country, NM: Crownpoint. Case Study." Published report commissioned by McKinley County, N.Mex.

Shorty, S. N. 1998. "Indian and Proud." *Navajo Times*, 22 January.

Shulist, S. A. 2013. "In the House of Transformation: Language Revitalization, State Regulation, and Indigenous Identity in Urban Amazonia." Ph.D. diss., University of Western Ontario.

Sider, G. M. 1994. *Lumbee Indian Histories: Race, Ethnicity, and Indian Identity in the Southern United States*. Cambridge: Cambridge University Press.

Silverstein, M. 1996. "Monoglot 'Standard' in America: Standardization and Metaphors of Linguistic Hegemony." In *The Matrix of Language: Contemporary Linguistic Anthropology*, edited by D. Brenneis and R. H. S. Macaulay, 284–306. Boulder and Oxford: Westview Press.

Simpson, A. 2014. *Mohawk Interruptus: Political life across the Borders of Settler States*. Durham, N.C.: Duke University Press.

Smaje, C. 2014. "Not Just a Social Construct: Theorising Race and Ethnicity." *Sociology* 31 (2): 307–27.

Smallwood, A. W. 1999. "A History of Native American and African Relations from 1502 to 1900." *Negro History Bulletin* 62 (2/3): 18–31.

Smedley, A. 1998. "American Anthropological Association Statement on Race." Understanding Race, May 17, http://www.understandingrace.org/about/statement.html. Accessed April 16, 2016.

Smith, A. 2003. "Not an Indian Tradition: The Sexual Colonization of Native Peoples." *Hypatia* 18 (2): 70–85.

———. 2008. *Native Americans and the Christian Right: The Gendered Politics of Unlikely Alliances*. Durham, N.C.: Duke University Press.

Smith, G. 1994. "Australian Country Music and the Hillbilly Yodel." *Popular Music*, 13 (3): 297–311.

Smith, L. T. 1999. *Decolonizing Methodologies: Research and Indigenous Peoples*. London: Zed Books.

Smith, N. L. 2010. "A Dream Come True: Two Grey Hills Native Wins Miss Navajo Nation Crown." *Navajo Times*, September 16.

———. 2011. "First Tribal ID Cards Issued." *Navajo Times*, November 17.

Smith, P. C. 2009. *Everything You Know about Indians Is Wrong*. Minneapolis: University of Minnesota Press.

Spruhan, P. 2006. "Legal History of Blood Quantum in Federal Indian Law to 1935." *South Dakota Law Review* 51 (1): 1–31.

———. 2008. "The Origins, Current Status, and Future Prospects of Blood Quantum as the Definition of Membership in the Navajo Nation." *Tribal Law Journal* 8 (1): 1–17.

Starn, O. 2004. *Ishi's Brain: In Search of America's Last "Wild" Indian.* New York: W. W. Norton.

———. 2011a. "Here Come the Anthros (Again): The Strange Marriage of Anthropology and Native America." *Cultural Anthropology* 26 (2): 179–204.

———. 2011b. *The Passion of Tiger Woods: An Anthropologist Reports on Golf, Race, and Celebrity Scandal.* Durham, N.C.: Duke University Press.

Starna, W. A. 1996. "We'll All Be Together Again: The Federal Acknowledgement of the Wampanoag Tribe of Gay Head." *Northeast Anthropology* 51: 3–12.

Stewart, K. 1988. "Nostalgia—A Polemic." *Cultural Anthropology* 3 (3): 227–41.

———. 1996. *A Space on the Side of the Road: Cultural Poetics in an "Other" America.* Princeton, N.J.: Princeton University Press.

Stimeling, T. D. 2013. "Narrative, Vocal Staging, and Masculinity in the 'Outlaw' Country Music of Waylon Jennings." *Popular Music* 32 (3): 343–58.

Strom, P. 2013. "Defining Dixie: Southern Political Discourse in Country Music." B.A. thesis, Rhodes Institute for Regional Studies.

Strong, P. T., and B. Van Winkle. 1996. "'Indian Blood': Reflections on the Reckoning and Refiguring of Native North American Identity." *Cultural Anthropology* 11 (4): 547–76.

Sturm, C. 2002. *Blood Politics: Race, Culture, and Identity in the Cherokee Nation of Oklahoma.* Berkeley: University of California Press.

———. 2011. *Becoming Indian: The Struggle over Cherokee Identity in the Twenty-First Century.* Santa Fe, N.Mex.: School for Advanced Research Press.

Sullivan, S. 2006. *Revealing Whiteness: The Unconscious Habits of Racial Privilege.* Bloomington: Indiana University Press.

Sutton, M. Q. 2008. *Introduction to Native North America.* 3rd ed. Boston: Pearson.

TallBear, K. 2003. "DNA, Blood, and Racializing the Tribe." *Wicazo Sa Review* 18 (1): 81–107.

Tang, P. 2007. *Masters of the Sabar: Wolof Griot Percussionists of Senegal.* Philadelphia, Pa.: Temple University Press.

Tapahonso, L. 1993. *Sáanii Dahataał, the Women Are Singing: Poems and Stories.* Tucson: University of Arizona Press.

Tate, S.A. 2016. *Skin Bleaching in Black Atlantic Zones: Shade Shifters.* London: Palgrave Macmillan UK.

Tedlock, D. 1983. *The Spoken Word and the Work of Interpretation.* Philadelphia: University of Pennsylvania Press.

Thomas, C. 1998. "On the Road with Miss Navajo Nation." Ruminations by Chip Thomas, http://www.chipthomasphotography.com/ruminations/miss_navajo_97.htm. Accessed April 16, 2016.

Thomas, D. 1997. "Interracial Marriages Have Deep Ties." *Navajo Times*, December 30.

Thomas, W. N. D. "Weaving in the Margins: Male Weavers of Diné Nation: Our Stories and Experiences." Museum of Indian Arts and Culture, http://www.miaclab.org/exhibits/maleweavers/male_weavers.html. Accessed May 15, 2013.

Thomas, W., and S.–E. Jacobs. 1999. "'. . . And We Are Still Here': From Berdache to Two-Spirit People." *American Indian Culture and Research Journal* 23 (2): 91–107.

Thompson, D. 1998. "Color Shouldn't Matter." *Navajo Times*, January 29.Thompson, K. F., and K. Jacobsen. Forthcoming. "The Right to Lead: Language, Iconicity, and Diné Presidential Politics." Article under review.

Thompson, K. F. 2009. "Ałk'idą́ą́dą́ą́' hooghanę́ę (They Used to Live Here): An Archeological Study of Late Nineteenth and Early Twentieth-Century Navajo Hogan Households and Federal Indian Policy." Ph.D. diss., University of Arizona.

———. 2011. "The Navajo Nation, Diné Archaeologists, Diné Archaeology, and Diné Communities." *Archaeologies* 7 (3): 502–17.

———. 2014. "Language Becomes Key Issue In Navajo Presidential Race." In transcript of interview for National Public Radio "Fronteras Desk," KNAU Flagstaff, September 22. http://www.fronterasdesk.org/content/9783/language-becomes-key-issue-navajo -presidential-race.

Tichi, C. 1994. *High Lonesome: The American Culture of Country Music.* Chapel Hill: University of North Carolina Press.

Tillet, S. 2009. "In the Shadow of the Castle: (Trans) Nationalism, African American Tourism, and Goréé Island." *Research in African Literatures* 40 (4): 122–41.

Tsosie, R. 2006. "Tribal Sovereignty and Intergovernmental Cooperation." In *Tribal Water Rights: Essays in Contemporary Law, Policy, and Economics*, edited by B. G. Colby, J. E. Thorson, and S. Britton. Tucson: University of Arizona Press.

U.S. Census Bureau. 2007. *American Community Survey*, https://www.census.gov/acs /www/guidance_for_data_users/comparing_2007.

Upchurch, J. 2005. "Potential Impacts Associated with Improvements to County Road 7950." Prepared for Chaco Culture National Historic Park.

Urban, G. 1988. "Ritual Wailing in Amerindian Brazil." *American Anthropologist* 90 (2): 385–400.

Urban, G. 1985. "The Semiotics of Two Speech Styles in Shokleng." In *Semiotic Mediation: Sociocultural and Psychological Perspectives,* edited by E. Mertz and R. J. Parmentier. Orlando, Fla.: Academic Press, Inc.

Van Gennep, A. 1909 [1960]. *The Rites of Passage.* Chicago: University of Chicago Press.

Veracini, L. 2010. *Settler Colonialism.* Basingstoke: Palgrave Macmillan.

Vosen, E. C. 2002. "Seventh-Fire Children: Gender, Embodiment, and Musical Performances of Decolonization by Anishinaabe Youth." Ph.D. diss., University of Pennsylvania.

Walker, Francis A. (Commissioner). 1872. "Report of the Commissioner of Indian Affairs, for the Year 1872." Washington, D.C.: Government Printing Office.

Walker, S. 1998. "Sovereign Racism." *Navajo Times*, January 22.

Wall, T. L., L. G. Carr, and C. L. Ehlers. 2003. "Protective Association of Genetic Variation in Alcohol Dehydrogenase with Alcohol Dependence in Native American Mission Indians." *American Journal of Psychiatry* 160 (1): 41–46.

Warburton, M., and R. M. Begay. 2005. "An Exploration of Navajo-Anasazi Relation-ships." *Ethnohistory* 52 (3): 533–61.

Webb, A., director. 2010. *Hearing Radmilla.* Documentary film.

Webster, A. K. 2009. *Explorations in Navajo Poetry and Poetics.* Albuquerque: University of New Mexico Press.

———. 2013. "The Validity of Navajo Is in Its Sounds": On Hymes, Navajo Poetry, Punning, and the Recognition of Voice." *Journal of Folklore Research* 50 (1): 117–44.

———. 2015. *Intimate Grammars: An Ethnography of Navajo Poetry.* Tucson: University of Arizona Press.

Weidman, A. J. 2006. *Singing the Classical, Voicing the Modern: The Postcolonial Politics of Music in South India.* Durham, N.C.: Duke University Press.

Weyermann, D. 1999. "Little Big Woman: Meet the Real Miss America, the Queen of the Navajo Nation." *Mirella,* October.

Wilkins, D. E. 1987 [2003]. *The Navajo Political Experience.* Lanham, Md.: Rowman and Littlefield.

Wilkins, T. J. 2013. *Patterns of Exchange: Navajo Weavers and Traders.* Norman: University of Oklahoma Press.

Williams, R. 1973 [1985]. *The Country and the City.* Oxford, UK: Oxford University Press.

Willman, C. 2005. *Rednecks and Bluenecks: The Politics of Country Music.* New York: New Press.

Wilson, O. 1999. "The Heterogeneous Sound Ideal in African-American Music." In *Signifyin(g), Sanctifyin,' and Slam Dunking: A Reader in African American Expressive Culture,* edited by G. D. Caponi. Amherst: University of Massachusetts Press.

Witherspoon, G. 1977. *Language and Art in the Navajo Universe.* Ann Arbor: University of Michigan Press.

Witmer, R. 1973. "Recent Change in the Musical Culture of the Blood Indians of Alberta, Canada." *Anuario Interamericano de Investigación Musical* 9: 64–94.

Wolfe, P. 2006. "Settler Colonialism and the Elimination of the Native." *Journal of Genocide Research* 8 (4): 387–409.

Wyman, L. C. 1957. *Beautyway: A Navajo Ceremonial.* New York: Pantheon Books.

Wyman, L. C., and C. Kluckhohn. 1938. *Navaho Classification of Their Song Ceremonials.* Menasha, Wisc.: American Anthropological Association.

Young, R. W. 1948. "What's in a Name?" *El Palacio* 55 (5): 86–88.

Young, R. W., and W. H. Morgan. 1987. *The Navajo Language: A Grammar and Colloquial Dictionary.* Albuquerque: University of New Mexico Press.

Yurth, C. 2012. "Census: Native Count Jumps by 27 Percent." *Navajo Times.* January 26.

Zolbrod, P. G. 1984. *Diné Bahane': The Navajo Creation Story.* Albuquerque: University of New Mexico Press.

Index

....

CPSIA information can be obtained
at www.ICGtesting.com
Printed in the USA
LVHW040517220623
750465LV00004B/507